*A*dventure Guide™ to
Trinidad
&Tobago

2nd Edition

Kathleen O'Donnell

with Stassi Pefkaros

HUNTER

Hunter Publishing, Inc.
130 Campus Drive
Edison, NJ 08818-7816
☎ 732-225-1900 / 800-255 0343 / Fax 732-417-1744
Web site: www.hunterpublishing.com
E-mail: hunterp@bellsouth.net

IN CANADA
Ulysses Travel Publications
4176 Saint-Denis
Montreal, Québec H2W 2M5 Canada
☎ 514-843-9882, Ext. 2232 / Fax 514-843-9448

IN THE UK
Windsor Books International
The Boundary, Wheatley Road
Garsington, Oxford OX44 9EJ England
☎ 01865-361122 / Fax 01865-361133

ISBN 1-55650-886-7
© 2000 Kathleen O'Donnell & Stassi H. Pefkaros

Cover photo: *Carnival, Trinidad,* © SuperStock, Inc.
Photograph on page 175 courtesy of Ricarda Solomon
All other photographs © 2000 Kathleen O'Donnell
Caribbean map on page 6 © Hunter Publishing;
all other maps by authors, unless otherwise indicated
Cartoon illustrations by Joe Kohl
Indexing by Nancy Wolff

Acknowledgements

We want to thank our special friend in Tobago, Gerry Johnston, who always engages us with his friendship and kindness. Without his support this book could not have been as well researched. Bertrand Bhikarry and Kay Seetal have been friends in Tobago for years now. They are always there when we need them and always giving of their time and resources. Thanks also go to Lambert Julian and Cecil Alfred who shared their thoughts on Carnival with us. We especially want to express our appreciation to Dr. Carla Noel, Director of TIDCO, for her support of our research on Carnival. Thanks also go to David Montgomery for contributing an essay on the first map of Trinidad, a new acquisition in his extensive map collection.

It is impossible to thank personally all those whose generosity made this book a reality. People opened their hearts, shared their insights and information, and advised us all along the way. We are grateful to every one of them.

Preface

We visited Tobago for the first time in 1995, after reading a short *National Geographic* magazine article about the island. That was the beginning of our love affair with this unique country. For our first trip, we couldn't find a guidebook we thought useful, so we decided to write one ourselves. We returned a year later to explore Trinidad so that it, too, could be a part of the book.

As it turned out, Trinidad intrigued us as well – pre-Carnival events, nature preserves, untraveled roads, wild ocean beaches, and kindness all around. In so small a place, there is much to enjoy.

Author Kathleen at Arnos Vale Waterwheel Park.

Our first guide was a great success. Readers wrote wonderful letters giving us kudos for what they thought was good and suggestions for what we might include in a new guide. They also told us what was wrong or in their experience was different from what we had written. We have included some of their comments in this new guide and have looked especially closely at any facility or activity that drew a negative response.

Our perception of a hotel or tour may vary from yours, and sometimes places change. If you travel frequently, you also know that occasionally things go wrong for no real reason. For this updated edition, we once again explored the islands. We've added new finds and deleted some of the old ones that didn't look so good anymore. We hope this new guide is even better than the first.

We have included the best information we could gather to make your visit to Trinidad and Tobago as informed and enjoyable as possible. There are listings of accommodations, restaurants, beaches, and things to do, but we have also tried to give you a sense of how wonderful this twin island country is. The people are open and friendly, the beaches beautiful, and the land enchanting. As the legend goes, Robinson Crusoe washed up in Tobago and found his tropical paradise. Well, it's still there, waiting just for you. Neighboring Trinidad awaits you as well, with its bewitching Carnival and its wondrous natural environment. We hope you have a wonderful time.

Author Stassi at Fort James

We researched this new book carefully to bring you the best of what we found, but no place is unchanging. We welcome your comments on the islands and on our guide. Please write to us at our home in Mexico at the following address, or send us e-mail.

Kathleen O'Donnell and Stassi H. Pefkaros
Adventure Guide to Trinidad & Tobago
Apto. Postal #280
Taxco, GRO 40200
MEXICO
☎/fax: 52-762-23-888
E-mail: krika2000@yahoo.com

CONTENTS

Introduction   1
   Why Visit Trinidad & Tobago?   1
   The People & Their Culture   4
   Geography   5
   Government   6
   Economy   7
   History   9
   Flora & Fauna   23
   Music   31
   Planning Your Trip   37

Trinidad   55
   Orientation   55
   Getting Here & Getting Around   59
   Where To Stay   62
     Hotels & Guest Houses   64
     Camping   74
   Where To Eat   74
   Sightseeing   81
   Beaches   98
   Adventures & Sports   101
     On Foot   101
     On Water   103
     Spectator Sports   104
   Touring   104
   Nightlife   112
   Shopping   114

Tobago   117
   Orientation   117
   Getting Here & Getting Around   117
   Where To Stay   123
     Hotels, Guest Houses & Houses   126
     Camping   145
   Where To Eat   145
   Sightseeing   156
   Beaches   168
   Adventures & Sports   173
     On Foot   173
     On Wheels   174
     On Water   174
     On Horseback   179
   Touring   180
   Nightlife   184
   Shopping   186

Carnival 189
History 189
Carnival Today 192
Fêtes 193
Masquerade 193
The Main Events 195
Competitions & Titles 201
Tickets & More Information 203

Yachting 205
A Safe Haven With Services 205
Directory of Facilities 209

Guide Services 215
Trinidad 215
Tobago 217

Eco-Tourism & The Environment 221

Bibliography 225

Index 229

Maps

Caribbean Islands 6
Trinidad 55
First Map of Trinidad 58
Port of Spain 61
Tobago 116
Crown Point 120
Boca de Monos, Chaguaramas Bay & Carenage Bay 208
Chaguaramas Facilities 210

Introduction

Why Visit Trinidad & Tobago?

Trinidad and Tobago is a country of twin islands, but they are fraternal rather than identical. The familial relationship is there, but each has grown in different and special ways. The British joined Trinidad and Tobago as one country in the latter 19th century, though each island has a very distinct history and culture. They also differ geographically: Tobago feels Caribbean in nature, while Trinidad feels more South American.

Tobago's history is one of estate plantations. Agriculture dominated the island's economy into the 1960s. It is still, in many ways, rural in character. Its people are mostly of African origin, while Trinidad's nature was shaped by the much wider variety of people who settled there. Trinidad has lush jungle in the north, a heavily developed central corridor, and swamps and savannah in the south. Though it, too, has an agricultural base, Trinidad also has almost a hundred years of modern industrial development.

Together, the two islands form a fascinating country with an intriguing history, wonderful people, and an array of unique places to explore and things to do.

The majority of visitors to the islands right now are British, Scandinavian, and German. Americans have long known of the bird watching opportunities in Trinidad, but have only recently discovered Tobago.

■ Visiting Trinidad

Many people travel to Tobago and fail to visit Trinidad. Probably equal numbers visit Trinidad for Carnival and fail to visit neighboring Tobago. There's not much excuse for that, since the two islands are connected by ferry rides or short flights. Each island has a very distinct appeal.

Though a small island, Trinidad is appealing to visitors from two very different perspectives. On one hand, it is cosmopolitan. The capital city, Port of Spain, has one of the best zoos in the Caribbean and one of the oldest botanical gardens. It has nightclubs and chic restaurants, and there is an air of hustle and bustle that is native to an urban environment. It is also home to one of the biggest parties in the world – Carnival, a spectacular event attracting visitors from all over the globe. There are calypso competitions and pan music, parades of fabulously costumed revelers, and dancing in the streets. Officially lasting only a few days, events leading up to the Carnival crescendo start at the beginning of the year. Carnival is the best-known reason to visit the island.

The lesser-known side of Trinidad is its wonderful natural environment. Within a short drive from the city, you'll find huge mangrove swamps, mountainous jungle rain forests, deserted wind-swept beaches, remarkable bird preserves, a pitch lake, island caves, mud volcanoes, and a wealth of micro-climates with an enormous variety of plants and animals. Each time we visit Trinidad, it seems even more remarkable.

Then there are the people of Trinidad. Here you will find a true melting pot. Cultures and races have mixed and remixed through the years, and a person's character has finally become more important than his or her color. "Trinis" are well-educated, politically informed, and sophisticated. They are kind, helpful, and open-minded. Wherever you go, you will be well treated.

Visiting Trinidad is a step into a world where people of all colors and cultures work hard at getting along. This may be the island's most special quality.

■ Visiting Tobago

Like so many Caribbean islands, Tobago offers an exquisite environment, but it has other major advantages. Until recently, Tobago's tourism industry was relatively undeveloped. There were only a few resort-style hotels on the island, and none were more than three stories high. Numerous small hotels and guest houses dotted the towns, and there was a very

Golden Grove Ranch, Caanan, Tobago.

low-key feel to the island. Tobago has now found itself on the tourist map, and hotels and holiday villa construction projects are in the works around the island or planned to begin in the next few years. Poised between the quiet life of local people and developing tourism, Tobago is still a very friendly and safe island. There are beautiful beaches, of course, but Tobago offers much more. It is a bird watcher's paradise. It also has the oldest national park in this hemisphere and some of the best scuba diving in the Caribbean for experienced divers.

Tobago offers visitors a true Caribbean getaway. It is very relaxed, with sunning and swimming its major attractions. Golf, tennis, and numerous water sports are available, including snorkeling, windsurfing, diving, sailing, and deep-sea fishing. The natural environment is perfect for hiking along nature trails in the rain forest, and people in Tobago are open and friendly. Like us and so many others, you'll find yourself wishing a part of Tobago could be yours forever.

Not much remains unchanging in this world of ours, and Tobago is no exception. With assistance and encouragement from the government, Tobago is making its mark on the world of tourism. Trinidad and Tobago has an advantage in being late to explore economic development through tourism; it has the rest of the Caribbean from which to study and learn. There is an unwritten law in Tobago that buildings may not be taller than a palm tree. That unofficial

Coastline, Crown Point.

rule is now becoming a part of development policy, and hotels may not be more than three stories high anywhere on the island. Attention is also being given to the delicate ecosystem and fragile nature of the land. While the number of hotel rooms will soon more than double, sites are being carefully selected to avoid damaging the very thing that makes the island special: its beautiful environment and clean waters.

As development continues, there is much discussion of what the future will bring. For now, Tobago is a delightful and welcoming destination.

The People & Their Culture

When visiting Trinidad and Tobago, remember that Tobago, especially, is still an island of villages and small-town friendliness. We got a lift from a farmer one day and as we rode along he talked about the strong village ties in Tobago. Village elders still try to keep everyone on the straight and narrow so there are fewer social problems in Tobago than in nearby, more urban Trinidad.

Tobagoins are accepting of visitors and seem to have unending patience with the interruptions in their daily lives caused by tourists. While open minded, the islanders are not sophisticated. Visitors, thoughtlessly sometimes, behave in ways that ignore local customs and, over time, this will certainly cause friction between the island's people and its visitors.

As a visitor to Tobago, pay a little more attention to dress than you may back home. Bathing suits belong only on the beach. Bring a wrap or shorts to throw on when you're leaving the beach and everyone will be more comfortable. Sunbathing belongs only on the beach or at the pool and sunbathing means in a bathing suit, top and bottom at all times. Public nudity is very offensive to local people and it is illegal.

Whether man or woman, remember you're the equivalent of a "city slicker" to the people who live here. Your presence can impress and distort local values on a short-term basis that may have long-term consequences after you leave. As a nation of travelers, we have become more sensitive to taking care of the natural environments we explore. We need to take equal care with the people we encounter.

Tobagoins are deeply religious and, though it may not be immediately evident, they are more straight-laced than you would expect. A local young man or woman who becomes romantically involved with a foreigner will have problems fitting in again when the visitor leaves. Be careful not to destroy what you came to see and enjoy.

Trinidad, though more sophisticated and urban in character than Tobago, is still a place where deeply held religious beliefs guide behavior. Dressing in a provocative manner will get you more of a response than you might expect (or want).

AUTHOR TIP

The people of Trinidad and Tobago are beautiful and you cannot help but want to take a few photos. However, always ask permission before pointing a camera at someone.

■ Language

Although the language of both Trinidad and Tobago is English, when the locals are talking among themselves it can sound like another language entirely. Here are some colloquial expressions you might find interesting.

- **"Lime"** is to spend time talking and socializing with friends. You'll see lots of fellows liming during the hotter parts of the day as you drive around the islands; work is done in the cooler morning and evening hours.

- **"Free up"** is to relax and let go of your inhibitions.

- A **"trace"** is a road or lane.

- **"Calabash houses"** are the old-style gingerbread houses you'll see as you explore the island.

- Locally, Trinidadians are called **"Trinis."** A new word, **"Trinbago,"** is being used more commonly now when talking about both islands together.

You will please many a person in Trinidad and Tobago if you use more formal greetings, such as good morning, good afternoon, good evening. The informal American greeting, "Hello, how are you?" doesn't seem to do the trick. You'll also hear "good night" used as a greeting, rather than as something to say when leaving for the evening.

Geography

The Republic of Trinidad and Tobago is the most southerly Caribbean country. Positioned just off the coast of Venezuela, Trinidad is seven miles from the mainland and Tobago is 21 miles off the coast of Trinidad. Rather than having volcanic or coral origins like many Caribbean islands, it is believed that these islands broke from the mainland and share many geologic features with Venezuela. Visible from one to the other because of their relatively high mountain ridges – 1,860 feet in Tobago and 3,085 feet in Trinidad – the two islands, though related politically, are worlds apart in physical characteristics.

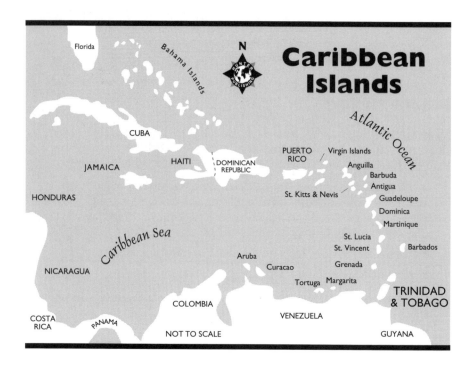

Government

■ Organization

The President of Trinidad and Tobago is elected Head of State by Parliament, but executive powers are held by the popularly elected Prime Minister and his Cabinet. Legislative power resides in the two houses of Parliament – the popularly elected 36-member House of Representatives and the appointed 31-member Senate. In addition to its representation in Parliament, Tobago has a voice in its local affairs through its 12-member House of Assembly. The current Prime Minister is Basdeo Panday, who is the first person of Indian heritage to hold that office. The current president is A.N.R. Robinson. New elections are being held in the year 2000.

■ History

Trinidad and Tobago gained political independence from Britain in 1962. Since that time it has held elections every five years, peaceably transferring the powers of government with each new ruling party. Because of its unusual history as a Crown Colony, Trinidad and Tobago has less political experience than other of Britain's colonies in the Caribbean. Most of Britain's other colonies enjoyed local political control and they developed political skills, becoming progressively more adept in managing the plurality that makes a democratic process. Crown Colony status for Trinidad meant that its government was appointed by the Crown and, until 1925, the citizens of Trinidad and Tobago were almost entirely excluded from the political process.

In the short period of time from the mid-1920s to the mid-1950s, their political control evolved from having only an advisory capacity to a British-appointed governor to full independence as a country with freely elected political parties and universal suffrage. Evidently their relative lack of experience in political and governmental processes did not greatly impede the development of their political sophistication.

The Red House (Parliament) at Woodford Square.

Economy

Trinidad and Tobago differ in their history and in their economic development. Tobago is decidedly rural – economically relying on locally consumed agricultural products, fishing, civil service employment, and, more recently, tourism. While also having a significant agricultural sector, Trinidad has diversified manufacturing and a petroleum products industry that developed early in the 20th century. Current oil reserves might not provide a rosy economic future for the country, though its reserves of natural gas and methanol may.

■ Oil

High worldwide oil prices in the 1970s created a financial boon for Trinidad and Tobago. Money was suddenly available for major infrastructure expenditures and ambitious projects were undertaken. Unfortunately, with the contraction of oil industry prices in the late 1970s, Trinidad and Tobago found itself in a financial squeeze. Like many smaller oil-producing countries, it had greatly over-extended public spending on development projects based on the widely accepted prediction of continued high oil prices. An economic crisis was averted, but severe cutbacks in public spending by the late 1980s and into the '90s sent waves of recession throughout the economy. With World Bank and IMF intervention, changes in economic policy have been implemented, including a loosening of restraint on foreign investment. The development of a tourism sector in the economy is also a part of these policy changes. Tourism in Trinidad and Tobago had never been a significant portion of the economy; it was not perceived as necessary or potentially beneficial.

■ Tourism

While tourism is cited as a major income-producing sector for many smaller Caribbean countries, it remains to be seen if tourism will appreciably improve or even help to maintain a desirable standard of living for people in Trinidad and Tobago. Given that the Republic of Trinidad & Tobago is seeking foreign investment, the top economic tier in the tourism industry may not end up being Trinidadian or Tobagonian at all. Extreme care must be taken to ensure that tourism dollars coming into the country do not drain out just as quickly. The drain of tourism capital is a significant problem, especially for small countries that lack the capacity to produce tourism-associated goods – wines and liquors, gourmet foods, televisions, rental cars, and a host of other similar products.

■ Yacht Services Industry

One of Trinidad and Tobago's burgeoning economic sectors with which we have first-hand knowledge is its yacht services industry. With more receptive attitudes toward tourism and an especially bad hurricane season in the more northerly Caribbean in 1995, the development of a sophisticated yacht services industry in Chaguaramas moved rapidly ahead. In 1990 there were only a handful of foreign yachts in the harbor, but by 1995 there were 2,500, demonstrating the phenomenal growth potential for this industry. It is important to note that the types of jobs prevalent in this field are skilled and technical, rather than service-oriented. This allows for the creation of well-paid employment opportunities, rather than the minimum wage unskilled jobs normally prevalent in the tourism industry.

■ Demographics

When compared to the aging population of the United States, Trinidad and Tobago's population is young; almost 30% is under the age of 15. Like the baby-boomers in the US, this group will have a significant impact on the country. The government will have to successfully address the education and employment needs of this portion of society if it is to continue improving the standard of living for all its people. The literacy rate may be estimated at a minimum of 80%, however, fully 30% of children 12 to 15 years of age do not have the option of attending secondary school. There is simply no place for them in the standard educational system. They must turn to opportunities for training or employment in one of the trades.

An accurate picture of any country's economy can't rely solely on data. With unjaundiced eyes and an open mind, it must be said that one of the more evident features of the economy is the lack of significant poverty. The extremes of wealth and poverty so prevalent in much of the Caribbean do not, for the most part, exist in Trinidad and Tobago, but they may be developing. There is a large, well-educated, sophisticated middle class and, although there are areas of the islands where development has failed to improve the standard of living, people do not appear to be in severe need.

All in all, Trinidad and Tobago is an impressive country. While certainly there are tensions among racial, ethnic, and economic groups, there is an upbeat forward movement. They also have a wonderful social mechanism for erasing barriers at least once a year when all groups, races, and classes join together in their national celebration – Carnival.

■ Doing Business in Trinidad & Tobago

Since our first guide was written in the spring of 1996, Trinidad and Tobago appears to have come upon very good times. The capital city of Port of Spain has had a face-lift in many areas. Imports and the general pace of business are on an upswing.

Trinidad and Tobago, appearances to the contrary, is a conservative country. Business dealings should always begin on a formal level and, although it's a tropical climate, you should present yourself in full business attire.

USEFUL BUSINESS CONTACTS

■ **Tourism and Industrial Development Company** (TIDCO), 10-14 Philipps St., Port of Spain. ☎ 868-623-6022/4, fax 625-0837.

■ **Trinidad & Tobago Chamber of Industry and Commerce**, Chamber Building., Columbus Circle, Westmoorings. ☎ 868-637-6966, fax 637-7425.

■ **Trinidad & Tobago Manufacturers Association**, 8A Stanmore Ave., Port of Spain. ☎ 868-623-1029/30, fax 623-1031.

■ **World Trade Centre of Trinidad & Tobago**, Mausica Rd., Piarco. ☎ 868-642-2270, fax 642-9134.

History

The Republic of Trinidad and Tobago shares much historical context with other Caribbean countries and that history has determined much of what it is today – its successes, its problems, its culture, and its orientation in the modern world. Understanding some of the historical antecedents of present day Trinidad and Tobago gives a richness to our experience of the country, patience with its flaws, and admiration for its achievements.

While each country in the Caribbean shares much history with its neighbors, each also had unique experiences within its colonial heritage. Trinidad's experience of colonialism differed remarkably from other British Caribbean and British American colonies. Britain's control of the American colonies was neither as extensive nor as long lasting as its domination in the Caribbean and, unlike the American colonies, the Caribbean colonies were home to relatively few European settlers. They had large slave populations and they were economically isolated and dependent on their European home countries. Many colonies had large indentured populations with racial divisiveness, and there was competition and jealousy among all the Caribbean colonies.

The Caribbean's place in history is not wholly unique. The way it was developed and exploited was the rule of the day. Its experience in history was an extension of existing European political, social, and cultural patterns. What is most interesting in reviewing the history of Trinidad and Tobago is the ways in which historical antecedents set in motion modern historical developments and helped to define this country's character in the world of nations.

■ Trinidad in the 15th-18th Centuries

Columbus discovered Trinidad and claimed it for Spain in 1498. The island at that time was inhabited by Amerindians. Though the Carib Indians seem to have left more of a legacy in Trinidad, it is likely that the island was populated by the peaceable Arawak Indians, who lived their lives in an agriculturally based economy. Nearby Tobago, where the Carib Indians probably did dominate, was apparently also sighted by Columbus, but not claimed for Spain.

For a few hundred years, Trinidad was largely ignored by the Spanish except as it provided opportunities for exploitation. Gold and removable resources were the main aim in Spain's control of the island, not residential colonial development. During this time, of course, the island's Amerindian inhabitants were seen as an exploitable resource and few survived the experience.

Spanish control of the island continued for 300 years, though little progress was made toward the development of a colonial settlement until the latter part of their period of influence. During that time the Spanish themselves were in conflict about the real goals of colonization. A policy of exploitation and subjugation certainly had its adherents, but there were other voices being raised. Within the Spanish hierarchy there were those who argued for religious conversion and better treatment of indigenous peoples and slaves. These latter voices were not strong enough, but probably did have a mild restraining influence.

To balance the humanitarian voices in Spain with the need for workers in the lucrative Spanish enterprises in the new world, the **Cedula of 1511** was issued. This edict was issued in an attempt to resolve the conflict between the former two forces within the Spanish hierarchy. By this law, peaceable Indian tribes such as the Arawaks were slated for conversion to Catholicism while the warlike and aggressive Caribs were to be exploited as slaves. Because of the distance and travel time between the New World and Spain and because of the on-site greed of explorers in the Caribbean, many Indian groups suddenly found themselves called Caribs, and the Arawaks in Trinidad were no exception.

Unlike the more lucrative Spanish incursions into South America, the occupation of Trinidad produced too little economic return for it to receive much attention from the Spanish crown. There were a few agricultural settlers, but the island showed little economic promise until 1718, when cocoa farming brought the island some brief prosperity. After a crop failure in 1733, Trinidad returned to a position of relative unimportance.

In 1772, Trinidad's total population was under 800, made up by a little over 300 Spanish settlers and about 400 Amerindians. In the **Cedula of 1783**, the Spanish opened Trinidad to Catholic non-Spanish immigration. Both whites and non-whites were enticed to immigrate, receiving economic benefits in land grants, tax reductions, and export rights. Whites were granted land parcels twice as large as non-whites, receiving 32 acres per family member and half that for each of the slaves they brought. Though free to immigrate, non-whites were at a disadvantage right from the start. All who came to settle were required to give their loyalty to the Spanish King and to follow the Catholic religion. Most of the immigrants were French, coming from neighboring Caribbean islands.

DID YOU KNOW?

The enticements of the 18th century are much like incentives to foreign investment today, and they were successful. The population of Trinidad grew enormously, as did the number of acres of land under cultivation.

By 1797, Trinidad's population had grown to over 16,000 – whites now numbered about 2,100, free Africans about 4,500, and slaves about 10,000. Trinidad was finally developing, but its character was becoming more French than Spanish, as the number of French immigrants began to dominate the culture. With its economic development it was coincidentally increasing its risk of invasion from without and rebellion from within from free Africans and slaves.

It was not until 1797 that the British took Trinidad from the Spanish. At the time, the colony was dominated by French culture, administered under Spanish law, and had a large population of Africans, one-third of whom were free. The British had to find the means to ensure its economic development, to put the stamp of British culture on an island with few English settlers, and to organize a legal and political structure.

Trinidad's economic future posed some tricky problems. The land in Trinidad had never been heavily exploited in sugarcane agriculture, as had many British colonies. These other colonies, realizing Trinidad's potential as a competitor, strongly opposed any program for the importation of slave labor to Trinidad. Without slave labor, the rich agricultural lands could not be fully exploited and Trinidad would not become a successful competitor. Along with opposition to slavery from other self-interested colonies, Britain's own social reformers were finally succeeding in turning public opinion against the practice. Under these pressures, Britain made it unlawful for agricultural slaves to be imported to Trinidad.

In creating governmental and administrative structures, Britain had to work with the fact that British landowners were a relatively small part of Trinidad's population. Strong French and Spanish influences and the large population of free people of color made it a complex situation. Still, the island had to be governed in a manner consistent with British interests.

Other British West Indies colonies were constitutionally organized and to a large degree self-governing. They might have provided a model for Trinidad, but there were differences. Trinidad had a large land-holding population of people of color. These people would have enjoyed the right to vote in a normally organized constitutional government, but this was a group with whom Britain had little experience. Granting a self-governing constitution might lead to developments in the island not consistent with Britain's perceived self-interest. Some alternative was needed and a solution was found.

Trinidad was given the unique status of **Crown Colony** – all significant decisions were to be left to the British Government. In establishing this administrative structure Britain denied the vote and political control to everyone on the island. Few islanders were British and the denial of political rights was not expected to arouse much opposition from other groups.

Britain's other colonies had significant numbers of free non-whites, but they did not own land and this meant they did not have the right to vote. They had no access to the political process. In creating the Crown Colony of Trinidad, Britain effectively denied the vote to non-whites in Trinidad who did own land and who would have had a political voice. That voice might have been heard by non-whites on other islands and might have caused problems. It was effectively silenced.

Crown Colony status remained in Trinidad until 1925 with few important changes.

■ Tobago in the 15th-18th Centuries

When first sighted by Columbus late in the 15th century, Tobago was home to Carib and Arawak Indians, though the Caribs dominated the island both by number and by their aggressive nature. The island was called Tabaco by its inhabitants, though Columbus was to call it Assumption.

Tobago was ignored by the colony collectors until early in the 17th century. First claimed by the **British** in 1626, it was later claimed so many times by so many governments that it more than made up for its late start. In 1646, just 20 years after the British claimed it, Tobago was claimed by France and by Holland. Even Latvia staked a claim in 1664, based on a land grant from the English King. While obviously claimed by one and all, Tobago was never settled or defended as a proper colony. Despite that, no one was willing to let go of it permanently.

Even the Spanish became involved. They feared the potential consequences to their colony in Trinidad if a coalition of Amerindians from Trinidad and Tobago were to develop and, in 1636, the Spanish invaded Tobago. They succeeded in destroying its small European settlements and in removing the islanders' store of ammunition.

In 1639, in what would be a long-lasting European political intrigue, one of the Baltic States, the **Duchy of Courland**, was granted rights to Tobago. In that same year, they made their first attempted settlement in what is now called Great Courland Bay. Though they abandoned their place on the island within a year, they returned in 1642. This time their settlement was to last eight years before failing. Tenacious, the Courlanders returned in 1654 and finally found the economic success that had eluded them in their other settlement attempts. They were soon joined in Tobago by a new Dutch settlement. Over the next 40 years, disputes between the Dutch and the Courlanders, political tradeoffs in Europe, and frequent attacks by Indians and other Europeans led the Courlanders to abandon their claim to Tobago in 1690.

In the latter half of the 17th century, the Caribbean was dominated by the French and the Dutch and both were interested in the small island of Tobago. After successive naval and land battles between these two forces, the French enjoyed a decisive victory and claimed Tobago as their prize in 1678. For all its troubles, Tobago was lush, its land was fertile, it had good water supplies, and it was located well out of the areas susceptible to hurricanes.

Though Tobago had an economic appeal to the French, other French-controlled islands in the Caribbean were still only sparsely settled and developed, which made them very vulnerable to attack. As well, markets for plantation products were still limited, so there was little motivation at the time for the French to attempt development in Tobago. Though late to enter the game, the British took advantage of this vulnerability, entering the competition for control of the area with its naval forces.

For half a century, France and Britain were repeatedly in conflict over territorial control of Caribbean islands, including Tobago. Finally, in 1749, France and Britain agreed that Tobago and a few other nearby islands would be neutral, but it was not a long-lived agreement. By 1756, France had allied itself with Spain and together they were at war with Britain. After seven years, the war was over, and Tobago was British. The British established a base for government on the island and made **Fort Granby** their military base.

Prospects for development in Tobago, however, did not materialize until 1781, when the French retook the island from the British. The French introduced financial incentives to lure immigrants from other Caribbean islands to Tobago. Between 1771 and 1791, just 20 years, the island's population grew from just over 5,000 to more than 15,000. Of this figure, the slave population was slightly greater than 14,000. A startling 94% of the population were African slaves.

Slavery formed the basis for the economies throughout the West Indies in the 18th century. But this situation was not free of risk. With a 9-to-1 ratio, even the most strictly controlled group might rebel. Slaves in Tobago proved no exception with uprisings in 1770 and 1798.

Amidst all of the battling for possession and economic supremacy, there was a serious concern among residents of the islands of the West Indies that no other island receive attention or benefits that might make it a successful rival. This competition that began in the colonial era continues as a legacy of colonialism and interferes even today in developing a lasting unity among the West Indies countries.

The pattern of claims and counter-claims, small invasions, and counter-invasions continued in Tobago until 1803, when the British took over the island from the French for the last time and finally kept it.

■ Tobago in the 19th Century

In 1834, at the time of Emancipation, Tobago was already in economic trouble. Despite all efforts, its financial decline continued throughout the 19th century. The **metaire system** was introduced as one means of sustaining the economy. Under this system, workers were not paid for their labor, but shared in the profits of the crop with the land owners. Everyone was highly invested in the success of the crops, which guaranteed a degree of social unity and stability because of the interdependence of worker and owner. Despite even this system, Tobago's economy declined further.

Politically, however, Tobago had an advantage over the nearby Crown Colony of Trinidad, because it had its own representative government. In the first part of the 19th century, Tobago's slave owners and the British government had clashed repeatedly over Britain's increasingly charitable attitude towards slavery. This attitude manifested itself in laws limiting the control and treatment of slaves by plantation owners and it was unwelcome in Tobago, at least by the elite.

In 1833, Britain placed Tobago, Grenada, St. Vincent, and Barbados under the rule of the Governor of Barbados in an attempt to reduce the cost of governing these small islands. Little changed. Tensions between Tobago and Britain continued, with planters refusing to give up control or grant rights to other islanders. In 1876, in the town of Roxborough, these tensions erupted in the **Belmanna Riots**.

Although Tobago had been in this loose political association with other islands since 1833, when Barbados separated from that union in 1885, Tobago made clear its interest in a future association with Trinidad. Britain was not adverse to a union of Trinidad and Tobago and subsequently offered Tobagoins two options for debate prior to taking action. First, Tobago and Trinidad could be joined under one government based in Trinidad or, second, Tobago might be annexed, but retain its own treasury and a subordinate legislature. Of course Tobago was more interested in the latter, especially where it related to their rights to collect taxes and expend funds.

Trinidad had nothing to gain from a closer association with bedraggled Tobago, but it was not given a choice. Tobago and Trinidad were politically associated, but Tobago retained its rights over internal fiscal affairs. As was their political habit, Tobagoins argued for the rights to further fiscal independence in this loose union. In response to Tobago's intransigence, Britain decided to bring the two islands more closely together rather than see the existing relationship fall apart. In 1898, Tobago and Trinidad were officially merged – financially and politically.

LOCAL LORE

A saying popular in Britain in the 19th century was to refer to someone being "as wealthy as a Tobago land owner," meaning someone who had money to burn. Acreage in Tobago had been grossly overestimated, and land was sold in Britain to people who never saw it and never profited from it. Sometimes the same lands were sold a few times over. Anyone who could throw away their money on an investment in Tobago obviously had cash to burn, hence the saying.

■ Trinidad in the 19th Century

With its political and administrative problems solved, Britain turned to addressing Trinidad's economic future. With the importation of agricultural slaves outlawed, Trinidad had to find other means of meeting its labor needs. Efforts to attract significant numbers of European settlers and colonists from other islands were unsuccessful. Never giving up, however, a strategy was devised for tapping an entirely new labor pool. Indentured laborers from China would be recruited. Initial efforts were successful and in the early 1800s over 300 Chinese workers arrived. Unfortunately, only men were recruited. Without their wives and families and largely shunned by other islanders, the men were not willing to stay.

Although it was illegal, ways were found to bring additional slaves to the island, but not in sufficient numbers to appreciably affect the agricultural labor pool. Despite labor shortages during this period, Trinidad progressed in its agricultural development, producing sugar, cotton, coffee, and cocoa, which was especially prized at the time.

In the years preceding the abolition of slavery, changing laws increasingly provided protection to the people forced into this degraded economic system of human ownership. But changing laws while keeping the basic system was not enough and, finally, with the **Emancipation bill of 1834**, slavery was abolished. Under this act, slaves were freed, but it was slave owners who were compensated for their losses. Compensation granted to slave owners in Trinidad was higher than in other West Indies islands because of the slaves' higher economic worth. Land in Trinidad was highly productive relative to other islands, therefore the loss of free labor had a greater financial impact.

While outright slavery was abolished, slaves were not yet really free. By law, there would be an apprentice period of several years during which freed slaves were required to work for their former masters at defined hours and wages. This obviously did not sit well with those who now considered themselves free, and in time the apprentices went on strike.

Other changes came with Emancipation. Britain had already had to solve the problem of non-white land ownership and voting rights. It had created Trinidad's Crown Colony status. With large numbers of freed persons of color, land ownership would have to be addressed all over again. A move was made to permit only large holdings ostensibly because large areas of land were necessary to make cane agriculture economically viable. This move had secondary benefits. It maintained a non-landholding labor pool dependent on plantation work for income. It also limited the size of the non-white landholding group to existing numbers.

Slaves for agricultural work had never been legally permitted to be imported to Trinidad so Emancipation was not the cause of labor shortage problems in Trinidad, but it did make existing shortages more severe. In response, a new labor recruitment plan was developed – India would be the new source of workers – and this labor program was successful. Between 1845 and 1917 almost 145,000 indentured Indian workers were brought to Trinidad to work in agriculture.

Correcting their previous recruitment errors with the Chinese, the Indian workers would be imported with all their cultural and social requisites. Trinidad would pay for transportation, provide medical services for the new arrivals, and police the newcomers during their time on the island.

For good or ill, indentured Indian workers were set apart from the mainstream in Trinidad. They had their own social service system, were governed by different laws, and they were physically isolated, tied as they were to particular estates. The initial assumption that they would return to India essentially left them out of consideration by the rest of the population. The result of this social isolation was that Indians initially made little adaptation to the local culture, though many aspects of their own culture were modified by their move from India.

Indian workers were transported without regard to caste and, on the estates, they were put to work as a group, again without regard to prior caste or class. Women, who did not enjoy high status in India at the time, were suddenly valued due to their relative scarcity. Workers came to Trinidad as individuals and marriage unions were no longer family affairs.

As part of its labor recruitment and management program, the British wrote laws governing everything related to immigrants and indentured workers. Reading these laws, one can't but feel they formed a whole new pattern of slavery. Plantation owners were granted protection from their workers and estate owners' responsibilities for providing work and remuneration were defined. Workers as well were given specific rights and responsibilities, but while provisions were made for adequate housing and working conditions, they were not enforced. Housing and sanitation facilities were extremely poor and illness was common, resulting in lost work hours. Wages for indentured workers were very low compared to other labor on the island and, with all the restrictions imposed on indentured workers, oftentimes their only viable option was passive resistance – work slowdowns and absences.

The grossly inadequate living conditions and lost work due to illness were often interpreted as evidence of the cultural characteristics of the Indians, not as their response to the appalling situation in which they labored. Indentured workers were blamed for the very conditions imposed on them.

Conditions were sufficiently intolerable that a large number of indentured workers opted to return to India when their servitude was completed. By law, return passage was to be paid for by the government. To avoid growing transportation expenses, it was decided to offer small plots of land to those who completed their indenture in exchange for return passage; usually they were given five to 10 acres. This decision was inadvertently one of the better and more lastingly favorable laws passed by the British because it developed a larger pool of non-white landowners. The land allotted for the Indians was usually based close to estate plantations as a way of providing an estate labor pool for the future, but it also gave them the opportunity to create communities with shared cultural values.

Though many of these new landowners opted to grow crops for local consumption, a sufficient number of them opted to plant sugarcane. They were successful enough in growing cane on their small plots to raise questions within the Crown Colony about the whole idea of a sugar plantation – that it had to be large and that a subclass of poorly paid workers was necessary to its economic success.

In time, Indians took their place among the more established ethnic and racial groups in Trinidad. With continued immigration and local births, at the turn of the century Indians made up fully one-third of the population, and their unique culture was having its impact on the overall culture of the island.

During the latter half of the 19th century, Trinidad's mix of people and races was dominated by upper-class whites whose behavior was emulated to one degree or another by most of the other groups. There was little mixing of races socially and even more rarely by marriage, though there was a middle class within each of the racial groups and they interacted comfortably in commerce. Though discrimination was an everyday affair, there was also a body of law developing to preclude outright racism, and there were educated members of the subgroups active in defending the rights of their own people. It must also be remembered that none of the social or racial groups in Trinidad, not even the top tier whites, enjoyed a political voice at that time.

Shortly before the turn of the century, in 1897, there was a collapse in the sugar industry throughout the West Indies. Sugar production in the Caribbean couldn't compete in a world market. It faced competition not only from countries with more fertile and more productive land, but Trinidad had also failed to keep up with developments in mechanization that improved yields. Britain's lack of concern for her Crown Colony was evidenced in the report produced by its commission sent out to study the problem. They recognized that sugar plantations had failed and recommended that islanders diversify.

Trinidad's Crown Colony status continued to preclude the development of island-based political and economic control, and why Britain held on is not very clear. There could not have been more than sparse economic benefits to the home country and there was not a large resident British population. Retaining the colony apparently became an end in itself.

■ The 20th Century

Trinidad and Tobago entered the 20th century as one country. Not long after, in 1910, oil was discovered in Trinidad. The country's value went from being a Crown Colony of little interest to one of the stars in the British colonial system. The new century brought other changes as well. After almost 100 years, the indenture system came to an end. Another change came with the end of World War I, when returning West Indian soldiers brought with them a new perspective of the world, of themselves, of their country, and their political rights. Out of these changes developed a movement for self-government and the creation of the Trinidad Labor Party. Change was not limited solely to Trinidad and Tobago, as the demand for political reform began to occur throughout the West Indies.

Voting rights were granted in 1925 under restrictive guidelines to some of the people of Trinidad & Tobago to elect a few of the people who would represent them. Along with these limited voting rights, 1925 brought the first election in Trinidad. The newly elected local officials, along with a group of appointees, acted as advisors to the British Governor, who still had ultimate control. It was not real political representation, but it was a beginning.

The year 1929 brought the sugar industry once again to the brink of bankruptcy, this time due largely to worldwide over-production and falling prices. Trinidad's cost of production was somewhere in the middle of overall producer costs, but Britain remained unwilling to commit financial support to Trinidad's sugar exports when it could buy sugar cheaper on the open market.

And time moved on. Though Trinidad's oil industry gave it the impression of a colony without the problems of other less resource-rich Caribbean colonies, that was far from an accurate picture. A 1937 British Commission sent to study problems in Trinidad and Tobago found an extremely low standard of living very common. The Commission recommended the construction of new housing and sanitation facilities, which were planned, but never built. People lived in squalor.

The Commission of 1937 was formed in response to disturbances in Trinidad that resulted not only from poverty, but from the absence of mechanisms by which labor could address its grievances. Labor had no legitimate voice and the result was as predictable as it was unfortunate. While sugar and oil production increased, other agricultural products failed and the economic division between the oil industry workers and agricultural workers widened. Slavery and the indenture system had guaranteed at least some rights to workers. With the advent of free labor, all rights were lost. The goodwill of the employer was the last and only resort for a worker.

In 1937 there was what could be called a general strike. A sit-down strike in the oil fields was the first spark. It resulted when police attempted to arrest an oil industry labor leader as he addressed the workers. Unrest and frustration was just below the surface and this event led to disturbances across the island.

Over the objections of Trinidadians, during World War II Britain granted permission to the United States to develop a naval base on the island. In exchange, Britain would receive warships from the United States. Chaguaramas was selected as the site, and the deal between Britain and the US was accomplished over the objection of even the British Governor of Trinidad and Tobago. The base was built under a 99-year lease agreement and became a long-term contentious issue between the US and Trinidad and Tobago, as well as adding one more strain to its relationship with Britain.

In 1946, Trinidad held its first election with universal suffrage. With little experience in the political process, no party won a majority and little was accomplished toward achieving the goals of reform and independence. Luckily, in the 1950s national spirit markedly grew in West Indian and other developing countries, and Trinidad and Tobago was no exception.

In 1956, a historically significant political conference led by Dr. Eric Williams launched the **People's National Movement** (PNM). This new party coalition, with its clearly presented political and social agenda, won a majority vote in the elections of that year and became Trinidad and Tobago's first party government. PNM held its dominant political position for 30 years, but it laid a solid foundation for a party system because of its acceptance of dissenting voices.

When PNM was created, whites held higher political offices and controlled the economy; blacks were in control of the civil service, police, nursing, and the army; and Indians predominated in agriculture. While there was not racial equity, there was equilibrium. Over time, PNM disturbed this balance and brought to the surface racial feelings formerly hidden in the status quo.

An Oxford-educated scholar and politician, Williams led the PNM with its ambitious and idealistic platform for reform. Their goals were to provide social services to all people in need as a "right," not as an act of kindness. They aimed to eliminate illiteracy with programs to promote education and centralize control of the schools, both public and private. They wanted not only to promote economic development, but to develop pride in their Caribbean culture – unifying the wide variety of races and cultures in Trinidad and Tobago. Williams also began with the goal of eliminating corruption with the aim of developing the political capabilities that would lead to a capacity for self-government.

PNM's economic goals were to diversify and enlarge the economic base in order to reduce income disparities and increase employment opportunities. As a nation, they needed also to develop internal food security and find ways to meet the basic needs of the population. Not focusing solely on more obvious economic development, they wished also to promote opportunities for exposure to the arts, culture, and recreational pastimes. Trinidad and Tobago had long been a dependency of Britain and it was going to be difficult to instill national pride and a real sense of nationhood in the population.

The next election took place in 1961 and PNM again won a majority with two-thirds of the seats in the general election. Their platform included political education, independence from Britain, morality in public affairs, equal rights for women, and a coalition of all races and religions. They looked forward to becoming an independent member of the British Commonwealth on August 31, 1962. Williams was elected as the country's first Prime Minister. He took office in 1962 and held the position until his death in 1981.

Williams was not naive in recognizing the extent of the problems they would have to overcome. Perhaps the most significant, widespread, and ingrained was the dependent colonial mentality and its attendant reluctance to make decisions and take risks. In the early years, Williams fostered a democratic mentality in the political process by dealing fairly with the press and with labor. He looked to political solutions rather than relying on the power of the police and military to maintain control. Unfortunately, Williams often relied on loyal party pals for advice, when he might more profitably have looked to individuals with genuine expertise, regardless of their political persuasion.

With its new measure of political sovereignty, Trinidad and Tobago moved toward a more practical conservative position in the next decade. Their economic survival was on the line and efforts were made to continue established international economic relationships. Even with this more conservative mood, Williams traveled extensively in Africa in 1964 and banned trade with South Africa in 1966. Side by side with these more liberal actions, Williams and PNM looked toward more paternalistic nations for relationships that would shore up Trinidad and Tobago's economy. Despite these efforts, by the early 1970s the rise in unemployment and political disaffection threatened the country's stability.

When PNM was formed, Trinidad and Tobago relied heavily on its single primary industry, oil. Though it is hard to believe, this lush country was a net importer of food and, despite investment in agriculture, with subsidies and infrastructure, little changed in the next 20 years. Manufacturing also played a very small role in the overall economy. Oil and its economic benefits created a solid resource base for Trinidad and Tobago, but the income derived from the industry created a skew in the economy. Those involved in the business of oil earned far more than those in other endeavors and there was a lack of drive to develop other parts of the economy when oil was so profitable. Oil has played a significant role in the economy, both positive and negative, and continues to do so today.

In the early years of PNM and independence, economic progress was marginal. The role played by the oil industry and by agriculture declined and manufacturing increased only slightly while imports of goods and services rose dramatically. The lack of progress in the economic sector was offset by liberal changes in social policies, such as changes in taxation which allowed some redistribution of income through subsidies for those with lower incomes.

As a measure of the changes in the quality of life for its people during these initial years of self-government, life expectancy rose by four years and there was a 60% decrease in infant mortality. Population growth slowed, but at 1.5% it remained high. Meanwhile, secondary school attendance rose from 24% to 70%. Some of these changes may have been responsible for the movement away from work in agriculture as people sought their piece of the pie in industry. As Indians predominated in agriculture and blacks in urban industry, movement of agricultural workers into urban communities opened areas of conflict between these two groups. And, if job opportunities are considered a measure of the quality of life, PNM failed. Unemployment was only 6% in 1956, but had risen to 15% by 1966 and to 17% by 1970.

None of the positive social changes occurred without attendant costs. Trinidad and Tobago's balance of payments required an increase in exports and a limit to the growth of imports. Investment had to focus on the long-term, not on expensive short-term quick fixes and the government had to find a way to promote profitable private investment.

PNM failed in its goal of eliminating corruption – it was rife throughout the party – and its aim of creating racial equality was more rhetoric than practice. Blacks dominated the political scene, whites retained their control of business and industry, while Indians did make some inroads in the government and commercial sectors.

The early 1970s brought severe social unrest. Following independence, people's expectations of rapid economic development had not been met, promises had not been kept, and there was widespread disaffection with PNM and with independence. In the **"February Revolution,"** thousands of workers joined by students took to the streets in protest and severely tested the political leadership and structure. In response, Williams brought more politically repressive techniques to the fore for the first time. The voice of the more radical press was silenced and labor strikes were banned. It now took police and military action to carry out the Prime Minister's policies, but PNM survived this social unrest and moved toward a more radical foreign policy.

During the next 10 years, Trinidad and Tobago took a more active role in establishing political and economic relationships with other nations. In 1972, Williams established relations with Cuba in a move away from dependence on their traditional, more conservative allies and trading partners and in the same era he personally visited both China and Moscow. PNM's economic policies in the 1970s favored a government-owned and directed economy requiring a 51% government ownership of all foreign investments.

The economic problems and resulting social unrest in the early '70s were magically resolved with windfall profits from the worldwide oil crisis. Shell Oil was purchased by the government and, with oil revenues, there was a move to reclaim other foreign-owned businesses. Changes in Trinidad and Tobago in the 1970s were remarkable. With profits from soaring oil prices, between 1973 and 1978 it loaned millions to other Caribbean countries. It took a leading role in Caribbean political and economic development and in 1976 became an Independent Republic with a fully democratic government. However, even with its move away from traditional economic relationships, in 1977 the United States was still its largest trading partner, consuming fully 74% of Trinidad and Tobago's exports.

In his book on the history of his country, Williams spoke proudly of the achievements of PNM that most significantly led to full internal self-government. After almost 20 years as Prime Minister, Williams died in 1981. The death of Williams and the precipitous decline in oil prices led Trinidad and Tobago toward new conservative policy directions in the 1980s.

In a book edited by Selwyn Ryan in 1987, Ryan rates PNM's overall performance in its 20-year dominance of politics. He gave it high marks for freedom of the press and judiciary, for political freedom especially to dissent, and to improved access to secondary and university education. On the down side, there was no progress in demonstrable cultural expression – no museums, no theater, no libraries. There was also no progress in overcoming the psyche of colonialism. All the resources devoted to education did not result in a more motivated and competent work force.

On Williams' death, the political power he wielded for so many years was up for grabs. Other political parties gained strength and in 1986, the National Alliance for Reconstruction was voted in over PNM, bringing Prime Minister Robinson into power. The 1980s brought serious economic problems following the 1970s boom and Trinidad and Tobago is only now recovering.

July of 1990 saw a coup attempt on the government of Trinidad and Tobago. The police station in Port of Spain was blown up and politicians, including the Prime Minister, were held hostage. Factions behind the coup were not widely supported in the populace and it was not successful. Normalcy returned shortly after and the government resumed its work. We discussed the coup attempt and its impact on the people of Trinidad and Tobago with friends in Port of Spain. Our impression is that their reaction was much like that of Americans following the bombing of the Federal building in Oklahoma City. We were outraged, but we did not fear a collapse of the government.

■ Looking Ahead

Trinidad and Tobago appears to be on very solid footing as it enters the 21st century. There is a stable democratic government and an improving economy. Divisiveness does still exist among workers, races, and classes, but it is one of the few countries where color matters less than character, where extremes of rich and poor are not prevalent, and where recovery from its colonial past is well underway.

Flora & Fauna

Trinidad and Tobago both provide extraordinary opportunities to explore nature in all its forms. There are over 400 species of birds, over 600 varieties of butterflies, monkeys, armadillos, caiman, lizards, over a hundred species of snakes, and a huge variety of fish and other marine life. All of these find homes in an astonishing variety of natural environments – saltwater and freshwater mangrove swamps, mountain and coastal rain forests, savannahs, coral reefs, deepwater caves, freshwater rivers, and city parks. There are over 2,300 varieties of flowering plants and it seems there are almost as many micro-climates to support them.

If you are staying in Port of Spain, you will have to travel by car to begin your hike or boat trip through natural preserves. Much of the terrain in Trinidad is rugged, though hiking to the more popular sites will not overly stress the average person. If you are looking for more adventure, though, it is easily found. On less traveled paths, the density of vegetation, the incline of the land, and the animal life you will encounter will provide all the excitement of a very genuine adventure. Some areas of Trinidad receive up to 120 inches of rain a year. With that much water and air temperatures in the 80s and 90s, plants grow phenomenally quickly.

Orchids in Tobago.

The natural environment in Tobago is more accessible than in Trinidad and the terrain is more gentle, less overpoweringly lush. This is not to say it is less entrancing. Bird song will accompany you throughout your days on this lovely island.

The terrain in Tobago begins as flatlands in the southwest with old coconut plantations, grasslands, and bush. The beaches are wonderful and the land has a gentle feel. As you travel east, especially on the Atlantic side of the island, the ocean and beaches become more wild and wind-swept. Mid-island, the land rises toward the east, culminating in the densely forested Main Ridge Forest Reserve. Each island has its attractions and neither should be missed.

■ Animals & Birds of Trinidad

The most unusual feature of Trinidad's natural environment is that it has not yet been packaged for tourism as have the natural wonders of some other countries – especially with the tourism industry's current marketing focus on eco-tourism. The environment here is right by the side of the road. Travel anywhere off the beaten track and you will be in midst of something truly wonderful.

The national bird of Trinidad is the **scarlet ibis**. One of the more popular excursions is a visit to the Caroni Swamp, where you will see thousands of scarlet ibis returning to roost for the night. There are two other internationally known bird sanctuaries in Trinidad that should not be missed – Asa Wright Nature Centre and the Pointe-à-Pierre Wildfowl Trust. We were told that it is not unusual for birders to add well over a hundred new species to their "life-list" during a short stay in Trinidad.

Unlike many of the forest animals that are common to both islands, **monkeys** are seen only in Trinidad. You may see howlers in the Nariva Swamp on the east coast or, oddly enough, at the Pointe-à-Pierre Golf Course on the west coast.

The armadillo, familiar to us in the States, is called a *tatoo* in Trinidad and Tobago, and it is considered a delicacy. You'll maybe see roadside stands advertising "wild meat," where *tatoo* will certainly be for sale. With its nocturnal habits, you probably won't see a *tatoo* unless you are in the bush at night. The animal we know as an opossum is called a *manicou* here, and wild pigs are called *quenk*.

The unusual **agouti** looks like a rodent and is about the size of a large cat. It eats fruits and vegetables and is very timid. While normally diurnal, it will become nocturnal if bothered during the day. Commercial farming of the agouti is being considered in Trinidad because the animal has long been hunted for food.

Snakes are common in Trinidad, and you'll find them in all sizes. There are even a few highly poisonous species – the bushmaster, pit viper, and two varieties of coral snake. Coming from a temperate climate where reptiles are less prevalent, we were surprised to see the wide variety of snakes in Trinidad and their common presence.

Behind the office desk at the Asa Wright Bird Sanctuary, where you might not expect it, is a terrarium with snakes. While we waited outside the office for the tour to begin, a worker came by and pointed up, laughing. Only a few feet over our heads was a resting tree snake. All curled up comfortably, taking the sun, it waited patiently for a head to drop onto. Thank goodness it wasn't mine!

Two of the more common flowering trees found in both Trinidad and Tobago are the **poui** and the **immortelle**. In January and February, you'll see the poui tree in bloom all over the islands in drier areas. Its delicate pink or yellow blooms do not last long, but they make a lovely show for the short time they are on the trees. With bright reddish-orange flowers, the immortelle stands out all over the hills. It was commonly planted amongst cocoa trees to provide shade.

■ Animals & Birds of Tobago

We did not begin our visits to T &T as avid bird watchers, but were seduced by the variety and beauty of all the birds we saw. Tobago is a bird watcher's heaven. You will hear bird songs all over the island, and will see a variety of birds, large and small. On any window ledge you can create a bird feeder with a little sugar or a banana. We made a birdbath for the tinier birds with a bowl of water, and it was endless joy to see hummingbirds, canaries, and parakeets dine and bathe.

The **cocrico** is the national bird of Tobago. Though not at all delicate, it is quite pretty, with a long tail, red feathers under the neck, and mahogany brown body. It's big and loud, and causes lots of trouble in the garden. We

Terrace visitor, Crown Point, Tobago.

laughed as the cocricos gossiped in the trees, sounding not unlike a shouting match in one of New York's neighborhoods.

One of the most interesting animals we found in Tobago was the "twenty-four-hour lizard" or **gommangalala** (you'll have to bear with us on the spelling). This unusual lizard is about 10-12" long, lives in trees, and is harmless until molested, when it will drop onto you and stick to your skin for 24 hours. After that it simply falls off (or so we were told). We saw lots of them at Englishman's Bay. Bring some sweet bread to feed them; they are quite friendly.

There are no poisonous snakes in Tobago, but watch for the "coco police" who live on cocoa trees and guard the chocolate pods.

■ Leatherback Turtles

Beaches in Trinidad and Tobago are nesting sites for the extraordinary and rare leatherback turtles. This largest species of marine turtle has been on the endangered list since the 1950s. Weighing over a half ton, females ready to lay eggs return to the beach of their birth from March through August. Arriving in the night and using their fins to dig a nest in the soft sand, each turtle will lay up to 100 eggs in under two hours. After covering the nest, these creatures, cumbersome on land, make their way to the sea again. The nest will protect the eggs during the two months they need to develop, when the emerging hatchlings will make their dash to the sea. Few will survive long enough to return.

In our world today there are many, far too many, endangered animals and plants. Luckily for some of the endangered animals and plants, we have found a self-interest in fighting for their preservation. The leatherback should, if it is not already, be in this lucky group. The major food supply for these turtles is jellyfish, especially the dangerous and proliferating Portuguese man-of-war. Anyone stung by one of these jellyfish should have a strong motivation to act on behalf of the leatherback. Those of us who have not been so unfortunate might find more altruistic reasons for respecting the life patterns of the leatherback. Seeing them in the act of creation is wondrous, but how would you feel seeing the last?

Leatherback turtles are extremely shy creatures. Their nesting behavior is instinctual, but any disturbance can break this pattern. They have been known to turn back to the sea before laying their eggs if the beach has been artificially lit. Nonetheless, they are a marvel to see and you can observe them by taking certain precautions. **Stay at least 50 feet away from a nesting turtle, and be very quiet. Use no artificial lights until the turtles have disappeared into the ocean.** Let your eyes naturally adjust to the darkness. Since nesting occurs during the dry season the night sky will not usually be overcast. As your night vision develops, you'll be able to see well without disturbing these magnificent creatures.

In Tobago, turtles nest on the Caribbean side of the island from March to August. Stone Haven Bay and Great Courland Bay beaches are good sites for observing the turtles as they arrive to lay their eggs anytime after dark. If you are staying at the Turtle Beach Hotel, the staff will let you know when a turtle is arriving. Otherwise, you can take your chances sitting on the beach in the evening, which is a nice thing to do in the good company of friends. Bring snacks and soft drinks and be prepared to wait. It is well worth your while.

AUTHOR TIP

In Trinidad, some of the beaches on the northeast coast have restricted access during turtle season. Contact the Forestry Department in Port of Spain, ☎ 622-3217, for permission to visit.

EARTHWATCH

Unfortunately, under the guise of eco-consciousness, leatherbacks have become featured attractions at some hotels. Hotel staff organize large group tours on the beach at night to see the turtles. Visitors are encouraged not only to approach the turtles, but to take turns touching them; bright lights are provided to allow everyone to take home a photo of the event. Most of the people engaged in exploiting these wondrous animals in their most fragile moments market themselves and their facilities as "ecologically involved." They are anything but. We hope you won't be fooled by their marketing ploys.

■ Coconuts

You may wonder, as we have, what is done with all the coconuts, especially if you've visited Manzanilla and Mayaro in Trinidad. You have part of the answer if you've had a fresh coconut served to you for its cool, wonderful water. These are green coconuts, and the familiar white coconut meat has not fully developed inside. Aside from its wonderful flavor, coconut water is extremely nutritious and is widely prescribed by doctors in Trinidad and Tobago as a drink for recuperating patients.

Drier coconuts with a brown husk provide not only the coconut shredded for desserts, but also a less well-known product called copra. Producers of copra wait until the dried coconuts fall to the ground naturally. The nuts are gathered, split with machetes, and laid out to dry in the sun, usually for two or more weeks. The dried coconut, now called copra, is collected and sold to processors in Trinidad who will produce coconut oil, soap, and animal feed. A 100-pound bag with approximately 100 dried coconuts will sell for just under $20, which makes this a very labor-intensive process.

■ Cocoa

Throughout Trinidad and in the Roxborough area of Tobago you'll see small, bushy trees with shiny, rusty-green leaves. Hanging from many of their branches and trunks will be yellow, purple, red, and brown pods, ranging in length from six to eight inches. This is chocolate. Or at least this is its beginning, cocoa.

In Trinidad, the heaviest concentration of cocoa estates are found in Toco, Paria, and Blanchisseuse, but cocoa can be found anyplace where there is an abundance of water. You will almost always find the orange-flowering immortelle tree growing among the cocoa, providing needed shade.

Cocoa has a long history in Trinidad and Tobago. Historically, chocolate was prized and cocoa plantations were highly profitable. Unfortunately, cocoa is tricky to grow, and crop failures were significant. In time, cocoa became a less fashionable agricultural crop, though it is still produced on a small scale in Trinidad.

From my point of view – I'm a chocolate lover also interested in plants – cocoa is an oddity. The large many-colored pods grow right from the main trunk, as well as from the branches. Where have you seen anything like that? Cocoa grows in dense rain forest and looks like it competes successfully with other plants, yet cocoa does not often take well to artificial fertilizers. Fallen leaves are left beneath the tree to keep the ground cool, yet the plant grows well in the tropics where cool is just a state of mind.

Cocoa pods are harvested from October to March. Pods are picked, split open, and wrapped in banana leaves for four to six days. After aging in the banana leaves, the fruit inside the pods is harvested and moved to the cocoa house, where it will dry in the sun for six to seven days. The ingeniously designed cocoa house has a movable roof, which sits on wheels and slides lengthwise off the building, like a sliding door. The cocoa is placed on the floor just under the roof and sits in the sun all day. In the evening workers slide the roof back into place over the beans, keeping evening dew or rain from dampening the drying beans.

Once the beans are aged and dried, "dancing the cocoa" will begin. The cocoa beans are given a touch of water or oil, and the workers begin the dance. Using their feet, they move the beans against each other until they are polished. Dancing the beans makes them shine, and glistening cocoa beans bring more profit. A good price for dried cocoa beans right now in Trinidad is a little over $1/kilo. The old cocoa estate plantations are great places to see flocks of green parrots. They love to eat cocoa as much as we do.

■ Special Plants

Seen in Tobago, but more common in Trinidad, **cashew trees** not only produce our favorite nuts, they do so in a very interesting way. When it was described to us that, "the nut is separate from the fruit," we didn't really get the idea. But it's true. The tree bears reddish-yellow, very soft fruits. At the end of each fruit is one cashew, so you now see why they are so expensive. As you're traveling around with a guide, ask him/her to point out a cashew tree. They are really quite marvelous.

Ginger lilies, common on both islands, are large-leaved, four-foot-tall plants with dangling stems of luscious pink flowers. The plant's roots are used for ginger beer and ginger ale.

Manchineel trees, often found growing by beaches, are highly poisonous. You are more likely to see them in Tobago because you'll usually be visiting beaches, so keep an eye out. Contact with the tree, its leaves, or fruits will result in very painful blistering. Oftentimes trees will be marked with a warning, but pay attention. To get a better idea of what they look like, watch for them on the left side of the road as you are heading into Pigeon Point in Tobago.

In Trinidad, if you travel south of Port of Spain, you will see **sugarcane** fields. We found it interesting that this prolific plant grows with no pesticides, only fertilizer. Cane is harvested every six months. Oddly, the fields are first burned, then the cane is cut and hauled to the sugar refineries. Refuse is left on the ground and in a short while the next season's cane begins to sprout. Fertilizer is added and the crop is on its way again.

The **buffalo tree**, which you will see in the Main Ridge Forest Reserve in Tobago, is very soft when felled and was used to make dugout canoes in times past.

■ Plants For Medicinal Purposes

Both Trinidad and Tobago have a wealth of beneficial plants. Each time we have visited we have spoken with one of the locals about these old-time cures. With the renewed interest in natural medicines, we thought you might find this information interesting.

Aloe, long known for its skin-soothing qualities, may also be used as an intestinal curative, providing relief from constipation, and for neutralizing an irritated bladder. Eaten in their natural state, **pumpkin seeds** are used to rid the intestines of parasites. The **paw paw** is a fruit useful for dieters, as its ingredient, papain, is said to help the body burn calories more quickly. Like aloe, it is also useful for constipation and, when mixed in a juice with sour orange, it will help reduce high blood pressure. Ordinary **carrots** are a curative for kidney and bladder problems and as a treatment for lower intestinal parasites. **Cherries**, which contain malic acid, are useful as a gargle to loosen phlegm. Applied to the skin as a paste, **turmeric** will rid you of irritating skin problems, like ringworm and eczema. Lime juice and turmeric mixed together and used as a poultice will provide soothing relief to aching joints. The lovely **hibiscus** is used as a treatment for colds and to relieve menstrual cramps.

These are just a few of the "cures" that we found listed in the *MotMot Times*. While in Trinidad and Tobago, if medicinal plants interest you, ask anyone for their favorite treatment and you'll learn a lot more. If you've got the time, send us a letter with what you've learned. We're always looking for more ideas.

Music

You can't mention Trinidad and Tobago without talking about its music, because it is a vital part of the culture and so integrated in the everyday lives of its people. Among the wide variety of musical forms are two internationally known and lauded musical styles – calypso and steel band. Both calypso, which is an older art form, and the 20th-century creation, steel band, have their origins in Trinidad and Tobago.

Although calypso and steel band music became well known throughout the world in the latter half of the 20th century, rhythmic music has a long history in Trinidad and Tobago. Both Africans and Indians contributed their own drums and rhythms, but together the mélange of sounds became something quite new.

As in any culture, the unique music here did not develop overnight; it has a long and involved history. Following Emancipation in the 19th century, freed slaves joined in the celebration of Carnival for the first time. They brought their drums and a more riotous character to the event, which of course sparked a reaction among the elitist land owners, who had always been the exclusive participants in Carnival. Efforts were made to level out the exuberance of the new celebrants and, eventually, in 1883, the use of drums in Carnival was banned.

Denied the use of drums, the common people searched for new rhythmic instruments and developed a style called Tambour-bamboo, played with varying forms of cut bamboo. The bass drum was a hollowed piece of bamboo about five feet long. Struck on paved ground, the bass established a deep rhythm. A foot-long piece of bamboo was held in each hand and struck together to create a counterpoint rhythm. This instrument was called the *foulé*. The third essential piece of bamboo was long and thin, and, resting on the shoulder, it was struck with a piece of hard wood. Called the "cutter," it tied the sounds of the other two together. Though the people were prevented from using traditional drums, Tambour-bamboo allowed a continuation of the rhythmic dominance of music in Carnival. It, too, was eventually banned, which led directly to the development of steel band music. With the advent of steel band as the new musical form for Carnival, the playing of Tambour-bamboo all but died out, though once in a while you may still be lucky enough to hear it performed.

In 1890, string bands were introduced to Carnival, bringing to the music a Spanish flavor from Venezuela. Instruments included guitars, the cuatro (a four-stringed guitar), mandolins, banjos, flutes, violins and maracas. Among upper-class revelers, these bands were very popular as an accompaniment to calypso singers. This music became known as **parang**, and its Spanish songs are still vital today. Oddly enough, it is now heard throughout Trinidad only during the two months before Christmas.

■ Steel Bands

History

Steel band, or pan, music developed in the Laventille and Picton areas of Port of Spain in the 1930s. A ban had been placed on public use of the bamboo instruments traditional to Carnival processions because the bamboo was more often used to pound heads than rhythms. With a deep need to make music, all sorts of things were tried as alternatives. Steel drums, later called pans, finally evolved as the instrument of choice. Due to an active oil and gas industry, there was an abundance of surplus and discarded oil drums. Used whole or in smaller parts, the pans were tuned and notes were played with skill.

DID YOU KNOW?

The steel pan has the distinction of being the only non-electronic instrument introduced in the 20th century.

Initial public reaction to pan music was not favorable. It was perceived as a musical form of the lower classes and considered inferior. With the support of a few very insightful politicians, a ban of pan music was averted, and eventually public acceptance grew. As with tambour-bamboo, steel band instruments come in three basic forms – the tenor pan, which carries the melody; the kittle, providing harmony; and the boom, which sets the rhythm.

It took three decades for public acceptance of pan music to reach a point where, in the 1960s, Prime Minister Eric Williams was able to encourage corporate and business sponsorship of steel bands. Williams had the foresight to find a way for anyone who wished to be in a band to do so. This proved especially insightful, as disadvantaged youths who might have found less appealing means for self-expression could now be part of something wonderful. By the early 1970s there were as many as 200 steel bands in Trinidad and Tobago, each averaging 25 members, though some had many more.

In Trinidad and Tobago steel bands are now everywhere, with five to a hundred members playing everything from soul-stirring solos to calypsos, pop tunes, and symphonies. The old oil drum has evolved; pans are now shiny with chrome and professionally tuned. You will hear steel band performances wherever you are in Trinidad and Tobago.

The Woodbrook Playboyz steel band.

Steel Bands at Carnival

Steel band is an essential part of Carnival, as well. Their music is the catalyst that keeps everyone dancing in the streets for hours, and steel bands also have their days to shine in Carnival competitions. Band members practice long nights for months and compete with other bands many times before the final judging at Panorama.

As in all Carnival competitions, Panorama sets high standards and has a surprising number of rules governing performances. For instance, each group plays for exactly 10 minutes and is penalized if their presentation is shorter or longer. The calypso songs that bands choose to perform are usually written specifically for the pan, allowing better exploration of the melody, but the music must also be written in the same year as the competition.

During the weeks of pre-Panorama competitions, the songs evolve in response to the reception they receive. In such a short time, and with so many people involved, a system for revising and relearning the music developed. Especially in large bands, the music arranger teaches section leaders the music, and they in turn teach the individuals in their sections. Surprisingly, much of pan music is played by ear, not only by individual musicians, but also by arrangers. The arranger for the band **Phase II** is well known for his talent and works entirely by ear, as he has no formal musical training.

We went to see the popular pan group, the **Amoco Renegades**, on Charlotte Street in downtown Port of Spain a few weeks before Carnival. Like many other steel bands, the Renegade's "pan yard," or practice area, has stadium seating for visitors, a snack bar, and hundreds of pans. Musicians arrived in what seemed a helter-skelter way, but before long, almost magically, everyone was in place and the music began. You may not hear a song completed in these practice sessions, but attending one prior to Carnival will give you a sense of the commitment the band members make to their music and the artfulness and organizational skills of the directors. We were very impressed. You can visit pan yards almost any evening around 9 PM or later.

PAN YARDS

Here is a list of pan yards to visit. Watch for all sorts of special events in the yards just before Carnival week.

- **Amoco Renegades**, 138 Charlotte St., Port of Spain.
- **Neal & Massy Trinidad All Stars**, 46 Duke St., Port of Spain.
- **BWIA (BWee) Invaders**, 147 Tragarete Rd., Woodbrook.
- **Phase II Pan Groove**, Roxy Roundabout, St. James.
- **Witco Desperadoes**, Laventille Rd., Laventille, Port of Spain.
- **Exodus**, St. John's Village, Eastern Main Rd., St. Augustine.

AUTHOR TIP

*If you are especially interested in steel pan music, here is a great opportunity to learn and see more. Contact **Hayden Browne** through his sister at ☎ 637-9513. Hayden not only plays steel pan, but will take you to his uncle's shop where the instruments are made and tuned. There you will see pans being made or tuned for Phase II and Starlift, among others. Hayden is articulate in explaining both the music and the instruments. Later, he will take you on a tour of some of the more popular pan yards, where you will hear the music being played. He will be a great resource in answering all your questions. Hayden is delightful and knowledgeable, and has an obvious love for steel pan music.*

Types of Instruments

In case you are like us and want to understand the music in order to fully appreciate it, here is some background on steel pan instruments. These are the types of pans and the part they play in producing the overall sound:

Tenor pan . . . . carries the melody
Double tenor pan . . . . harmony with melody

```
Alto pan . . . . . . . . . . . . . . . . . . . . maintains rhythm
Guitar pan . . . . . . . . . . . . . . . . . . . maintains rhythm
Cello pan . . . . . . . . . . . . . . . . . . . . maintains rhythm
Bass pan and tenor bass pan . . . . . . . . . carries the bass line
Drum sets . . . . . . . . . . . . . . . . . . . . . . add scratches
Iron . . . . . . . . . . . . . . . . . . . . . . . . . . drum brakes
```

Tenor pans with holes are experimental and have a lighter sound, more like an echo. Today, some pans are chromed to beautify and preserve them, but that process also modifies the sound.

DID YOU KNOW?

Like pianos, pans need to be tuned once a year; the cost of tuning is based on the number of notes. Each pan or group of pans carries 28 to 32 notes.

■ Calypso

In the United States and elsewhere in the world, calypso enjoyed a heyday of popularity; it was a musical style that made one think of warm climates and easy living. In the 1950s, many of the most popular songs in the States were adaptations of calypsos written in Trinidad. The Andrews Sisters popularized one, called *Rum and Coca-Cola*, which was written by a Trinidadian calypso artist who received no compensation for this work until he took them to court.

History

Calypso has a long history and is still a very vital part of the music scene. The calypsonian is the town crier of politics, the gossip of the neighborhood, the commentator on everything that's happening and everyone that's making it happen. From the neighborhood, to national and international politics, to the people in the audience, or to anyone who calls their attention, no one is safe from the witty, sharp tongue of the calypso singer.

Traditionally, calypso always has been more about words than music; the heart of it is commentary. Cultural sources for calypso are many and there is no doubt slave communication was one antecedent. In fact, the West African word **kaiso** is now sometimes substituted for calypso in Trinidad. In the late 18th century, French settlers had their slaves sing extemporaneous songs to entertain guests. These songs typically flattered the owners and satirized their enemies. This type of entertainment may have evolved naturally from the slaves' own West African tradition of singing songs of witty commentary.

Before and continuing after Emancipation, stick-fighting matches were a common way to let off steam in Trinidad and, of course, there had to be music. In form, this music called for the participation of the audience, a singer perhaps providing the verse and the audience the chorus. These songs too, were sharp-tongued comments about one and all. Whatever its many sources, calypso is still today a vehicle for expression – a means by which a people find their voice.

Calypso Today

Calypso is also a vital part of today's Carnival tradition, as singers compete for the formal title of **Calypso Monarch**. To win the title, the song must be new, written by the performer, and its verses must fit within the structure that defines calypso. These songs are often highly political, and no topic is too hot to touch. Social commentary, humor, biting anger hidden in the stylish turn of a phrase – all are characteristics of calypso.

The runner-up for Calypso Monarch in 1999 was **Sugar Aloes**. His song, *This Stage is Mine*, caused a major ruckus in Trinidad, as it was particularly critical of the Prime Minister's wife. Whether the song was truly in bad taste or simply an unappreciated truth-telling, calypsonians have always been in trouble with the law, or at least with the elite, and this was no different. Aloes' song was very popular throughout Trinidad.

Singing Sandra, named Calypso Monarch in 1999, is one of only two women ever to win this title. The songs she sang for the competition were political and social, commenting on poverty and racism, but they were also theatrical, as is the tradition for calypsonians. Their songs, their dress, and their theatrics are all part of the performance. Even their names are part of the show: Chieftain Douglas, Atilla the Hun, Lord Executor, Roaring Lion, Lord Invader, Growling Tiger, and Mighty Zebra, to name a few.

Calypsonians also have a chance to earn a second title during Carnival, that of **Road March King**. This title goes to the writer of the song that is the most popular music for dancing and parading in Carnival. In response to the parading crowd's need for stronger rhythms and simpler lyrics, these songs have evolved into a new musical form called **soca**. Based on dance rhythms and volume, this is definitely party music. Not remaining static, Soca has incorporated Indian musical themes to become **chutney soca**. Still not satisfied with their accomplishments, musicians in Trinidad are now combining their oral and musical traditions with that of rap in the United States, creating **rapso**.

Apart from Carnival competition performances, calypsonians sing in what are locally called tents. While tents were originally used for calypso presentations, today performances are given in halls of all sizes, and audiences remain an active part of the evening's entertainment. As they respond to the calypsonian's verses, the singer must create a response right there. Hopefully the audience is pleased and won't be tossing toilet paper toward the stage. One of the most popular tents is a music hall called **Spektakula Forum**, on Henry Street in the center of Port of Spain. If you are in Trinidad you must spend an evening at a performance of this wonderful music.

CALYPSO TENTS

Here are just a few of the calypso tents to visit, where you will be thoroughly entertained:

- **Spektakula,** Henry Street, Port of Spain.
- **Calypso Revue,** SWWTU Hall, Wrightson Road, Port of Spain.
- **Kaiso House,** NUGFW Hall, Henry Street, Port of Spain.

Planning Your Trip

■ Banks & Money

The value of the TT$ floats in the international currency market and the exchange rate varies. At press time, it was running at about $6.18 TT to $1 US for traveler's checks exchanged at banks. Sometimes US dollars will get you more TT dollars than traveler's checks, sometimes less.

While it is almost always better to use traveler's checks for security, you can comfortably pay with US dollars in many places. Since the exchange rate for dollars usually is less than for travelers checks, your purchases will end up costing a little more. It ends up being just a few cents per dollar and for the convenience, it's often worth it. Hotels will almost always quote prices in US dollars for accommodations and you can readily pay with traveler's checks or credit cards.

Credit cards are welcomed for most major expenses. Check ahead of time to see which of your cards will give you a more favorable exchange rate. Of the two cards we have used in Trinidad and Tobago, one saved us a few dollars on each transaction and you can guess which one we use now. Charges you make in Trinidad and Tobago will appear on your credit card bills almost immediately, which is not always the case when you make credit card purchases while abroad.

Exchanging traveler's checks in Trinidad is most convenient in Port of Spain, where there are many banks from which to choose. All are open from 8 AM to 2 PM, Monday through Thursday, and 8 AM to noon and 3 to 5 PM on Fridays. Generally, there are not long lines so it goes fairly quickly. Should you run short of cash, you will find banks in almost all towns.

To exchange traveler's checks in Tobago, it is usually more convenient to use **Republic Bank** at Crown Point Airport. It is open from 8 AM to 3 PM Monday through Thursday and, on Friday, hours change to 8 AM to 1 PM and 3 to 5 PM. They are closed on weekends and holidays. Republic has two locations in Scarborough on Main and Carrington Streets and there are several other banks there as well. All have similar hours, but parking is a problem. Hotels will almost always exchange traveler's checks for you, but the rate will not be as good as at the bank.

AUTHOR TIP

Exchanging money at the bank is a problem if you are staying in the northeastern end of the island; there are no banks there, so plan ahead.

■ Climate

Trinidad & Tobago is relatively close to the equator and could be oppressively hot, but it's not. Tempered by cooling trade winds, the average year-round temperature in Trinidad is 83°F or 29°C. In Tobago, the average daily temperature is 84° and 74° at night. If your hotel room has good cross ventilation and screens, you'll be able to enjoy the cooling night time breezes and forget all about air conditioning; you won't need it.

CAUTION

The sun is very strong in this part of the world, so you'll need a good sunscreen; also remember to drink lots of water.

Both islands have distinct **dry and rainy seasons**, though rain does sometimes fall during the dry season which is January through May. Rain will come on fast and leave just as quickly, but for a few moments it's a refreshing break from the sun. Rainy season begins in June and lasts

View across the rolling hills, Belle Garden, Tobago.

through December. These months tend to be cooler than the dry season, which is hottest in April and May.

Trinidad and Tobago differ in annual **rainfall** and even within these small islands, rainfall differs significantly from place to place. Some areas are lush year-round, with an average of 90 inches of rainfall. Others are quite dry, like the grasslands in Tobago. A visit to either island in spring will provide you with lots of greenery to see, but not as much as a rainy season visit.

Trinidad and Tobago are both out of the vulnerable Caribbean hurricane belt, which makes planning your vacation fairly secure. There have been only three hurricanes to hit Tobago in the recorded history of the island. The last of these occurred in 1963, and it was very destructive.

■ Crime

Unlike many areas of the world, Trinidad and Tobago is not a dangerous place. It is in fact surprisingly free of crime and unpleasant human interactions. It is not as safe as it once was, but what is? When Tobagoins talk of their idyllic past it seems a fantasy land. They complain of changes and make comments like, "You can't leave a camera on the beach anymore while you go to lunch." Are they kidding?

There is more crime in Trinidad than in Tobago because of its population density and more urban development. Still, we found it to be a very friendly and safe place to travel.

Crime has become a problem for all of us and our awareness of the potential for problems has made us sometimes overly cautious. Take the precautions you would at home and you will have no problems at all. Don't leave your camera on the beach while you go to lunch, don't leave money and valuables in your hotel room (check them at the desk), and don't walk alone in lonely dark areas. If someone should pester you with something to sell or for any other reason, make it clear in simple vocal terms that you are not interested and go on with your business. Use only registered guides and check that their licenses are up to date.

While we feel Tobago to be especially safe relative to many places, increasing tourism and the gulf between the simple life on the island and the affluence of tourists has led to some problems in popular visitor sites. We recommend that you go in groups of two or more or with a guide to the following areas: Grafton Bird Sanctuary, the rain forest trails, waterfalls, forested areas, deserted beaches, and Sunday School. When leaving your rental car it should always be locked and valuables put out of sight. If you don't give someone a reason to break into your car, they won't. You need not be concerned that your car will suffer any external damage in your absence; a case of petty vandalism would be very unusual in Tobago.

We are not very comfortable writing about crime in Trinidad and Tobago because we found it such a safe and friendly environment. People were always helpful and kind. Let's hope that visitors to these islands don't encourage or invite a change in the islanders' very civilized and generous traditions.

A very good pamphlet providing safety information was written by the Tobago House of Assembly, and is available in Tobago's tourism offices at the airport and at NIB mall in Scarborough.

It is a crime to be publicly nude (or partially nude for women) anyplace in Trinidad and Tobago, including beaches.

■ Drugs

Recreational drugs are illegal in Trinidad & Tobago, as they are around the world. However, here the police do not turn a blind eye as they do in many places. Foreigners are prosecuted the same as locals, the sentences are stiff, and the prisons unattractive, to say the least. Do not even think about trying to carry drugs out of the country; inspections of departing visitors can be very thorough.

■ Embassies

The area code in Trinidad and Tobago is 868.

AMERICAN: Embassy of the United States, 15 Queen's Park West, Port of Spain. ☎ 622-6371.

CANADIAN: High Commission for Canada, 3-3A Sweet Briar Rd., St. Clair, Port of Spain. ☎ 622-6232.

BRITISH: High Commission for United Kingdom and Northern Ireland, 19 St. Clair Ave., St. Clair. ☎ 622-2748.

GERMAN: Embassy of the Federal Republic of Germany, 7-9 Marli St., Newtowne. ☎ 628-1630.

DUTCH: Embassy of the Kingdom of the Netherlands, 3rd Floor, Life of Barbados Building, 69-71 Edward St., Port of Spain. ☎ 625-1210.

■ Equipment To Bring

BICYCLES (Tobago) – Much of Tobago is perfect for riding, though with the poor road conditions, a mountain bike is definitely a plus. You'll need to keep the climate in mind, make sure to drink enough water, and use a good sunscreen. Bikes can be rented on the island for about $7/day. Though the quality of what's available is improving, if you love your own bike, bring it.

Airlines charge about $45 to ship a bike each way from the US to the Caribbean. Air Caribbean now charges about $16 to transport a bike box weighing up to 66 lbs between Trinidad and Tobago. You can put two bikes in one box and still be under the weight limit.

BINOCULARS (both Trinidad and Tobago) – These are a must if you're a bird watcher, but wonderful for everyone else too. You can watch sailboats and fishermen come in to harbor and see the small animals and birds that are so abundant in Trinidad & Tobago.

CAMERAS AND FILM (both Trinidad and Tobago) – Above and below the water you'll find a wealth of shots to take. Please first ask permission if you want to take photos of local people. Don't neglect to bring fast film because many of the locations where you will be taking photographs will be deeply shaded by foliage. Underwater cameras can often be rented at dive and snorkeling shops.

COOKING TOOLS (Tobago) – If you'll be staying at a hotel or guest house with kitchen facilities or renting a house, you may want to bring your favorite wooden spoon, a knife sharpener, and a good frying pan.

SNORKEL, MASK AND FINS (Tobago) – These are available for rent on a daily basis for about $7, but it's great to have your own at hand when the mood strikes. The quality of equipment you might own yourself is likely to be superior to what you'll find commonly available for rent. If you wish to purchase the equipment in Tobago, stop by Mt. Irvine Watersports shop (see *Guide Services*, page 219).

LAMP SHADES (Tobago) – Your authors' pet peeve. In some of the smaller, less expensive hotels and guest houses, you'll find bare light bulbs, which are awful to look at and impossible to read by. The problem is easily solved if you bring Japanese or Chinese paper lanterns to soften the light and cut the glare.

■ Expenses

There is a wide variety of hotel styles here, from posh to primitive. One thing you won't find is noticeable friction between visitors and locals. That means you are free to select a hotel and go about the islands finding local restaurants and seeing the sights. You need not feel concern that you will run into something unpleasant when you leave your hotel. So, rent a car, visit the sights, stop for a snack, laze on a deserted beach, and settle in for dinner at a place you find appealing. Be at home.

For all this freedom, you'll find yourself spending less than you might have spent if you stayed in a fully enclosed resort, and you'll be having more fun.

Trinidad and Tobago are still bargains by Caribbean standards. With tourism just now developing, there is much competition for your business and bargaining is as worthwhile as it is entertaining.

ESTIMATED DAILY EXPENSES
Dinner for two at an average restaurant . . . . $40 to $80
Mid-range hotel for two . . . . $50 to $125
Car rental and gas. . . . . $40 per day
Taxi (private) . . . . $4 per trip

NOTE: *Expenses in this book are given in*
US dollars unless otherwise noted.

■ Health

EMERGENCIES: If you should have a serious medical problem, return to your native country as soon as possible for treatment. You will be more comfortable and familiar with the medical system at home. Minor problems can be handled locally. Ask at your hotel for the physician they recommend. Usually they will have a doctor on call who is comfortable dealing with foreigners.

The **Port of Spain General Hospital** (☎ 623-2951/52/53) is at 169 Charlotte St., right in the downtown area. Hopefully, you will never have to use it.

The **Tobago County Hospital** is in Scarborough, ☎ 639-2551.

PRESCRIPTIONS: If you take prescription medicine, bring a good supply in labeled bottles. Pharmacies in Trinidad and Tobago are required to have physician's written prescriptions before selling regulated medicines.

SEX: If you might be sexually active while in Trinidad & Tobago, bring along a good supply of condoms. If you have them on hand you are much more likely to use them. You don't want to bring home an unattractive souvenir or pass one along yourself. AIDS is a serious problem in Trinidad and Tobago and you should not take the possibility of exposure lightly. There is now an **AIDS hot line** open 8 AM to 8 PM at ☎ 625-2437. Donations currently cover the costs of being open these hours. Coordinator Helena Joseph or Miya will answer your call and will give you help with an HIV-friendly doctor, information on support groups, referrals, confidential testing, and comfort. They will most sincerely appreciate any donations. Their goal is to be open 24 hours a day. Donations may be mailed to the following address: National Aids Hot Line, PO Bag 472, Woodbrook, Port of Spain, Trinidad & Tobago, West Indies.

SUNBURN: The sun in this part of the world will burn you much faster than you think. Bring a good sunblock and use it liberally; you'll still get a tan, you just won't look fried.

■ Immigration & Customs

Although we have heard of travelers encountering problems while clearing customs, we have never experienced any ourselves. Customs and immigration officers in Trinidad and Tobago seem professional, though the process is very slow, especially in Tobago, compared with other countries we've visited.

You are allowed to bring a carton of cigarettes, one quart of liquor per person, and about $200 worth of gifts into Trinidad and Tobago without paying duty. Books, new or used, make great gifts for the library in Scarborough, Tobago.

To avoid confiscation of any fruit, vegetables, plants, or seeds you may wish to take back home, contact the Plant Quarantine Officers at the Botanic Station in Scarborough, ☎ 639-2234, or at Crown Point Airport, ☎ 639-0634. They will answer your questions and give you written permission for any approved materials.

For US citizens returning to the States, the duty-free allowance is $400, but we'd be surprised if you can find that much to buy.

■ Maps

Unless you are looking for some very specialized maps, tourist maps are adequate for getting around. There just aren't that many roads to choose from on either Trinidad or Tobago, and few of the roads are sign-posted anyway.

■ Newspapers

Newsday and two other dailies – *The Guardian* and *The Express* – are widely available and many people read at least two. There are also a number of weeklies, such as *Punch*, *Heat*, and *Mirror*, which provide local gossip, lots of pictures of women in bathing suits, and sensational news, if you miss your source for this information back home.

■ Religion

Religions in Trinidad and Tobago are as varied as its people. Almost a third of the population is Catholic, descendants of the French and Spanish; 24% is Hindu; 6% are Muslim (people of both Indian and African heritage); 11% are Anglican, demonstrating the British influence here; and the rest are protestant with several evangelical groups. Finally, there are some traditional African faiths still practiced. One of these is Orisha, a tradition maintained by the Yoruba people.

■ Special Interest Groups

Organizations and associations supporting specific interests:

D.R.E.A.M., ☎ 636-8986; distance running.

Heritage Committee, ☎ 639-4441; Tobago Heritage Festival information.

National Carnival Commission, Queen's Park Savannah, Port of Spain; ☎ 627-1530.

National Chutney Foundation of Trinidad & Tobago, ☎/fax 628-2174; for concert information.

National Parang Association, Arima, ☎ 667-3348; traditional parang music.

Pan Trinbago, 75 Edward St., Port of Spain, ☎ 623-4486; steel band information.

Power Boat Association, ☎ 634-4427.

Trinidad & Tobago Cycling Federation, ☎ 636-2547.

Trinidad & Tobago Game Fishing Association, ☎ 624-5304; game fishing and tournaments.

Trinidad & Tobago Golf Association, ☎ 622-2909.

Trinidad & Tobago Rally Club, ☎ 623-7840; car rallies.

Trinidad & Tobago Powerboats Association; ☎ 634-4227.

Trinidad & Tobago Yachting Association, ☎ 634-4519; yacht races and regattas.

Wildlife Division, Forestry Department, ☎ 622-7476; for turtle sighting in Trinidad.

Windsurfing Association of Trinidad & Tobago, ☎ 637-3567.

■ Telephones

The **area code** for Trinidad and Tobago is 868. From the USA, dial 1-868 and the seven digit number. From Britain, dial 011-868 and the seven digit number. There is no area code used between the two islands. Local calls are very reasonably priced, costing under 20¢.

As in the US, coin-operated public phones here are becoming a rarity. You can buy phone cards in denominations of TT$ 20, 60, and 100 (US $3.44, $10.34 and $17.24), plus tax, at the TSTT company, 18 Park St. in downtown Port of Spain, Trinidad. Hours are 8 AM to 4 PM, Monday through

Friday. You can also purchase phone cards at many hotels, guest houses, and shops on both islands.

AUTHOR TIP *Look at the back of the phone card before buying. If it has nothing written on it, this is the one you want. Otherwise, you will have to enter a series of numbers in order for the card to work, before entering the specific number you are calling.*

Long distance calls from Trinidad and Tobago to the US or UK are least expensive if you purchase and use the local TSTT phone card. Numbers that are toll-free in the US can be called from Trinidad and Tobago by dialing 880 instead of 800. You will be charged about $1 per minute locally for calling the number from Trinidad and Tobago.

Recently, telephone service in Trinidad and Tobago has been problematic. Numbers are changing and sometimes the system just doesn't seem to work. You'll have to be patient, as there's just no other option. Write and let us know if the situation is better when you are there.

■ Television

Cable TV with a wide variety of channels is now offered in many hotels. Satellite TV service has also progressed and offers the same fare as in the rest of the world. If your hotel does not have either of these services, you will have access to only the three local stations.

■ Tipping, Service Charges, Taxes

Americans (Europeans already live with this) will find an onerous tax in Trinidad and Tobago, called VAT (Value Added Tax). I've never understood what value gets added, but they get to nick you for from 10 to 15%. It applies to all of your major expenses while in the country – hotels, restaurants, and car rentals. If you don't see it on a bill, assume it has been included.

Don't confuse VAT with the 10% service charge, which is also automatically added to most of your bills in hotels and restaurants. The service charge is collected and divided among staff. If you get particularly good service in a hotel or restaurant, don't hesitate to acknowledge it with a small additional gratuity. And don't forget the maid who cleans your room; $2 a day will be genuinely appreciated.

■ Tourist Information

The following telephone numbers and contact sources have been set up by the **Tourism and Industrial Development Company** (TIDCO) in Trinidad to provide you with up-to-date travel information.

TOURIST INFORMATION
In Trinidad 1-868-669-5196
In Tobago (airport information office) 1-868-639-0509
In Tobago (Scarborough information office) . . . 1-868-639-2125
From the UK. . . . . 0-800-960-057 (toll-free)
From the US. . . . . 1-888-595-4TNT (toll-free)
From Germany . . . . 0-130-81-1618 or 49-06131-73337
From Italy . . . . 1-678-70272 or 1-678-77530
Web site. www.visittnt.com
E-mail . . . . tourism-info@tidco.co.tt

There are tourist information offices in both Trinidad and Tobago. The most useful one we found was at the **Piarco International Airport** in Trinidad (☎ 669-5196). On all of our visits there, staff were well informed and very anxious to help. When we told them the sort of accommodations we preferred and gave them a price range, they made a few recommendations, answered our questions, and called ahead to make arrangements for us. They also have a wealth of printed material on everything you might need. Pick up a copy of *Discover Trinidad & Tobago*, a publication of the Hotel Association, which is well written and covers all the basics. This office is your best bet for late reservations for Carnival. If there is anything available, they will know about it.

In Tobago, tourist information services are improving. Just across the street from the Crown Point Airport you'll find the **Tourist Bureau** (☎ 639-0509), where they will do their best to answer your questions. A list of B&Bs with phone numbers, locations, and prices is provided and there are also names and phone numbers of hotels and tour services posted on the wall. There's another tourist office in Scarborough at the NIB mall, but unless you are already in the area it is not worth a stop. Currently, neither of these offices in Tobago can provide you with the wealth of printed information available at the Piarco International Airport office. If you don't find what you're looking for at the tourist information services in Trinidad or Tobago, don't be discouraged. Locals are more than willing to impart whatever information they can.

In Tobago pick up a copy of ***MotMot Times***, a delightful bi-monthly tourism magazine published by the Tourism Department. There are interesting articles written by a variety of authors. Another good resource is the bi-monthly paper ***Tobago Today***. The articles are well written and the advertisements are a great way to see what's new and what's happening.

Just Facts

AREA	**Tobago** – 116 square miles, about the size of Martha's Vineyard. **Trinidad** – 1,864 square miles, about the size of Rhode Island. Together they are about the size of Delaware.
POPULATION	Tobago – 47,000 (as of 1994). Trinidad – 1,250,000 (as of 1994).
ELECTRICITY	110/220 volts, 60 cycles – good for American and European appliances.
PASSPORT & VISA REQUIREMENTS	All visitors to Trinidad and Tobago, including US citizens, must have valid passports. Visitors from some countries other than the US are required to have visas. Everyone must have a return-trip ticket, though no one has ever asked us to produce one.
EMERGENCY NUMBERS	Police: ☎ 999 or 639-1200 Fire: ☎ 990 or 639-2108 Ambulance: ☎ 639-2222 Port of Spain General Hospital: ☎ 623-2951/52/53 Scarborough Hospital: ☎ 639-2551 Coast Guard: ☎ 639-1461
TIME ZONE	One hour ahead of EST.
LANGUAGE	English
MAILING ADDRESS	Republic of Trinidad and Tobago, West Indies. When mailing from the United States, it is best to spell out West Indies to avoid having your mail go to WI (Wisconsin).
AREA CODE	Area code from the US is 868; dial 1-868-xxx-xxxx.
WHAT TO PACK	Comfortable, cool clothing. The islands are very informal. Even in the evening at resort hotels, women can rely on casually elegant clothing. Long pants are required for men in the evening in some places. Port of Spain is the only place where dressier (but still informal) clothes might be appropriate. Clothing that might be considered scanty will attract unwanted attention.
WATER SUPPLY	Tap water is drinkable. Bottled water is readily available.
DEPARTURE TAX	The equivalent of about $16 US or $100 TT. It is necessary to pay in TT dollars.
TAXES	Hotels charge 10% room tax and 10% service charge (though this can vary). Elsewhere you will pay 15% VAT (value added tax) and in restaurants typically an additional 10% service charge.
TELEPHONES	Local assistance: ☎ 6211 Operator assistance: ☎ 0

■ Holidays & Special Events

While traveling on national holidays can present logistics problems in some countries, in Trinidad and Tobago it should not, but there are a few exceptions. The busiest time of year is during Carnival when visitors arrive from all over the world to witness or participate in this extravaganza and you will not find a hotel room without prior reservations.

AUTHOR TIP

If you want to be in Trinidad for Carnival, you should reserve at least six months in advance or you risk not finding a place to stay. The next busiest times are Christmas and Easter, especially in Tobago, where many Trinis spend these holidays. Summer can also present problems in Tobago because it is an ideal family vacation spot for Trinis.

Holidays with indeterminate dates are usually religious in nature. Exact dates are determined late in the year and it should not affect your holiday. If you have a special interest in one of these holidays, contact the Trinidad & Tobago Tourism Department to confirm dates (☎ 888-495-4TNT) and get more detailed information.

You may be astonished at the variety and frequency of celebrations in Trinidad and Tobago. These are truly a people who know how to party and they have abundant stamina for having fun.

January

■ **New Year's Day, January 1, Public Holiday** – Aside from the worldwide tradition of making resolutions, Tobago's celebration includes some charming folkways. All clothes must be washed before morning, or dirty clothes will plague the new year. Being at home with your family at dawn will assure you aren't drawn to whomever's house you were in when dawn arrived. Attending church for two hours on the eve will ensure you forgiveness and, if the morning finds you working, you will be blessed with employment the year-round.

■ **Panorama, Events from January through February** – This is a nationwide pan music competition with bands of up to 100 members playing up to 400 pans.

February/March

■ **Pre-Carnival Festivities** fill the entire month prior to the festival. Carnival is not an official public holiday, but if Carnival isn't a holiday, I don't know what is. On these two days, every office is closed, many restaurants aren't open, and there is little or no public transportation. Festivities culminate on the Monday and Tuesday before Ash Wednesday, but the preceding week is filled with related activities.

CARNIVAL DATES	
2000	March 6-7
2001	February 26-27
2002	February 11-12
2003	March 3-4
2004	February 23-24
2005	February 7-8

■ **Spiritual Baptist Liberation Shouter Day**, March 30, Public Holiday.

April

■ **Good Friday** (date varies)

■ **Easter Sunday** (date varies). Easter in Tobago takes on a special flavor. There are goat and crab races and festivities all over the island on Easter Sunday and the few days following. Believe it or not, residents actually breed and train racing goats, and have done so for over 75 years. Easter Sunday brings a big party at Buccoo starting at 10 PM and continuing till dawn.

■ **Easter Monday** (date varies) Public holiday.

■ **Carib Tournament** (date varies) – International game fish classic.

May

■ **Angostura Yachting World Regatta Race Week** (date varies) – Governed by the International Sailing Federation, this is a category B event. In the tradition of Trinidad & Tobago, winning isn't so bad, but having fun is the real goal. There are parties at Store Bay in Crown Point all week long.

■ **Indian Arrival Day**, May 30, Public Holiday – This day is set aside to honor the arrival of the first indentured workers from India, after their months-long grueling journey.

June

■ **Whit Monday** (date varies).

■ **Phagwah** (date varies) – Hindus celebrate the advent of spring and the coming harvest with this holiday, which over time has developed an almost carnival atmosphere. The day's festivities culminate in a street parade where celebrants arrive in white clothing and join in squirting one another with heavily tinted water; Trinidad's answer to tie-dye.

■ **Labour Day**, June 19, Public Holiday.

■ **Corpus Christi**, June 22, Public Holiday – This is a special day for Catholics, who plant their crops on this day each year.

July

■ **Tobago Heritage Festival** (date varies) – Begun in 1987, this two-week celebration of the island's village traditions brings many Tobagoins home from all parts of the world. The festivities include theater, dance, special foods, the re-enactment of an old-time wedding, and all the things of times past in Tobago.

■ **The Great Speedboat Race** (date varies) – This speedboat race is one of the biggest events of the year. It covers the distance between the Gulf of Paria in Trinidad and Store Bay, Crown Point, Tobago. In 2000, the race will celebrate its 32nd consecutive year.

August

■ **Emancipation Day**, August 1, Public Holiday – This is a special holiday for those of African heritage for obvious reasons, celebrating freedom from slavery in 1834. There is food, music and dancing, and crafts.

■ **Independence Day**, August 31, Public Holiday. Celebrated largely in Trinidad, this day marks the achievement of independence from Britain in 1962.

■ **Santa Rosa Festival** (date varies) – Descendants of the Carib Indians in the Arima area celebrate their heritage during this special event.

■ **Eid-ul-Fitr** (date varies), Public Holiday – Celebrated by the Muslim population in Trinidad, when the new moon marks the beginning of the Islamic New Year, Eid-ul-Fitr. This day marks the end of the month-long Ramadan Fast and is a time of feasting and prayer. Donations are given to the poor and gifts are exchanged between relatives and friends.

September

■ **Republic Day** (date varies).

October

■ **Divali** (date varies), Public Holiday – This is the Hindu festival of lights, honoring the goddess Lakshmi. Devout Hindus place thousands of little earthenware lamps around their homes and temples; music, dance, fireworks and sparklers add to the festivities. Evolving with the party spirit of Trinidadians, there are now competitions for the best light display and for Divali queen. Chaguanas and San Fernando, in Trinidad, are the best places to be for Divali.

■ **Hosay** (date varies) – This Muslim religious festival featuring booming tassa drums and colorful processions is celebrated in the mohorram month of the Muslim calendar, 10 days after the new moon. On the last of the three days of this not very solemn occasion, paraders march through the streets singing and carrying *tadjahs*, very large and elaborately decorated models of the tombs of Mohammed's grandsons, Hussain and Hassan. Hosay is celebrated almost exclusively in Trinidad.

November

■ **Pan Jazz Festival** (date varies) – Pan music and jazz combine in this three-day celebration of music.

December

■ **Christmas Day**, December 25, Public Holiday – Christmas is celebrated in Trinidad with parang music, a mark of the Spanish heritage in Trinidad and Tobago. In Tobago it is preceded by a whirlwind housecleaning and repairing, followed by a community outpouring of shared foods, music, song, and the exchanging of small gifts.

■ **Boxing Day**, December 26, Public Holiday – Boxing Day becomes a great day for anniversaries as it is a tradition to marry on this holiday.

■ Transportation

Airlines

Air traffic from North America and Europe to Trinidad and Tobago is increasing rapidly and departure gates are becoming more varied too. We have listed flight information below, but things change frequently. Please check with your travel agent or the individual airline for up-to-date information.

FLIGHT TIMES TO TRINIDAD & TOBAGO
From Miami . . . . 3½ hours
From New York . . . . 4½ hours
From London. . . . . 8 hours

Air Canada (☎ 800-422-6232 or, in Trinidad, 669-4065) has four daily flights to Miami connecting with BWIA for flights to Port of Spain, Trinidad, and Crown Point, Tobago. There are also three weekly non-stop flights to Port of Spain.

Air Caribbean, in Port of Spain (☎ 623-2500, in Tobago ☎ 639-2500, reservations ☎ 625-3543/7/9. E-mail aircarib@ttemail.com, Web site www.aircaribbean.com). Air Caribbean makes the short hop between Trinidad and Tobago. Lasting only 20 minutes, the flight may remind you of what flying used to be: with leg room, adequate aisle space, and no bad smells. Flights are generally on time, and scheduled daily from Tobago to Trinidad at 6:40, 8:40, and 11 AM and 1, 3, 5, 7, and 9 PM. Flights from Trinidad to Tobago leave at 6, 8, and 10 AM, 12 noon, and 2, 4, 6, and 8 PM. The cost is now about $80 round-trip for foreigners. Locals pay about half that. Air Caribbean also has flights to nearby Barbados and Grenada.

American Airlines, ☎ 800-624-6262 or, in Trinidad, 669-4661. AA has one daily non-stop flight from Miami to Port of Spain, Trinidad. They also have one flight leaving from New York with a stop in Miami, but with no change of planes. The Port of Spain American Airlines office is at 63-65 Independence, but service there is extremely slow, as is service at the **American Eagle** counter at Crown Point Airport in Tobago. American Eagle currently has one daily flight each way between Tobago and Puerto Rico, which makes connections to the United States easy. Flight times change every few weeks, so check with the airline for the latest information.

British Airways, ☎ 800-247-9297. British Airways offers direct flights between Britain and Tobago once a week.

BWIA, North America, ☎ 800-538-2942; reservations in Trinidad and Tobago, ☎ 627-2942. Web www.bwee.com. Currently there are daily flights from Miami to Port of Spain, Trinidad, and flights to Tobago twice a week. From New York, BWIA has daily flights to Port of Spain and a once-weekly flight to Tobago. They also have flights to Port of Spain originating in Toronto, connecting with Air Caribbean for the flight to Tobago. BWIA's European departure gates are in Zurich, Switzerland, and Munich, Germany.

Caledonian Airways, ☎ 800-338-2410. Flights to Tobago originate in the UK, flying out of Gatwick on Monday and Saturday mornings.

Liat, ☎ 627-2942 or 625-1010/9 in Port of Spain or 639-0276 in Tobago. This local airline makes short hops among Caribbean islands.

Ferry Service

A ferry plies its way between Port of Spain in Trinidad and Scarborough in Tobago on a daily basis. Because of prevailing winds and currents between the islands, the trip from Tobago to Trinidad is much calmer than the reverse. The ferry, *Panorama*, leaves Tobago at 11 PM, arriving in Port of Spain at 5 AM. On this overnight trip, you can stretch out in an airline-style reclining seat or get a cabin. Each area is comfortably air conditioned and, in first class, there are cushioned armchairs and sofas. If you'd like a drink, there's a bar on the first-class deck. For snacks, there's a place on the second deck, but pickings are pretty slim. If you can, bring some food along with you; that's what locals do.

The *Panorama* is large and accommodates both passengers and cars. The ride is best on the first deck (first class) and will cost around $5 each way. Cabins are $13 each way.

To take the ferry from Port of Spain to Tobago, buy your tickets in advance between 7 AM and 3 PM at the Government Shipping Service Passenger Terminal opposite the twin towers in Port of Spain. Be there for boarding by 1 PM. The ferry leaves at 2 PM and arrives in Scarborough at 8 PM. They no longer accept reservations by phone, but information is available at ☎ 639-2417 in Tobago, ☎ 626-4906 in Trinidad.

The trip from Port of Spain can be a problem for anyone inclined to seasickness. I didn't find the trip troublesome, but many passengers on board were uncomfortable at one time or another and some were truly distressed. Though I'm a devoted ferry fan, this is a relatively long trip. Its only advantage is the price, since airfares for foreigners have doubled since 1996.

Driving

Check your insurance policy and credit card privileges before leaving home to determine the coverage you have on a rental car. You may save money if you don't need to buy additional insurance from the rental car company. If your policy doesn't cover foreign rentals, be sure to get the extra coverage. If you should have an accident, get license and insurance information from the other driver, if one is involved. Contact the police and call your rental company immediately. Remember to rent from a reputable company and make sure the license plate begins with an "R." Keep your rental information and license with you in the car while driving. The police in Tobago have instituted a program of road checks, and it is very likely you will be stopped at least once.

Trinidad & Tobago has left-hand driving as in the UK and other Commonwealth countries, and I found it disconcerting seeing traffic coming at me from all the wrong directions. It takes a little getting used to, but drivers are pretty reasonable and you can always pull over and let people pass if you're going slowly. Oddly enough, people walk on the left side of the sidewalk, too. Getting down the crowded sidewalks in Port of Spain was very awkward until we figured out what was happening.

Although left-hand drive is the norm, middle-of-the-road drivers are not uncommon. When approaching a blind curve be especially cautious; hit the horn.

A current driver's license from the US, Canada, France, Germany, or the Bahamas will entitle you to drive here legally for up to 90 days. An international driving permit will allow you to drive here for a year.

Gasoline will cost you about 40¢/liter. And the wonderful thing is that service stations actually provide service at no extra charge. It's like stepping back in time in the US, and what a pleasure! Gas stations in Tobago are harder to find than in Trinidad, so pay a little more attention to the gas gauge than you normally might to avoid being left on empty with no gas station open or close by.

Remember to use your seat belt – it's the law.

Picking up hitchhikers requires common sense. In smaller towns on either island, you can readily give a lift to women, a worker, or a couple of schoolchildren on their way home. Young men can be more of a problem; use your discretion.

Trinidad

Orientation

Trinidad is a fascinating mix of lands and micro-climates in a very tiny package. The island is only about the size of the State of Rhode Island and combined with its twin, Tobago, the entire country reaches only the size of Delaware. Roughly a wide rectangle, Trinidad is 50 miles long and 37 miles wide.

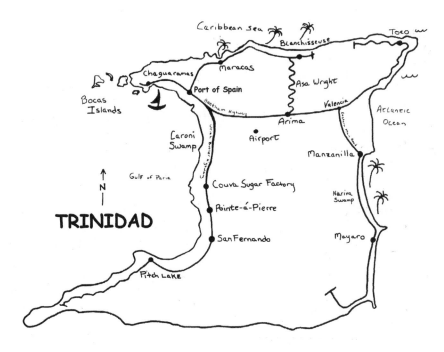

The 3,000-foot **Northern Range** of mountains runs across the northern coastal edge of Trinidad. Covered in tropical rain forest, the mountains lead down to the sea and all along the coast provide a dramatic backdrop. The north coast is accessible only from one end or the other, unless you're hiking. There is no through-road yet. At the eastern end are **Toco** and several other small villages. On the northwestern coast are some of Trinidad's most popular beaches, and the lovely town of **Blanchisseuse**.

On the inland side of the mountains, from Port of Spain across to Arima, is a strip of mixed commercial and residential development. The central area of the island is more level than the north, but is still favored with rolling hills. This central area is home to mixed development – agriculture, small towns, and manufacturing.

The west coast is generally less attractive from a tourist's point of view than other areas of the country, except for its specific destinations. It is home to one of the country's best-known bird sanctuaries – the **Caroni**. With its dense mangrove, this brackish swamp is the roosting home to thousands of scarlet ibis, the national bird of Trinidad and Tobago. Just south of Caroni is congested residential development, sugarcane agriculture, and the petrochemical industry, which surprisingly is the home of **Pointe-à-Pierre**, a wildfowl preserve. Farther south is **San Fernando**, the country's second largest city. South of San Fernando is the **Oropuche Swamp** and the **pitch lake**, which is the best reason to drive this far on the west coast.

The northwest coast is a burgeoning yacht haven and has some of the better restaurants and entertainment near to Port of Spain. It is also the access point to offshore islands. The south coast is largely inaccessible.

"THE FIRST MAP OF TRINIDAD"

by D. Montgomery, Port of Spain, Trinidad and Tobago

It is the year 1595 and Queen Elizabeth is on the throne. The King of France has just declared war on Spain, Mohammed III is on the throne of Turkey, fighting the Austrian Hungarian Empire to the West, and the Dutch are beginning to colonize the East Indies. Spain will soon land troops in Cornwall, burning Penzance and Lousehole before being defeated. The Armada of Spain is in the making and will set sail in two years time. Shakespeare is writing both *Richard II* and *A Midsummer Night's Dream*. Trinidad, the small West Indian island owned by Spain, is governed by Don Antonio de Bereo.

Onto this world stage comes the first mapmaker of Trinidad, Robert Dudley, Earl of Warwick and Leicester and Duke of Northumberland. A favorite of Queen Elizabeth, he was only 20 years old when he set sail for the New World "for gold, for praise, for glory." Sadly, he got none of the former and little of the latter.

Dudley was born at Sheen House in Surrey on August 7, 1574, and matriculated from Oxford in 1588, when only 14 years old. Our hero was obviously a court favorite, dashing, charming, good-looking and, as his portrait shows, a sharp dresser.

With permission of the Queen, Dudley sailed to Trinidad, leaving Southampton on November 6, 1594, on his flagship of 200 tons called *Great Bear*. He had with him Captain Wyatt and Abram Kendall who was master of *Little Bear*. There were also two pinnaces, small sailing ships used as tenders on the expedition, called the *Frisking* and the *Earewig*. It was this small company that left England to seek the gold called "calcuri" by the Amerindians in Trinidad.

On January 30, 1595, Dudley sighted the island at what is now called Point Galeota, but called Cape Carao on Dudley's map. He anchored at Curiapon Bay, now known as Icacios.

Dudley described the Amerindians, probably Arawaks, as being fine shaped, gentle, naked, and painted red. Their red coloring came from the pulp of the local shrub *roucou*, whose seed pods yield the dye which is still used locally as a food coloring. Charles Kingsley, 250 years later, in his travel book about the West Indies, said, "The Indian of the Orinoco prefers paint to clothes, and when he has 'roucoued' himself from head to foot, considers himself in full dress."

Dudley bartered with the locals, offering hatchets, knives, hooks, bells, and glass buttons, in exchange for hens, hogs, plantains, potatoes, pines, and tobacco. The latter was a well-known product of Trinidad at the time. He also obtained information about the gold he was seeking. The locals said it existed in large quantities at a site nine miles to the east. Sadly, Dudley's search party found only a mine of marcasites – fool's gold.

Dudley's next problem was whether or not to attack de Bereo, the Spanish Governor. Though Dudley had 50 men and the element of surprise, de Bereo had good defenses at the capital, St. Joseph, and about 300 soldiers. Our hero cheated and, after inscribing a message on a lead plate, he hung it on a tree, and departed.

The map [which follows] is number 13 in the atlas, *Secrets of the Sea*, the first to be compiled using the Mercator projection. This complete atlas was lithographed over a period of 12 years and published on August 26, 1645. Looking at the map today, you will see that most of the place names have changed from Dudley's time, though the pitch lake is there as "Terra di Brea." Remarkably, for producing such a detailed map, Dudley spent only about three weeks in Trinidad.

A copy of Dudley's complete works is kept in the Bodleian Library in Oxford.

Trinidad

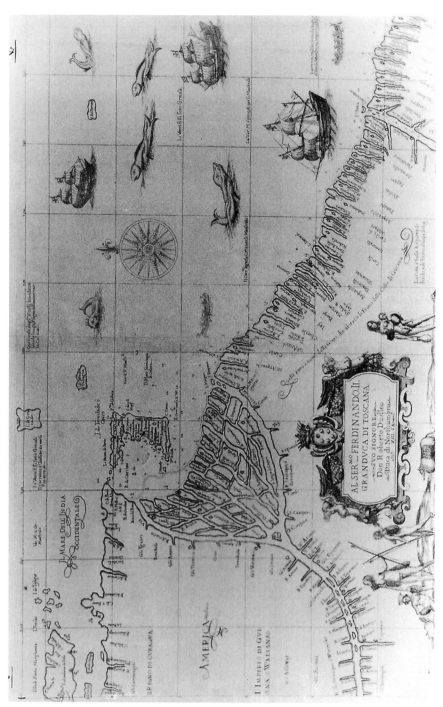

The First Map of Trinidad. *Photograph courtesy of David Montgomery.*

Getting Here & Getting Around

■ Airport Facilities

Piarco International Airport, Port of Spain, Trinidad. This is a small airport with duty-free shopping on your way in or out of Trinidad. The **Tourist Information office** here is an excellent resource, providing plenty of information, and even calling ahead to make hotel reservations for you if necessary. Don't miss it.

Piarco is 20 or 30 minutes from downtown Port of Spain. A trip into the city by taxi will cost you $20 before 10 PM and $30 after, as taxi fares rise 50% after 10 PM. If you're going to one of the Port of Spain suburbs the fare will be slightly higher. Negotiate and agree on a price before leaving. There is some sort of public transportation from the airport to Port of Spain, but unless you are dead broke, it's not worth the time and trouble to buy your ticket and find the bus.

■ Car Rentals

Most hotels and guest houses will arrange car rentals for you and generally they will discount the cost. If you prefer to arrange a rental independently, here are two of the better agencies, both located at Piarco Airport.

CAR RENTAL AGENCIES

■ **Econo-Car Rentals**, ☎/fax 669-2342, e-mail econocar@trinidad.net.

■ **Thrifty Car Rental**, ☎ 669-0602. Rentals will be about $46/day inclusive, rising to about $50/day during Carnival. One advantage at Thrifty is that they'll sometimes accept discount coupons from the States.

■ Taxis

Private taxis are available at the larger hotels or may be summoned to pick you up, since they don't normally cruise the streets for fares. Private taxi fares can be quite expensive, but Trinidad has a terrific alternative in its route taxi system. Route taxis are great; they ply specific routes all day, picking up and dropping off passengers along the way. Simply flag cars with "H" license plates heading in your direction and ask if they'll be passing your destination. They're very inexpensive and a smart alternative to the huge (and usually half-empty) buses we have in most US cities. Small vans called maxi-taxis also ply the roads, but they stick more to prescribed pick-up and drop-off points.

If you are heading out of Port of Spain, you can get route taxis, as well as buses, at the bus station near South Quay.

■ Areas of the Island

Remember that Trinidad is small. From any location, you can leisurely drive to the farthest point in three hours or less. Trinidad is only now developing for tourism so most of the hotel and restaurant services are congregated in and around the capital city of Port of Spain. If you are visiting for Carnival, we highly recommend staying as close to the Savannah as you can get.

Those who like places with a yachty flavor will enjoy Chaguaramas, on the northwest coast. Raw nature in a village setting can be found in the northeast (Grand Rivière), and nature with a gentled touch is found in Blanchisseuse, on the northern coast. Bird watchers might be happiest at Asa Wright, in Arima, or the Mount St. Benedict Guest House in Tunapuna.

Port of Spain

Port of Spain is a busy, bustling center of activity by day. By night, most areas of the city are extremely quiet, except in Carnival season. The city streets are organized on a grid system and were it not for the one way streets, it would be extremely easy to negotiate. Once you get the hang of which street heads north and which goes south, it is very simple.

The city is not large and much of it has a residential character with offices located in old homes. Port of Spain sits between the ocean and dock area on the south, where the highway has been constructed, and Queen's Park Savannah on the north. The Savannah is a very large city park, but it is not remarkable in itself. Surrounding the park, however, you'll find many of the city's key attractions – the magnificent seven, the Emperor Valley Zoo, and the Botanical Garden. Just past the Savannah are the suburbs, only a few minutes from downtown – Maraval, St. Ann's, and Cascade, to name a few. All in all, the central city is small and very manageable on foot or by car.

Blanchisseuse

This small fishing village is on the sloping northwestern coast. It is sandwiched closely between dense rain forest and ocean and is as quiet as it is beautiful. You will find a few pretty guest houses and pleasant restaurants. Trails into the forest abound, and Paria Waterfall is just a short hike away.

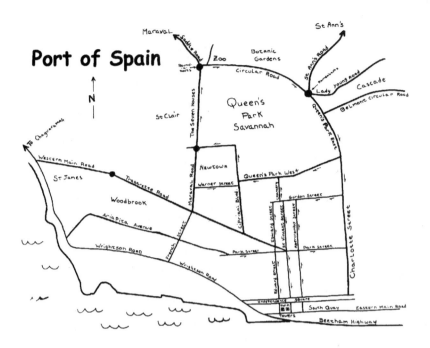

Chaguaramas & The Bocas Islands

The coastal area of Chaguaramas and the Bocas Islands are in the northwest corner of Trinidad. The small group of islands, sometimes called the Dragon's Mouth, leads to and protects the Gulf of Paria. Lying between Venezuela and the coast of Trinidad, this sheltered gulf area is being extensively developed for yachting services. Chaguaramas, on the mainland, and the offshore Bocas Islands are rich in history and offer many opportunities to explore the natural environment. Each of the offshore islands has unique attractions – Gasparee's caves, Chacachacare's leper hospital, salt pond, and iguanas, and Centipede Island's centipedes. Good swimming beaches can be found on the islands, but beaches are less accessible on the mainland. We have listed a few hotels and restaurants in this area, all with a yachty feel.

Toco & The Northeast

In the northeast corner with Toco at the point, you'll find exuberant rain forest and wild ocean beaches. Just about every fellow you'll see will be carrying a machete – they are used every day. The waters in this area are primarily for surfing, but you will find a few spots for swimming. There is one guest house in Toco that we have listed (see *Where To Stay*), but more are sure to follow as this area is developed for tourism. As of now, however, there are not many hotel or restaurant options.

Manzanilla & Mayaro, The East Coast

The east coast is largely undeveloped, although there are some small towns along the road. One of the major sights here is the Nariva Swamp just about halfway down the coast. The Nariva is quite large, like the Caroni, but it is a freshwater mangrove swamp; home to monkeys, caiman, and all sorts of other small wildlife. The east coast boasts coconut farms and miles of windswept empty beaches. The only town of substantial size on this coast is Mayaro; we found a hotel there that looks fine for a night or two. As with Toco, this is a likely area for development, though as yet not much is happening.

Where To Stay

 Until recent years, there were relatively few tourist accommodations in Trinidad. Even in Port of Spain most of the larger hotels catered to business travelers, but that is changing rapidly.

■ Practical Information

Tax & Service Charge

An important question to ask when making reservations is whether the price you are quoted is inclusive of taxes and service charges. A tax of between 10 and 15% and a standard service charge of 10% will add significantly to your hotel and restaurant bills. We have listed prices and noted where taxes are included, but you may avoid an unpleasant surprise if you confirm prices in advance.

Credit Cards

Most hotels and restaurants accept credit cards, but make sure they accept the one you carry. In small towns, you will most likely have to pay in cash.

Handicap Access

We have listed a few hotels with wheelchair access, but there is great sensitivity to individual needs in Trinidad and Tobago and there may be other hotels that would suit you just fine. If you have special needs, be sure to ask in advance if they can accommodate you.

Airport Transfer

The cost of a taxi ride from the airport to Port of Spain will be at least $20, and there is a surcharge of 50% after 10 PM. Hotels will arrange to have you picked up at the airport, but you will be charged the regular fare.

There is currently no reasonable alternative public transportation from the airport to Port of Spain. If you are planning to rent a car, it is probably best to pick it up at the airport.

Cooking Facilities

Few hotels in Trinidad offer cooking facilities, but some do. When making reservations, ask specifically what is provided when a kitchenette is offered. It can vary from a hot plate to a full kitchen.

Choosing a Location

PORT OF SPAIN: In Port of Spain you have a choice of good standard hotels, all offering the amenities that make for a comfortable stay. Prices, even for the better hotels, are quite reasonable, though prices will vary with the degree of luxury. There are also small hotels in the city, locally called guest houses, but most of these are budget-style accommodations. Bed and breakfasts, or host homes, in the suburbs are a good alternative to the larger hotels, giving you a comfortable place to stay and offering the friendliness of a private home. Wherever you stay in or near Port of Spain, the island is so small that everything you'll want to see is within a two- or three-hour drive from the city.

When you glance at a map, Port of Spain may not seem a central location. Remember, though, the island is only about the size of Rhode Island, the smallest of the United States, so the city makes a good base from which to explore the rest of the island. Port of Spain is not very close to beaches; the most popular ones, Maracas and Las Cuevas, are about 30 to 45 minutes away, and most people go for the day rather than staying in these areas. Trinidad has much more diversity than many Caribbean destinations; you may want to spend beach time in Tobago where you can easily locate right next to the water. Central Port of Spain is definitely the place to be for **Carnival**.

AUTHOR TIP *Private and route taxis are extremely difficult to find during Carnival. Pick your hotel location carefully to be within comfortable walking distance of the Savannah and downtown areas, where you will find most of the action. During Carnival you can expect to pay up to three times the normal hotel rate and you will usually have to book a minimum number of days.*

Though one of the best reasons to visit Trinidad, Carnival is not the only reason to be there. Trinidad is more than just another touristy Caribbean island, it is a very distinct country with a diversity of attractions for so small a place – steel band music competitions, Moslem and Hindu celebrations, wildlife sanctuaries, yachting facilities, miles of deserted beaches, and a variety of cultural activities in the city.

AWAY FROM PORT OF SPAIN: The few towns outside the city that might be appealing enough for a short stay have good small hotels. One of these towns is **Blanchisseuse** on the north coast, which has a few pretty guest houses and good restaurants. Included in our accommodations listings are places that have a special appeal, such as Asa Wright, and a few in outlying areas where, for convenience, you might decide to stay a night.

If you want to be close to the city and have easy access to the rest of the island, think about staying in **Chaguaramas**. New and stylish hotels and restaurants have opened here in response to the dramatic increase in the number of marinas and yacht repair facilities. Some of the more popular night spots are also in this area, and you are only a half-hour's drive from Port of Spain.

Bed & Breakfasts (Host Homes)

Host homes offer the same wonderful alternative that has grown so popular in Britain and the States. All are registered and offer accommodations ranging from modest to luxurious. This is probably one of the best ways to get to know the kind people of this country. Breakfast is included in the base price, which ranges from about $30 to $50 double. For the most up-to-date listings, call ahead or visit the Tourist Information office at Piarco International Airport upon your arrival (☎ 669-5196).

READER'S COMMENT

*The Koudeles of Portland, Oregon, decided at the last minute to attend Carnival and found accommodations at **Lynch's West Hill B&B** through the Tourism Information office at Piarco International Airport. The Koudeles couldn't have been more enthusiastic; they thoroughly enjoyed their stay with the host couple, a chef and the sister of an American Olympic swimmer.*

In Trinidad and Tobago, a small hotel with less than 16 rooms is called a **guest house**. This may be confusing to Americans who generally think of a guest house as a family home with rooms devoted to overnight guests. Sometimes a guest house is just what you imagine; sometimes it's a small hotel. Keep that in mind as you look through the following list so you won't be disappointed to find yourself in a hotel rather than a home, if that's what you're looking for. Remember, all prices are quoted in US dollars.

Hotels & Guest Houses

■ Downtown Port of Spain

THE ABERCROMBY INN, 101 Abercromby St., Port of Spain; ☎ 623-5259 or 627-6658, fax 624-3858, e-mail aberinn@carib-link.net. Owner

James Thompson personally manages this small budget-style guest house in downtown Port of Spain. Deluxe rooms have AC, TV, phone, and refrigerator, and cost $35 single, $45 double, including continental breakfast. For the very budget minded, there are economy rooms with bath at $23 single, $30 double and, for those who need to really scrimp, James has rooms with shared bath for $20. Prices do not include 10% tax and 10% service charge. Continental breakfasts are served on the small dining patio on the second floor. The Abercromby is a good location for Carnival on the cheap because it's just a few blocks from the Savannah, where many events are held. They may be expanding, adding about 20 better-quality rooms.

Amenities: AC, TV, phone, complimentary continental breakfast.

Good for: Budget-minded singles or couples who want to be in central Port of Spain, especially during Carnival.

Comment: The location is central.

PAR-MAY-LA'S INN, 53 Picton St., Port of Spain; ☎ 628-2008, fax 628-4707 (see also Sundeck Suites; their guest house just down the street). This small guest house is best suited for attending Carnival very economically. Rooms are not small, but they are simply furnished. The guest house is on the second floor and there's a large veranda for catching the evening breeze. This guest house is located in a quiet residential area in the city and there are small restaurants nearby. Including an American or local-style breakfast, rooms are $30 single or $50 double. An extra person or child over 12 is an additional $15. Rates do not include 10% tax and 10% service charge. Reasonably priced car rentals are available to guests and tours can be arranged.

Amenities: AC, TV (local stations), phone, breakfast included, car rentals, tours.

Good for: Budget-minded singles or couples for Carnival.

Comment: This is an inexpensive centrally located small guest house.

HOLIDAY INN, Wrightson Rd., Port of Spain; ☎ 625-3366, toll-free in the US ☎ 800-HOLIDAY, fax 625-4166, e-mail holidayinn@trinidad.net, Web site www.trinidad.net/holidayinn. This is a 235-room business hotel in the city center. It is exceptionally secure and has all of the services of a standard Holiday Inn. Single rooms are $154 and doubles are $172, including breakfast, taxes, and service charges. Suites are also available. One of its more interesting features is a revolving restaurant at the top of the hotel. Built during the 1960s, the hotel has been well maintained, offers views of the harbor and is a good bet for the business traveler. Their rain-or-shine protected tennis courts are a nice amenity.

Amenities: AC, TV, phone, pool, tennis courts, exercise room, restaurants, bar, free parking, business services.

Good for: The business traveler.

Comment: For the business traveler, the location of this hotel gives it an edge over other hotels.

SUNDECK SUITES, 42-44 Picton St., Port of Spain; ☎ 622-9560, fax 628-4707. Owned by the folks at Par-May-La's Inn, this new guest house is located on a quiet residential street. It has 15 suites with minimal kitchenettes, each with a small balcony. Rates are $35 single and $56 double, not including a tax of 10% and service charge of 10%. Three suites are designed for handicap access.

Amenities: AC, TV (local stations), kitchenette, patio.

Handicap: Yes, three suites.

Good for: Singles or couples on a tight budget.

Comment: Looking more like a small apartment building, this provides a good alternative. between host homes (B&Bs) and more expensive full-service hotels.

TRINIDAD HILTON, Lady Young Rd., Belmont Hill, Port of Spain; ☎ 624-3211 or 624-3111, ☎ 800-HILTONS (in the US), fax 624-4485, e-mail hiltonpos@wow.net. This is a large hotel with close to 400 rooms. It sits high on a hill overlooking the Savannah with views all the way to the sea. It is only a short distance from the business district. Business services such as fax and computer hookups are available and they also have 24-hour Telex, worldwide courier service, and secretarial and translation services. Rooms are pleasantly furnished as you would expect, and some have great views from their small terraces. The hotel has all the usual amenities of a standard Hilton, along with a large pool and lighted tennis courts. Rack rates, or published rates, for standard rooms are $205 single and $235 double; deluxe rooms are $220 and $250. Room rates do not include tax and service charges.

AUTHOR TIP

The Hilton's room rates do not dramatically increase during Carnival. At any other time of the year do not hesitate to ask about discounts, which are readily available.

Amenities: AC, TV, phone, mini-bar, restaurants, large pool, tennis courts, business services.

Good for: Carnival visits, tourists, and business travelers.

Comment: If you like Hiltons, you'll like this one. Its location is great, especially for Carnival.

■ Greater Port of Spain

ALICIA'S GUEST HOUSE, 7 Coblenz Gardens, St. Ann's, Port of Spain; ☎ 623-2802, fax 623-8560. This guest house was suggested by readers of our first guide. It has 17 rooms, a pool, and Jacuzzi. Rates are about $35 single and $50 double.

KAPOK HOTEL, 16-18 Cotton Hill, St. Clair; ☎ 622-5765, 800-74-CHARMS (US and Canada), fax 622-9677, Web site www.kapok.co.tt. One of our favorites, the Kapok is run with every attention to detail. The 95 rooms in this nine-story hotel all are quite spacious and have good views. The Tiki Village restaurant on the eighth floor has windows all around and it is well worth a stop late in the afternoon to see the sunset and the spectacular views. See *Where To Eat* for a further description. Standard rooms cost $86 single, $99 double. Rooms with kitchenette are $89 and $102. Suites are $115 and $128. Prices do not include 10% VAT. The standard 10% service charge is not automatically added to your bill, so remember to recognize extra services with a tip. Just a few minutes from downtown and near Queen's Park Savannah, the Kapok is an excellent choice for anyone visiting Trinidad, but it also gets an extra vote of confidence from us for the business traveler. Rooms have voice mail, direct dial phones, and a dataport for fax/modem access. Business services include fax, secretarial, computer access, copying, and several meeting and conference rooms with state-of-the-art presentation equipment. There is always a taxi at the front door. Make reservations two weeks in advance or six months in advance for Carnival.

> *Amenities: AC, TV, phones, kitchenettes, pool, shops, restaurants and bar, pool, excellent business services, free parking, car rentals, and tours.*
>
> *Good for: Carnival, couples, friends, business travelers.*
>
> *Comment: We were very impressed. Staff is friendly and professional and the rooms are large and pleasant. Recently renovated.*

NORMANDIE HOTEL, 10 Nook Ave., St. Ann's, Port of Spain; ☎ 624-1181, fax 624-0108, e-mail normandie@wow.net. A family-owned hotel, the Normandie strikes us as a delightful holiday hotel. Their 53 rooms are attractive and nicely appointed. There's a very pretty pool, and relaxing after a day of touring the island would be easy here. Standard rooms with double or twin beds are $62 single, $72 double, but don't have much of a view. Superior rooms with two double beds are $77 single and $87 double; we think they are the best choice. Loft rooms at $87 single and $97 double would be good for families. Prices do not include taxes of 20%. Business services include fax, copying, typing, and meeting rooms. For the business traveler in a hurry, there are more responsive places to stay. On the grounds you'll find small craft and specialty shops, a bakery, and the nicely designed La Fantasie restaurant serving international, local and creole cuisines. MAP per person is $26; tours and car rentals can be arranged.

Trinidad

One of the unique features of the Normandie is its commitment to cultural entertainment. They have a large outdoor space called "Under the Trees," where musical and theatrical performances are held.

> *Amenities: AC, cable TV, phones, attractive pool, restaurant, shopping, tours and car rentals.*
>
> *Good for: Singles, couples, families.*
>
> *Comment: The Normandie is not a resort, but it sure made us feel like we were on vacation. It's a great place to stay and experience Carnival.*

PELICAN INN HOTEL, 2-4 Coblentz Ave., Cascade; ☎/fax 627-6271. This very funky place is grouped with the popular Pelican Bar and a squash court. Manager Deborah De Souza seems to handle whatever comes up with a smile. Their 20 air-conditioned, simple rooms have private baths and cost $36 single and $48 double, including all taxes and service charges. Weekly rates can be negotiated. Rooms vary a lot, so have a look around before settling in. Rooms 22 to 25 are new. Full breakfast is available for guests only, and lunch and dinner are served in the English pub-style bar.

> *Amenities: AC, central location, pub-style bar / restaurant, squash court.*
>
> *Good for: Budget-minded young social singles or couples.*
>
> *Comment: This is for the not-too-finicky young and lively crowd. We think this is the best bet for a budget location because it "feels right" – friendly, safe, and comfortable – and it's improving.*

ROYAL PALM SUITE HOTEL LTD., 7 Saddle Rd., Maraval; ☎/fax 628-6042 or 628-5086, e-mail royalpalm@trinidad.net. All rooms in this older, 70-room hotel are spacious and comfortably furnished, but the suites win hands-down. They are attractively arranged, large, and include a fully equipped kitchen – perfect for small families in town for Carnival or as a base from which to see the island. The Royal Palm is also surrounded by restaurants and shops and is only a short ride from downtown. Standard rooms are $75 single and $85 double. Executive suites are $165. Prices do not include tax of 10% or service charge of 10%.

> *Amenities: AC, cable TV, phone, kitchenettes, small pool, restaurant and bar, car rentals, and tours.*
>
> *Good for: Singles, couples, families.*
>
> *Comment: Good location and one of the better suites we found.*

■ Elsewhere On The Island

Arima

ASA WRIGHT NATURE CENTRE AND LODGE, Spring Hill Estate, 7½ mm, Blanchisseuse Rd., Arima. ☎ 667-4655, fax 667-4540. In the US and Canada call Caligo Ventures, ☎ 800-426-7781; e-mail asaright@ tstt.net.tt. Asa Wright is best known as a nature preserve, and anyone with an interest in the natural rain forest environment would find a comfortable stay here. Their 24 rooms are $107 single and $162 double from April 16 to December 15. In the winter season, December 16 through April 15, rates are $139 and $210. Prices include all meals, service charges and taxes, as well as afternoon tea and a rum punch in the evening. Situated in the forest at 1,200 feet, this former plantation of 191 acres is a non-profit preserve, providing a home for hummingbirds, toucans, bellbirds, manikins, tanagers, and the rare oilbird. See *Sightseeing*, page 95, and *Guide Services*, page 216, for more information.

Groups are often booked from the United States, spending a week at Asa Wright and a final few days in Tobago. Their busiest months are December through April, the dry season. During this period you need to make reservations one or two months in advance – maybe longer if you want one of the two rooms in the estate house. All rooms are priced the same, but those two are very pretty, though it can be noisy there in the early morning. Each guest receives one free tour a day; after a few days you will learn the trails well enough to go off on your own. There is handicap access to a degree, but it will be rigorous. Talk to them in advance if you have special needs.

Meals are very good (see Asa Wright under *Where To Eat*). Although the food may appear to be vegetarian from their literature, it is not. They even serve pretty good wines. Asa Wright is a lovely setting for a visit – there are staff who are knowledgeable and helpful, a perfect tropical forest setting, and sounds of the forest to soothe you to sleep or puzzle you in an interesting way if sleep eludes you.

Amenities: Rain forest setting, restaurant, guided tours.

Good for: Singles, couples, families with an interest in the natural environment (and heaven for bird watchers).

Comment: We were very impressed. Asa Wright is well-known to birders, but we could have whiled away a week or so very happily.

Blanchisseuse

BLANCHISSEUSE BEACH RESORT / LAGUNA MAR NATURE LODGE, 65½ Mile Marker, Paria Main Rd., Blanchisseuse; ☎ 628-3731, fax 628-3737. This German-style guest house currently has 12 rooms with bath and a separate four-bedroom cottage with kitchen; more units are planned. Rooms are $55 single, $75 double, not including service charges and a 15% tax. Located toward the end of Paria Main Rd. at the Marianne River, fishing is good and ocean swimming is nearby. The German owners, the Zollnas, have created order in a tropical setting. The guest house consists of two white buildings with six rooms each. There is a large veranda for relaxing and rooms come equipped with mosquito nets. Across the street they've opened the small Coco's Hut Restaurant and Bar. See *Where To Eat* for more information.

Amenities: Restaurant.

Good for: Singles, couples, small families.

Comment: If you want only rain forest views in this oceanside town, this is the place.

NORTH STAR/BOUGAN VILLA, L.P. #4, Paria Main Rd., Blanchisseuse; ☎ 637-4619. Bertram Blackman and his sister Sandra built this small guest house under the guiding influence of their gracious parents. The house sits by the water with five rooms, three up and two down, all with shared baths, for $35 a day. The best option is either of their two new apartments built right over the water for $50, all-inclusive. Rooms are comfortable and attractive, there's a fully equipped common kitchen, and a grassy lawn with steps leading down to the beach.

Amenities: Beachfront, kitchen facilities.

Good for: Singles, couples.

Comment: These are very nice people and they'll do their best to help you enjoy your stay.

READER'S COMMENT

"We stayed in the [Bougan Villa] apartments hanging over the water. They were great!" Greenberg and Angelucci, Mahwah, NJ.

SECOND SPRING BED & BREAKFAST INN, Lamp post 191, Blanchisseuse; ☎ 669-3909, fax 638-7393. Owned by Frenchwoman Ginette Holder, this guest house offers four nicely designed apartments, all with ocean views, terraces, and kitchenettes. The one cottage rents for $50 single, $60 double, and $70 triple. The studio units are $40 single and $50 double. Prices include continental breakfast and service charge. The setting is high on a hill at the edge of the rain forest. There's no AC, but with the sea breezes you probably won't need it. With tiles and wood and touches of antiques, this is a lovely spot. If you're having trouble finding it, just ask for directions to Mrs. Holder's guest house when you get into town. (Ginette promises to have a sign by the time you get here.) If you would like complete meals, Ginette will prepare them for an extra charge. If you're really lucky, she'll have figured out a way to open an antique shop like the one she had in Port of Spain. It was wonderful.

Amenities: Great views, stylish setting, continental breakfast.

Good for: Singles, romantic couples.

Comment: Blanchisseuse offers both rain forest and ocean. Second Spring gives you both in style.

SURF COUNTRY INN, North Coast Rd., Blanchisseuse; ☎/fax 669-2475. Owned by Mr. Andrew Hernandez, Sr., the Surf Inn is a charming and romantic guest house perched on a hill. Only three rooms are currently open, but they are planning to build a few more. Rooms have either balconies overlooking the bay or terraces by the garden. They are not large, but offer a small fridge, a hot water pot for tea or coffee, fresh flowers, a mosquito net, and ceiling fan. Rooms are $60 single or double, inclusive of tax and service charge, and the price also includes a full breakfast. See *Where To Eat.*

Amenities: *Mini-fridge, flowers, hot water pot, restaurant.*

Good For: *Singles, couples, especially romantics.*

Comment: *We thoroughly enjoyed our stay. Blanchisseuse offers more in the way of romantic accommodations than other places, and Surf Country Inn is no exception. Flowers in the room, pretty views, and candles are just the needed touches.*

Chaguaramas

THE BIGHT, Western Main Rd., at Peake Yacht Services; ☎ 634-4427, fax 634-4839, e-mail pys@cablenett.net. Five of their 10 comfortable rooms face a furnished patio beside the yacht harbor. Swimming is not advisable, but the view is pleasant. Rooms are quite nice and the price is $45 off-season, $55 during their busy season (September 29 through November 30), and $70 during Carnival. If you're having work done on your boat, room prices are discounted. There's a good restaurant on the second floor (see *Where To Eat* for more information).

Amenities: *Quiet, AC, restaurant/bar, shared patio and lawn right by the yacht harbor.*

Good for: *Singles or couples.*

Comment: *The Bight is one of the newer places in Chaguaramas. It's small, comfortable and affordable and makes a good base for hikes in the area or for visiting offshore islands. Be sure to ask for a room facing the water.*

CREWSINN, Chaguaramas; ☎ 634-4384 or 634-4385, fax 634-4175, e-mail crewsinn@trinidad.net.tt. This brand-new 42-room, four-suite hotel is a part of the upscale CrewsInn yachting complex. Prices range from $90 to $150 for a double with small fridge, cable TV, phone, sitting area, and water view. Non-smoking rooms are available. Guests have access to their pool, gym, and recreation area. Located just a half-hour from Port of Spain, this is a very good place to stay, even if you're not a yachty. There is an open-air upscale restaurant with mid-range prices, a bank, shops, and all the other services you might need while in Trinidad. Yachties with boats in the harbor receive a 35% discount.

Amenities: *AC, phone, cable TV, restaurant/bar, pool, yacht harbor view, non-smoking rooms, gym.*

Good for: *Anyone who does not actually need to stay right in Port of Spain.*

Comment: *This reminds me very much of yacht harbors on the coast of New England, but with a decidedly Caribbean flair.*

Las Cuevas

LAS CUEVAS BEACH HOTEL, Northern Main Rd., Las Cuevas; ☎ 669-5045. With 18 very basic rooms, they cater to the young beach crowd. This is a no-trouble, fun place for the young traveler. Rooms have private bath and a water view. A single room is about $8 or $14 with meals; doubles are about $12 or $26 with meals, all-inclusive. Meals provided are breakfast and dinner. Lunch is available, but not included in the room price. Food is local style with lots of fresh fish.

> *Amenities: Funkiness, restaurant.*
> *Good for: Young beach crowd on a budget.*
> *Comment: You're only a few minutes from the beach in this small town; this is the only hotel we found in the area. See the manager to arrange fishing trips.*

Maracas Bay

TRINIDAD MARACAS BAY HOTEL, Maracas Bay; ☎ 669-1914, fax 669-1643. Though the rooms are spacious and face the beach, the furnishings are very basic and quite musty. There is currently not much to choose from in this area if you want to stay a night. The hotel has a restaurant and a bar on the premises. The cost of a double room, $165, includes meals and taxes. If you choose to stay here for some reason, ask for a second-story room; at least you'll have a good view.

> *Amenities: AC, beach view, restaurant, bar.*
> *Good For: An overnight.*
> *Comment: We first saw the Maracas Bay Hotel under renovation and are disappointed that it didn't turn out better.*

Mayaro

AZEE'S HOTEL AND RESTAURANT, 3½ Mile Mark, Grand Lagoon, Mayaro; ☎ 630-9140, fax 630-4619. Only about a block from the beach down a sandy road, this very clean, modern, small hotel has AC and cable TV. Rooms are about $45, single or double, all-inclusive. There's a surprisingly formal restaurant/bar, as well, with great AC. Lunch or dinner will cost between $6 and $10. Breakfast is about $4.

> *Amenities: AC, TV, restaurant, beach access.*
> *Good For: Couples, friends.*
> *Comment: There's not much available on this coastline and Azee's came as a surprise. It's not a destination in and of itself, but if you're passing by and want to stay in the area, you should be comfortable here.*

Grand Rivière

MT. PLAISIR ESTATE HOTEL, Grand Rivière, one hour from Toco; ☎ 670-8381, fax 680-4553, e-mail info@mtplaisir.com. This Italian-owned guest house is easy to miss, but if you are looking for something in the northeast corner of Trinidad, it's one of the very few accommodations available. There are 10 attractive suites on the beach; including meals, a single is $105, a double $142. You should definitely consider including the cost of all meals as there is not yet much of a dining alternative in this area. Tours in the local jungle or up the nearby rivers can be arranged, as can visits to nearby isolated beaches.

> *Amenities: Beach, isolation, good restaurant.*
> *Good For: Anyone wanting good accommodations in this area.*
> *Comment: This as yet undeveloped part of Trinidad offers wild abandoned beaches and stunning rain forest.*

Tunapuna

PAX GUEST HOUSE, Mt. St. Benedict, Tunapuna; ☎/fax 662-4084, e-mail pax-g-h@trinidad.net, Web site www.paxgguesthouse.com. Pax is an independently owned guest house, located on the extensive grounds of a Benedictine monastery. Their 18 rooms are monastically furnished with large windows and great views. Only seven have private baths and three have AC. Including breakfast and dinner, single rooms with bath are $55, doubles $85. Set high in the hills, Pax is best known to bird watchers because of the nearby trails where you may see trogans, manikins, honeycreepers, and many others of the 120 species found on the grounds. Behind the guest house they have planted a hummingbird garden where you may see nine different species of hummingbirds, including the very special ruby topaz. Built originally as housing for the monastery, Pax is now nonsectarian, but it still has the feel of a spiritual retreat. Tours to other sights in Trinidad can be arranged and car rentals are available. They do not accept credit cards. On our last visit to Trinidad, we met an American couple who had stayed at Asa Wright and then at Pax. They were so thrilled by the kindness of the people at Pax that they stayed another week.

> *Amenities: Great views, restaurant, bird watching trails, car rentals, tours, some AC rooms.*
> *Good for: Bird watchers.*
> *Comment: This is not a place to kick up your heels, but for a calming environment you can't find better.*

Trinidad

Camping

Camping in the backwoods areas without a guide can be risky. Your sense of direction in these dense jungle areas may not serve you well and there are some very dangerous snakes that you certainly do not want to stumble upon. The good news is that there are now new guide services that will take you on adventurous camping/hiking treks. See *Guide Services* for more information. The deep forest of Trinidad holds challenging hikes and many wonderful surprises, but it is not without risks. You should not elect to go it alone until you are familiar with the area.

We're avid campers and found a place right on the beach in Blanchisseuse that seemed just fine, though a little primitive. Here you can pitch your tent or drape your mosquito net for under $2 per night. In the winter and early spring, the beach has rough waters which might be suitable for surfing, and there are good swimming areas nearby both in the ocean and in the Marianne River. If you're there in late spring or summer the ocean is quite calm and you can pop right out of your tent and go for a swim.

The campsite we're referring to is on Paria Main Road and hard to miss. As you are driving through upper Blanchisseuse heading toward the Marianne River you will find it on your left, just before reaching Coco's Hut Restaurant. Food supplies for an extended stay may be had as follows: Thursday the chicken man drives in, Saturdays the fresh vegetable man, and there's always great fresh fish. Tiny local shops can provide you with Cokes, rum, and other sundries. The name of the place is roughly "**Marianne camping, car park**." We met Evette Olivierre there. She is a very knowledgeable local guide and can take you up into the hills or to Paria waterfall. Just ask around and you'll find her. Camping facilities are minimal.

Where To Eat

■ About The Food

We don't travel to Trinidad and Tobago thinking about food (as we do when we set off for Italy), but there are good things to eat and places where the food matters less than the setting, especially in the Chaguaramas area. There you'll find the romantic, waterside restaurants you are dreaming of in a cold winter up north. The food in many of these places is pretty good, but it's the ocean and yachts and the tinkling of rigging on masts that will make your evening unforgettable.

Local Dishes

Aside from perfect settings, we also love food, and Trinidad and Tobago's roti is wonderful in all its forms. **Roti** is a large, very thin, flat bread, like a tortilla, filled with curries of all kinds and then folded up as a package. Unlike a filled tortilla, which is eaten rolled up, the roti package is first opened on your plate. You then tear off pieces of the bread and use them to pick up the filling. This we learned by accident. As we live in Mexico, I thought it was another type of burrito and picked up the whole thing and took a bite. I bit down hard on a chicken bone, and I figured out right away I was doing something wrong. Sometimes you'll find the roti wrapper itself filled with dried chickpeas. Our first time eating this style of roti puzzled us because the chickpeas kept falling out. It was good, but a little messy. Roti is available everywhere, and it was one of our favorite foods in Trinidad and Tobago.

Seafood is plentiful in Trinidad and Tobago, and the second real treat of the island is "**shark and bake**." This is a beach specialty with fried shark sandwiched between two halves of a piece of fried dough. You can dress it with lettuce and tomatoes and a choice of hot sauces for variation. It's absolutely delicious. We even brought a friend's "bake" recipe home and use it for burger buns, as we live in the mountains, far from the sea and fresh fish.

Natalie's Bake and Shark kiosk at Maracas Beach.

Our favorite foods are "local style," served in the less fancy restaurants. One staple local dish is actually several different varieties of stews in combination with a wide range of vegetables. Often served with rice, plantains, and sweet potatoes, the stews are rich with flavor, whether beef, chicken, pork, or fish. Just ask for "stew beef" or "stew chicken," etc.

Chinese food is also considered local. It is different from US-style Chinese food and you ought to give it a try. I can't put my finger on the exact differences, but even so it's good and widely available.

AUTHOR TIP *MSG is used in many of the Chinese restaurants here. Locally it's usually called **vetsin**, and you can ask for your food prepared without it; sometimes they can accommodate your request.*

Fast Food

Fast food has overtaken Trinidad and most of the restaurants Trinis recommended to us served some variety of fast or already prepared food. Surprisingly, for no apparent reason, Chinese fast food is about 50% more expensive for what you get than other types of fast food in Trinidad. With a high percentage of the population being of Indian heritage, we were disappointed when we didn't find lots of Indian restaurants where food is prepared to order.

If you're looking for familiar fast food, you'll find Pizza Hut and KFC franchises all over the island, but the local chains are really much better. Try Mario's, and especially Pizza Boys, for pizza, and Royal Castle for fried chicken.

Beverages

Fruit drinks are very popular in Trinidad, and if you like yours lightly spiked, fruit-flavored beers called **Shandys** come in wonderful flavors – sorrel, ginger, and lime. Like wine coolers, Shandys are low in alcohol and very popular. Made by the same company that produces **Carib beer**, Shandys are exported to other Caribbean islands, such as Jamaica. **Local wines** are made from a wide variety of plants and fruits and you can sample them at any of the Savannah food and drink stands or buy a bottle at the Port of Spain market on George St.

AUTHOR TIP *If you are going to be traveling around the island, you may want to consider taking beverages and a picnic lunch with you. You won't always find good places to stop for a meal and, if you do find one, it might not be open.*

Restaurants

■ Port of Spain & Suburbs

One of the areas of the city where you'll find new, upscale restaurants, bars, and night spots, is along Tragarete Road, which runs out of the center of Port of Spain by Newtown. Some of the more established restaurants are in this area too, but they come and go with surprising speed. Let us know if you find something you think is really special.

BREAKFAST SHED, Waterfront, Wrightson Rd., Port of Spain (near the Cruise Ship Complex); ☎ 627-2337. Local specialties are served at breakfast from 6 AM through lunch with prices from $3 to $5 for a delicious meal. Similar to the several small eateries in Store Bay, Tobago, you'll find a choice of offerings, all authentic and all wonderfully filling. This is a local landmark and a great place to try stew beef or chicken.

LA FANTASIE, Normandie Hotel, 10 Nook Ave., St. Ann's; ☎ 624-1181. The Normandie presents entertainment in it's outside courtyard; having dinner at La Fantasie first would be a great start to the evening. They serve nouvelle creole food in a very stylish and attractive restaurant. Dinner for two will be under $50 and sometimes you can take advantage of their special three-course dinners for under $12. Tax and service charge will be added to your bill.

HONG KONG CITY RESTAURANT, 86A Corner Tragarete Rd. and Maraval Rd., Newtown, Port of Spain; ☎ 622-3949. Good Chinese food at reasonable prices. They have a second location at Piarco International Airport.

HOT SHOPPE, various locations. This is a very popular local chain serving good rotis. Shrimp is $3.50, beef or chicken are $2.50, and vegetarian rotis are about $2. The food is great and the price is right at these crowded local places. The surprising thing is that the roti is not spicier than in other places, but they really are served hot.

INDIGO, Second Level, Rear West Mall, West Moorings (no phone). It is next to MOBS (see page 113). Opened a few years ago with an ambitious menu, Indigo introduced tandoori cooking in this small very stylishly decorated restaurant. Current menu favorites are Indigo Chicken pâté for an appetizer at $4.50, and roasted chicken in herbed coconut at $11.25 for an entrée. All main courses are served with fresh vegetables of the day. Lunch is served Monday through Friday between 11:30 and 2 PM; dinner is from 7 to 11 PM, except Sundays.

JOHNNY'S, West Mall, West Moorings (no phone). The mall food court has several eateries, and Johnny's is the best. Serving a fresh, inexpensive, and good-tasting variety of local foods, Johnny's is popular with Trinis.

Trinidad

MARIO'S PIZZA, two shops in Port of Spain at either #1 Cipriani Blvd., ☎ 627-5464, or at 57 Independence Square, ☎ 623-5464. This is a local chain with locations all over Trinidad. They serve pizza and other fast food to eat in, take out, or be delivered. Including a 50¢ charge for delivery, a family-size pepperoni and green pepper pizza and two large Cokes will be under $10 delivered, and it's pretty good.

MONSOON, 72 Tragarete Rd. at the corner of Picton, Port of Spain; ☎ 628-ROTI. Monsoon's lavender neon sign outside is an indication of the chic modern interior. It's open for lunch and dinner from 11 AM to 10 PM; closed Sundays. On Wednesday evenings they offer a special buffet with several main dishes, vegetables, rice, coffee and dessert for $12, including tax, but not service. You'll need reservations, but same day is fine. Their normal fare is a wide variety of curried meats and fish served with vegetables, rice, and potatoes, offered as a roti, which they call dhalpuri, from $2 for chicken to $3.50 for conch. The same offering of one meat and three vegetables with "busted up bread" or "bus up shot," called paratha, will cost $3 for chicken and $5.50 for conch. They have soft drinks, and also serve beer. Either the dhalpuri or paratha is a filling and good-tasting meal.

PATRAGE, 159 Tragarete Rd., St. James (next to the Invaders steel band pan yard); ☎ 622-6219. Patrage has another location (most say it's even better) in El Socorro on Back Chain St., but it's out of the way, and the food at the Tragarete Rd. location was just fine for us. Specializing in roti, it's another favorite Trinidadian take-out style restaurant. You can have your roti there or take it with you for about $3, and it's a very satisfying meal.

PELICAN INN PUB, 2-4 Coblentz Ave., Port of Spain; ☎ 624-RHUM. Serving English pub-style food with lots of different beers, the Pelican is a great gathering place for locals and visitors. It's very informal, the drinks are cheap, and on Fridays there is standing room only. Usually this is the first stop on a typical Friday evening round of entertainment – after this it's on to dancing.

PIZZA BOYS, Park Street, Port of Spain; ☎ 627-2697. With locations all over Trinidad this local fast-food chain serves burgers, chicken, Chinese food, pizza and ice cream. The decor is 1950s style with decorative juke boxes at the table and other paraphernalia of that time. The pizza is quite good and everything seems fresh and inexpensive. Delivery hours are from 10 AM to 11 PM. With all the writing we did in the evenings, we often ordered one of their pizzas for a late-night treat.

RAFTERS, corner of Woodford St. & Warner St., Newtown, Port of Spain; ☎ 628-9258. Rafters is actually two restaurants in two buildings right next to each other with one entrance. The first is a more formal restaurant with traditional white tablecloths and subdued decorations. The second building was originally a dry goods store. They left the best of the old building and turned it into a very chic bar/restaurant with great neon signs for lighting, an attractive bar, and bar stool-style seating at colorful tables. In all, they created a bit of home away from home for Americans and Europeans, and the place is popular with Trinis as well. The food is decidedly

American-style and they do a close approximation. Service is excellent. In the restaurant, they offer a roast beef buffet dinner for $21, inclusive of taxes and service. It includes soup, salad, entrée and vegetables, coffee and dessert. You'll recognize everything on their à la carte menu, with appetizers from $4 to $5, steaks $18, and seafood from $11 to $22 (for lobster thermidor). They are open for lunch and serve dinner until about 10 PM. Uncomplicated good food is their specialty. An enterprising fellow outside directs parking. He's an independent and will watch your car if you give him $1.

TIKI VILLAGE RESTAURANT, at the Kapok Hotel, 16-18 Cotton Hill, St. Clair; ☎ 622-6441. Chinese specialties are served at lunch and dinner and Dim Sum, a Chinese brunch, is served from 11 to 3 PM weekends and holidays. Reservations aren't required, but suggested if you want a window table. This stylish restaurant is on the next to the top floor of the hotel and has great views from its large windows, especially at lunch. Their pot stickers are very good and the entrées are all freshly prepared. You can ask for food free of MSG (vetsin). Service is excellent, and dinner for two costs about $30. Free parking is available in the hotel lot next door.

VENI MANGÉ, 67-A Ariapita Ave., Woodbrook, Port of Spain; ☎ 624-4597. Local Trinidadian specialties are served at lunch only from 11:30 AM to 3 PM, but they are open for dinner on Wednesday evening at 7:30. Lunch, with one of their special fruit juices, will be under $20 for two; dinner about $30 for two. Of their three lunchtime offerings, one is always vegetarian. Friday is the best day for "liming," because it is a very popular social gathering place to start the weekend with drinks and light snacks. It's owned and managed by two very popular sisters, Alison and Roses Hezekiah, who are both considered bright lights in Port of Spain.

■ In Nearby Chaguaramas

THE ANCHORAGE RESTAURANT, Pt. Gourde Rd., Chaguaramas (West of Port of Spain); ☎ 634-4334. The Anchorage has an international menu, specializing in seafood and steaks. Located right on the water, they've taken every advantage of the view and sea breezes. The restaurant is entirely open air with lots of rustic wood, but still has formal touches such as white tablecloths. They are open seven days a week, serving lunch from 11 AM to 3 PM and dinner from 4 to 11 PM. Friday and Saturday they have music, dancing, and "liming" and it's a busy night spot for foreigners and Trinis alike. The menu is varied, with all dishes given colorful names like "Dance the Moon" (butterflied shrimp in a curry and coconut sauce) and "Buccoo Bacchanal" (grilled fish lapped with a mushroom and wine sauce). They have some interesting appetizers, along with the usual shrimp cocktails, and a variety of salads and vegetarian meals. Dinner entrées range from $12 to $21; an average meal might end up at about $30 US per person with drinks. Tax of 15% and service of 10% will be added to your bill.

THE BIGHT HOTEL AND RESTAURANT, at Peake Yacht Services, Chaguaramas (West of Port of Spain); ☎ 634-4427/4423/4420. This popular place has a sports bar/restaurant inside and more formal dining on the large outside terrace overlooking the yacht harbor. Open early for breakfast, it is busy throughout the day and into the night. The drinks are strong and the food is as good as it is reasonably priced. Their snack menu includes spicy wings at under $2 and fish and chips for $3. All are delicious, but portions are snack-like as advertised in the menu. The fish served as "fish and chips" is fried in a batter with herbs. It was the most unusual batter-fried fish I've had and one of the best. Don't miss the accra, fried dough with bits of salt fish served as an appetizer. It may not sound great, but it is. The Bight is part of a marina and serves the yachty crowd and Port of Spain yuppies.

THE LIGHTHOUSE RESTAURANT, at CrewsInn Yacht Complex, Chaguaramas; ☎ 634-4384/5 or 634-4542. If you like upscale, casual, yachty places, you'll love this. The open-air restaurant sits right over the CrewsInn harbor filled with beautiful boats. The service is good and the food is too. From the stuffed crab back appetizer at under $4 to a dinner of coconut curried chicken at under $7, both the quantity and quality are sure to please just about everyone. This is a very pretty place. It felt much like my favorite places on the coast back home in New England, but with a Caribbean twist.

■ Away From The City

Blanchisseuse

COCO'S HUT RESTAURANT AND BAR, Blanchisseuse (no phone). This is a small restaurant across the road from the Blanchisseuse Beach Resort guest house. The menu offers local food with a German touch; our pork chops were reminiscent of schnitzel. Be sure to specify how you want your meat cooked. The service is very slow, but the food is freshly prepared and, in Blanchisseuse, what's your hurry. Lunch or dinner with a drink will be $12 to $15 per person.

SURF COUNTRY INN RESTAURANT, North Coast Rd., Blanchisseuse; ☎ 669-2475. The inn serves local and international dishes in a bar and restaurant on the hill overlooking the bay. It is a very romantic setting, like their guest house, and the food is quite good. Good enough, in fact, to have been written up in several European and American magazines. We had fish with sweet potato pie, black-eyed peas, rice, vegetables and salad for two for about $35, inclusive. Everything was freshly prepared and delicious. This is not a late-night place, so plan to dine relatively early.

Maracas Bay

NATALIE'S BAKE AND SHARK, Maracas Bay Beach. Fried dough is cut in half and filled with freshly fried, fileted shark. They cost about $1.50 each and taste great. This is the most memorable food we ate in restaurants in both Trinidad and Tobago. Also try **Richard's Bake and Shark** across the street in the parking area.

Sightseeing

■ Port of Spain Area

 BOTANICAL GARDENS, Circular Rd. (locally called Zoo St.), Port of Spain. Across the street from Queen's Park Savannah, next to the zoo, the publicly owned Botanical Gardens dates from the early 19th century. This 70-acre property is open during daylight hours. On first inspection it looks neglected, but despite the lack of care, with a knowledgeable guide it offers a view of some unusual tropical plants and trees. One thing that may save the gardens is that they lie just outside the President's official residence. If he likes gardens, we may all be in luck.

Inside the park-like setting you'll find a small graveyard where past colonial governors have been laid to rest. There is only one space left, reserved for the wife of former Governor Solomon Hochoy. Hochoy was a great friend to the people of Trinidad, a British political appointee who rose above politics on behalf of the people. During the week, it is often possible to find a government guide at the gardens when a cruise ship is in port (cruise ship travelers are often brought to see the gardens).

AUTHOR TIP

At the entrance to the Botanical Gardens, look for Anthony Graves, a tall (about 6'4"), very thin, bearded black fellow. He'll give you a great guided tour of the gardens, explaining what you're seeing, describing medicinal uses of some of the plantings and, once in a while, throw in local political gossip. He's very well informed and charges only about $10 per person for a tour of an hour or longer. We thoroughly enjoyed meeting Anthony and taking his tour.

Some of what you'll see includes the **queen of the flowers tree**, the national flower of Beijing, which has delicately scented red and yellow flowers, and **screw pines**, with inedible pineapple-size fruit resembling the surface of the brain. The fruit's bristles were once used for toothbrushes. Another cosmetically useful plant, the **roucou**, produces nuts that contain red seeds that were originally crushed and used as skin decorations by the Amerindians and later on as lip color. The **cassia fistula** provides long, string-bean-like fruit used during Carnival to join in the music-making. **Samum trees** are the largest-growing variety of tree in Trinidad and Tobago and usually are home to a great many epiphytes. The bush-like **jatoo plant** has not only pretty purple trumpet-shaped flowers, but its seeds are later boiled for a tea. The tea is intoxicating and is said to re-create a young man's libido in an older man's body. **Chaconia** is here, too, a beautiful red-flowering bush that is the national flower of Trinidad and Tobago.

The **bloody beef tree** is an oddity. A scratch on the surface bark gives the appearance of red beef and, surprisingly, the tree repairs these scratches almost immediately. The tree is originally from Peru, where it enjoys religious significance. The **blood wood tree**, as distinctive as the bloody beef, exudes a blood-colored liquid that was once used as a dye. The popular **cinnamon tree** is surrounded by a fence to protect it from greedy cooks. The fence is not enough, however, as cinnamon bark and leaves are heavily used in Trinidad and Tobago cooking. **Heliconia**, which grows freely on the island in the rain forests, is a beautiful plant with heavy red, yellow, and green flowers, the colors of the Rastafarians. You'll often see Rastafarian photographs with this flower included. **Date palms** provide not only needed shade, but when the berries turn red they are harvested for wine and palm oil.

There is a small area with plants that have medicinal qualities. One of them is the **wonder of the world plant**, whose leaves are scraped to remove their outer skin, then heated and placed on the body to reduce swelling and inflammation. The **chanallaner**'s leaves are used to make a tea to treat headaches and fever. The **wild sugar apple** is a fruit about the size of a large lemon, with a speckled, warty surface. While on the tree it is poisonous. When it falls from the tree, it is ground up into a white powder and either mixed with water as a drink or rubbed directly on a wound to relieve pain.

EMPEROR VALLEY ZOO, Circular Rd. (locally called Zoo St.), Port of Spain; ☎ 622-3530. Located across the street on the north side of Queen's Park Savannah next to the Royal Botanical Gardens, the zoo has a good collection of local animals and birds and a fascinating reptile house, but the aquarium is disappointing. There are several types of small monkeys and a good representation of birds. The zoo is privately owned and appears very well-managed. Animal enclosures are clean, and most were well de-signed to accommodate each animal's needs. The terrain of the zoo is hilly and, since the land was formerly part of the Botanical Gardens, the plants and trees are quite interesting. We spoke casually with park staff, who seem very committed to public education and to continually improving conditions for the animals maintained there. They are doing a great job. The zoo is a must-stop for families and those interested in seeing some of the smaller wildlife of Trinidad and Tobago and other Caribbean islands. It is open from 9:30 AM to 6 PM; admission for adults is under $1.

LAPEYROUSE CEMETERY, between Tragarete Rd. and Ariapita Ave., central Port of Spain. This is an old cemetery full of history and is well worth a visit.

Lapeyrouse Cemetery, Port of Spain.

MAGNIFICENT SEVEN, Circular Rd., Port of Spain. Along the west side of Queen's Park Savannah, you'll see seven large, architecturally exuberant, colonial buildings. One of the best is Whitehall, which was restored recently at a cost of millions and is now the office of the Prime Minister. Whitehall is officially open to the public by appointment, but you can probably stop in without reservations and take a look if you're interested. If you're in Port of Spain for a few days, you'll ride by these buildings almost every day.

NATIONAL MUSEUM, 117 Frederick St. at the corner of Keate, Port of Spain; ☎ 623-5941. The museum has exhibits on island geography, history, and art, and also houses a collection of Carnival costumes. Foreign embassies are also staging temporary exhibitions here. Open 10 AM to 6 PM, Tuesday through Saturday, and 2 to 6 PM on Sunday. Admission is free.

OLD POLICE STATION, opposite the Red House on St. Vincent between Sackville and Queen Streets, Port of Spain. This 1876 structure, now in ruins, appears to have been a church or convent. However, it was designed to be, and always was, the Port of Spain police station. During the coup attempt in 1990 the building was blown up and extensive damage was done. The new police station is across the street. You may notice a Star of David on the building with a dove at its center. This is the police symbol in Trinidad and Tobago, and we were told the story of this oddity. Apparently the first police commissioner in Trinidad was Jewish, and he convinced people that the Star of David he wore was a good luck symbol. It was accepted for the police insignia long ago and is still used. Until recently, the Star of David was also found on the four corners of postage stamps in Trinidad and Tobago.

QUEEN'S PARK SAVANNAH, northern side of central Port of Spain. This city park of 199 acres, once a sugar plantation, is home to cricket fields and the grandstands where many of the spectacular Carnival events take place. If you happen to be nearby, you can always get a refreshing drink from any one of several fresh coconut-water vendors at the Savannah every day.

RED HOUSE, Abercromby St., between Knox and Hart Streets, Port of Spain. This is the familiar name for the Parliament Building across from the old police station and in front of Woodford Square.

WHITEHALL – See **Magnificent Seven**, above.

WOODFORD SQUARE, Abercromby St., Port of Spain. In front of "Red House" or Parliament, this public park, similar to the park in front of the White House in the US, is host to voluble speakers with strong opinions. Otherwise, it's just a park.

■ Central Trinidad

MUD VOLCANOES, Piparo and Devil's Woodyard. These are sights I thought I would never see. Even on this trip, when we planned a whole day just to find them, we got hopelessly lost. The start of the trip begins easily enough at the Trintoc/Pointe-à-Pierre turnoff on the Uriah Butler Highway on the west coast, where you turn left after the exit (away from the refinery). While lost, we drove to and fro on very bad roads, through beautiful lands with cane fields and a teak forest. Much of this area is now abandoned plantations, but you can still see the coffee and cocoa trees in the dense vegetation. Eventually we found the site of the most recent eruption of mud in the town of **Piparo**. It was initially very disappointing, as all we could see was a huge pile of dried mud, but lively children quickly arrived to give us their tour and all the facts.

The volcanoes at Piparo erupted in February 1997 and covered 15 acres with mud in under 10 minutes. According to our child guide, mud flew 350 feet in the air and poured down to cover 11 homes, damaging another four. No humans were injured, but animals were not so lucky. They lost "four dogs, three goats, two cows, and a baby calf... and chickens and ducks." There's not much to see other than a whole lot of mud, which still oozes, oddly cold, from two small hills. Thinking this over, I'm not so sure why I find this phenomenon so interesting, but there you are. Take a look if you like.

Having seen the volcanoes at Piparo, we gave up trying to find Devil's Woodyard, but readers of our last guide sent wonderful information to us in a long letter. Here is a snippet of what they had to say.

Trinidad

READER'S COMMENT

"After about an hour's drive from San Fernando we did arrive at the Devil's Woodyard. As you turn off the road there is a small carpark with a tin sign announcing it and a board giving information about the volcanoes. The site is about an acre in size with several volcanoes slowly oozing mud from craters a foot or so high. There are streams of dried mud and the impression is of a dried-up lake bottom.... The whole site had a deserted and unused feel to it, we being the only people there, and it is in one of the most remote inland areas of Trinidad.... even with my Trinidadian sister-in-law driving it was quite hard to find." David & Pat Ayling, Surrey, UK

SAN JUAN ESTATE, in Gran Couva, is a cocoa estate still in operation. Apart from the fascinating processes that bring us chocolate, you can see the old estate house and tended grounds with their beautiful samaan trees. The cocoa production season is from December to June. Cocoa plantations are ideal habitat for birds, and the San Juan Estate is no exception. You will see dozens of species in just one visit.

■ Along The East Coast

NARIVA SWAMP, Bush Bush Wildlife Sanctuary, between Manzanilla and Mayaro. Located about half-way along the east coast of Trinidad, Nariva is a freshwater, seemingly impenetrable, mangrove swamp – there are no local signposts or readily visible entry points. Home to howler and capuchin monkeys, water-snakes and caiman, the swamp itself is undeveloped for tourism. In years past, Nariva suffered destruction of habitat by rice growers who cut areas of the swamp for agriculture, but recently restrictions on these encroachments have been enforced. An important activity new to the swamp is the Manatee Project, which has set aside protected habitat for this endangered species. You can make arrangements to explore the area with a tour guide (see the *Guide Services* chapter) or contact the Wildlife Division of the Forestry Department (☎ 622-7476). Asa Wright also provides bird watching excursions in the swamp and they're worth a call. While touring here, bring binoculars, camera (we recommend fast film), and strong insect repellent.

CAUTION

If you take any tours in Nariva Swamp, do not wear perfumes or anything scented, as it will attract bees.

Mangrove trees at Nariva Swamp.

TAMANA TRAIL AND BAT CAVE, near Sangre Grande, has been the focus of nature films by the prestigious BBC and National Geographic. Thousands of insect- and fruit-eating bats nest here, flying out at sunset to feed. This area is also home to many bird species, though the bat cave most certainly is the high point of the trip. Make arrangements with a good guide; see listings in the *Guide Services* chapter.

■ Along The North Coast

PARIA WATERFALL, North Coast. The falls are accessible from Blanchisseuse either on foot or by boat. The trail is wide and comfortable, and it will take about an hour and a half to reach the falls, where hardy souls can bathe in its chilly waters. In Blanchisseuse, ask for Evette Olivierre at the Marianne Camping/Car Park on Paria Main Rd. She knows the trail well and will lead you for about $10 a person for two; ask about group rates. It will cost approximately $52 for the boat, round-trip.

■ Along The Northeast Coast

TURTLE EGG LAYING – The shoreline east of Blanchisseuse, which is not accessible by road, provides a nesting home to leatherback turtles in late spring and early summer. (See *Flora & Fauna*, pages 26-28, for detailed information.)

■ Along The West Coast

CARONI SWAMP NATIONAL PARK AND BIRD SANCTUARY, West Coast, off Uriah Butler Highway. A favorite with bird watchers, Caroni is a huge, brackish-water, mangrove swamp. The vegetation is unvarying and the boat trip through the channels to the swamp lake is dull. However, Caroni has its own special attraction – it is a roosting home for thousands of **scarlet ibis**, Trinidad's national bird.

DID YOU KNOW? *Until the mid-1960s the scarlet ibis was hunted not only for its meat, but especially for its feathers, which were highly prized in making Carnival costumes. It is now protected in Trinidad and Tobago.*

You can arrange to visit Caroni either at dawn, when the birds fly out en masse, or in the late afternoon, when they return in small groups to roost for the night. On the trip to the lake, you'll see herons and egrets, but the scarlet ibis is the star attraction – it is a vibrant, scarlet red and resembles a small flamingo.

A new visitor center has been in the works for years, but on our recent visit it still wasn't open. Caroni tours cost $10 per person. You can also be picked up and returned to your hotel for an additional $20 to $25 per person. **Nanan's** (☎ 645-1305) is the most commonly used tour guide to the swamp, but everyone charges about the same as Nanan's and delivers similar services. Another tour operator to call is **James Madoo** (☎ 662-7356). His tour fees are the same as Nanan's, but he will pick you up at your hotel at $20 for two.

The trip is made in large boats carrying about 30 people; sit toward the front to escape the motor-exhaust fumes. Unfortunately, the noise of the outboard engine scares off much of the wildlife you might otherwise see along the way to the lake. Once there, they tie up, turn off the engines, and everyone awaits the ibis.

Special Needs: Binoculars and a telephoto lens for your camera.

Getting Here: Leave Port of Spain on Beetham Highway, heading east. Take Uriah Butler Highway south toward San Fernando, getting off at the Caroni exit. It's about a 20-minute trip.

AUTHOR TIP *Caroni Swamp is the perfect place for a canoe or kayak tour, because the noise of motorized boats scares off most of the wildlife you would otherwise see.*

Nick & Davy
6/18/2000

Trinidad

PITCH LAKE, La Brea. In the southwest corner of Trinidad, about an hour and a half drive from Port of Spain, there's a pitch lake. Touted as a "wonder of the world," which it really is, its appearance can be disappointing. This peculiar small lake supplies road-building tar to countries around the world. It has been recorded in history and reportedly supplied the pitch for corking vessels during the time of colonial exploration. Widely believed to replenish itself, in reality it grows smaller each year.

At the parking area you'll encounter lots of people asking to be your guide. Arriving in the afternoon will free you from the sometimes unpleasant competition for your business. To avoid problems with would-be-guides, go to the security booth and ask for assistance in selecting someone or see below for our recommendation.

AUTHOR TIP

To avoid hassles with guides at the lake, call ***Marvin Billy***, ☎ *648-7720. Contact him in the evening a day ahead to make an appointment with him to be your guide. When you arrive at the lake, simply ask for him by name at the security booth. He was our guide and we found him informative and easygoing. An hour-long tour will cost about $5, and tips are appreciated – unemployment is high in this area of Trinidad.*

Marvin Billy, guide at the pitch lake.

The lake is a puzzling oddity. In small areas, the pitch is liquid, while in others it resembles dry elephant skin. In small pools of water you'll find delicately fragrant lotus flowers. It would be a shame not to see it while you're in the area.

> ***Getting Here:*** *From Port of Spain, take the Beetham Highway east to the Uriah Butler Highway, heading south. Pass through San Fernando, staying on Southern Main Rd., also called Trunk Road. Follow the signs to La Brea, the small town on the edge of this peculiar sight. You'll know you're there by the deterioration in the road surface and by the smell, and by the feeling that you are on a moving surface. The trip will take about 1½ hours each way.*

POINT-À-PIERRE WILDFOWL TRUST, Trintoc Oil Refinery, Pointe-à-Pierre; ☎ 637-5145/662-4040, e-mail wildfowl.trust@petrotrin.com, Web site http://users.carib-link.net/~wildfowl. Reservations necessary. This private volunteer organization has the unique distinction of finding itself deep in the heart of oil refinery property. That is unusual, but the people involved are no less unique. Committed to education, preservation, and an ambitious endangered species breeding program, president Molly Gaskin and vice president Karilyn D. Shephard are impressive people. Both are deeply concerned with wildlife and habitat preservation. They are also aware that compromises will have to be made and better solutions found in a developing world where human encroachment on the natural environment is unavoidable. Believing that genuine education leads to positive action, they are committed to finding constructive solutions.

The preserve began with the idea of providing habitat for water birds, which an oil company executive had noticed were declining in numbers. In the 1920s, two man-made ponds were created and the 67-acre preserve was on its way. Later, the breeding program was introduced to ensure the survival of endangered species. Some of these, like the scarlet ibis, formerly nested in Trinidad. Point-à-Pierre has six breeding pairs of the ibis, and has been very successful in releasing chicks into the wild.

On the preserve 80 bird species are commonly found, although it may take you a while to record all of them. Some that you may see are the wild Muscovy duck, the blue-winged teal, silver pintail, or hooded mergansers. Wading birds and songbirds also make their home in the preserve. Staff are also breeding blue and gold macaws, and they have several natural breeding habitat enclosures. There is a habitat for caiman, which are native to the area, and another for one of the water snakes found in the preserve, a rainbow boa constrictor. Aside from birds that are native to the area, 35 of the 38 tropical bat species find a home here – insect, fruit, and vampire varieties.

The initial tour takes a little over an hour and will costs $1 per adult. They like to have two or three days notice, but can be flexible if that isn't possible. There is a small building with film and video presentations on the second floor; the first floor houses a gift shop and displays of animals and historic artifacts.

Special needs: Binoculars, walking shoes, fast film for your camera. Trails are not readily wheelchair accessible, although much can be seen from accessible areas, especially with a good pair of binoculars.

Getting Here: From Port of Spain take Beetham Highway east. Turn south on Uriah Butler Highway and take the Pointe-à-Pierre exit. Turn right over the highway. The entrance is directly ahead. The trip will take about 45 minutes.

RUM DISTILLERY TOUR, Caroni 1975, Ltd. Tours can be easily arranged by calling the Public Relations Department, ☎ 636-2311, ext. 2700 or 2701; fax 636-4976; e-mail prcaroni@tstt.net.tt. Two prime rums, one called Superb White Magic, a white rum aged seven years, and a premium rum called Premium Old Cast, aged 10 years, are produced at this facility. The year 2000 represents the 25th anniversary of the private ownership and many special events are planned.

SUGAR FACTORY TOUR, owned and operated by Caroni 1975, Ltd. You may visit either of their two factories. **Brechin Castle**, locally called the BC Factory, in Couva, or **St. Madelin**, on the outskirts of San Fernando. Tours can be easily arranged by contacting the Public Relations Department, ☎ 636-2311, ext. 2700 or 2701; fax 636-4976; e-mail prcaroni@ tstt.net.tt.

The **BC sugar processing plant** is over 100 years old and operates only during the four- or five-month harvest season, January to mid-May. There are great opportunities for camera buffs, but be sure to bring very fast film for the low interior light. Caroni is the largest landholder in Trinidad and Tobago, and sugar is a big part of their business. Cane is harvested either mechanically or manually and brought to the factory in trucks around the clock for processing during the season.

Your guide will take you through every process, from raw cane being delivered to the final drying of table sugar. We found it fascinating, and it would probably be a great tour for extremely well-behaved children over eight years of age. Remember, this is a busy factory and there are no special safeguards for children. They process about 300 tons of cane a day and produce brown table sugar, molasses, and a less sweet product for the production of rum.

BC is conscious of conservation, and we were impressed by their recycling and reuse of all the by-products of sugar production. Our guide was a senior level lab assistant who began working at BC as a laborer after college; he made a lot of progress in a few years. We also met the sugar boiler, who took time out to explain the crystallization process in a way we could understand. Everyone we met along the way was proud of what they were doing and pleased to have curious visitors. The tour took about two hours and we were excited the whole time. It's a great opportunity to see where all that sweet stuff comes from.

Although heavily invested in sugar, Caroni is diversifying into citrus, rice, livestock, and aquaculture. If you're interested, ask if you can visit their aquaculture unit at the old Orange Grove Sugar factory, just off the Beetham Highway between Port of Spain and the airport.

> ***Getting Here:*** *From Port of Spain take Beetham Highway east to Uriah Butler Highway, and head south toward San Fernando. After about 15 or 20 minutes you'll see sugarcane fields. Begin to watch for the Couva/Preysal exit. At the end of the exit, turn right over the highway and take your first left. After about five km take a left at the palm-lined entrance to the factory. If you're feeling lost, just follow the trucks full of fresh-cut sugarcane.*

SEWDASS SADHU SHIV MANDIR, on the west coast in Waterloo, is a temple built in the sea because its devout Hindu builder owned no land. We didn't see this, but wish we had. It has recently been restored, and has always attracted religious pilgrims. If you are in the area, take a look and let us know what you find.

■ The Northwest

Bocas Islands

CARERA ISLAND – Long considered escape-proof because it is surrounded by shark-filled waters like Alcatraz, Carera was home to one of Trinidad's prisons.

CENTIPEDE ISLAND – One of those small ice-cream-scoop-shaped islands passed on your left as you head out to the larger islands in this group. Centipede, as you can imagine, is known for its centipedes – they are said to be very large, though we didn't see any. It is also a roosting site for pelicans, and the trees are covered with these large birds each evening. Hawks are also commonly sighted here.

CHACACHACARE – Still bearing its Amerindian name, Chacachacare was formerly a leprosarium and is now an island preserve, covering 900 acres. The leper hospital and its associated buildings have been looted, but you will still see much of the larger equipment and facilities that were there when it was closed in the mid-20th century. The island was also Simon Bolivar's jumping-off point for the invasion of Venezuela. There is a good swimming beach on the island, a lighthouse, and salt pond; manta rays swim offshore. For permission to visit Chacachacare, contact the Chaguaramas Development Authority (CDA), ☎ 634-4364. For five people or fewer, the CDA charges $50 for the boat and guide. Expect to spend about four hours. CDA will arrange to take groups out to the island on their boat or will give you permission to visit on your own by arranging transportation through the Home Owners Association boat ferries in the same area.

GASPAR GRANDE ISLAND (CAVES), commonly called Gasparee, features a very interesting network of underground caves. It is open from 9 AM to 2:30 PM; the best time of day to visit is between 10 AM and 1 PM. Elwyn Francis was our guide to the cave system and he is as knowledgeable as he is agreeable to be with. After paying about $2 per person, we walked across a wide lawn to the cave entrance. There are stairs leading down and lighting that accentuates the cave formations. The rock is limestone, which over millennia was dissolved by slightly acidic rainfall seeping through the rocks from above. At the entrance you'll see (and smell) some of the 500 or so nesting fruit bats that make their home in the cave. As you descend, the quality of the cave formations – stalactites and stalagmites – become more impressive until you reach the base of the currently developed system. There you'll see a pool of saltwater as clear as glass. If you watch carefully, you'll see leaves float very subtly this way and that, indicating that the cave is connected to tidal action of the surrounding sea. The cave tour is limited to safe areas, but experienced spelunkers may contact the Chaguaramas Development Authority, ☎ 634-4364, for a guide to the undeveloped and more dangerous parts of the cave system.

AUTHOR TIP

Ramish Darmoo *can be contacted directly to ferry you to any of the outlying islands. He's a good boatman and knowledgeable about the area. His home number is ☎ 634-4331, or you can page him at 625-5472. You can also leave a message and he'll get back to you to make arrangements.*

Some of our friends and many other Trinis explored the caves as brave and foolish boys prior to 1972, before there were stairs or any safe way back to the surface. Diving into the underground pool between two large rock formations was the game to play for the eight- to 15-year-old crowd, and many have stories to tell of close calls and near misses. You won't have those problems now, and the pleasure of seeing the caves will be undiminished.

Getting Here: *Leave Port of Spain on the Beetham Highway heading west and stay to the left when there's any choice. You'll find yourself on Western Main Road. Follow that for about 15 minutes, passing several boat yards, and you'll come to the Island Property Owners Association on your left (if you get to the National Guard base you've gone too far). Stop and ask for the island ferries. Prices are posted.*

Trinidad

Arrival at Gasparee with Ramish Darmoo.

ISLAND PROPERTY OWNERS ASSOCIATION - PRICES	
Gasparee caves	TT$90 / US$15.50
Gasparee	Fantasy Island TT$55 / US$9.50
Monos	TT$55 / US$9.50
Balmoral	TT$60 / US$10.50
Domas	TT$65 / US$11.25
Parking at the Association	may cost you US$2

CHAGUARAMAS DEVELOPMENT AUTHORITY (CDA), Chaguaramas; ☎ 634-4364/4227, fax 625-2465. This office manages the natural environment of the Chaguaramas area, offering educational programs and tours. Bright and engaging Dr. Jesma McFarland is park planner, and Kathleen Pinder is head of product marketing and development. A subdepartment responsible for tours and events is headed by Sharon Sharpe Gomez. Permissions for touring the area are granted when you hire a CDA guide. Permissions and guided tours on trails or to the nearby Bocas Islands are all under $20/person, some of the most reasonable tour prices you'll find.

You'll be advised to contact this office for tour information or permissions for several of the sights listed in this section. But, if you're in the area, feel free to stop by and see their new guest, Julius, the five-foot boa constrictor, locally known as a *macajuel*. Julius is replacing Fred, their boa who died a few years ago. Fred was quite a remarkable animal; surprisingly "she" foiled repeated attempts to release her into the wild by showing up looking for human company in the backyards of CDA's neighbors. She had lived at CDA since a baby and was named when presumed male. Boas are protected in Trinidad, and Julius will be a great part of the educational efforts being made on behalf of these often-mistreated creatures.

> *Getting Here: Leave Port of Spain on Beetham Highway heading west. Stay to the left when there's a choice and you'll find yourself on Western Main Road. Follow along past the police station on your left until you see large greenish buildings on your right – the convention center. CDA is behind the convention center.*

CHAGUARAMAS MILITARY HISTORY AND AVIATION MUSEUM, Chaguaramas; ☎ 634-4391. Open from 9 AM to 6 PM with a small entrance fee, this museum might be a good stop for military history buffs.

COVIN RIVER – Contact the Chaguaramas Development Authority, ☎ 634-4364.

DIEGO MARTIN ESTATE AND WATERWHEEL, Diego Martin. Unfortunately, we visited the waterwheel when it had been defaced by a fellow advertising his construction business in spray paint all over the site. There's not much else there to see except some historical photos of plantation farming in an old estate building across the road.

> *Getting Here: Head west out of Port of Spain on Beetham Highway. Just as you see West Mall on your left, bear to the right and follow that till you come to a gas station. Ask for directions there. (We got lost and can't recreate any plausible directions for you.)*

EDITH FALLS TRAIL – Contact the Chaguaramas Development Authority, ☎ 634-4364. Although in dry season the water flow is restricted, the height of the falls is spectacular – 180 meters (about 590 feet). This trail is a gentle 1.5 km (a little under one mile), good for beginners or getting your feet wet as a hiker in the tropics.

FORT GEORGE, just to the west of Port of Spain, off the highway. Once a signaling site for ships at sea, the fort now has the remains of a jail and several cannons. The trip to the top is not long by car and offers panoramic views. Otherwise, it's not particularly interesting. It closes at 6 PM and has no entrance fee.

MANGO VALLEY – Hikes are arranged through Chaguaramas Development Authority. Contact them at ☎ 634-4364.

THE SADDLE – This is a common name for the pass dividing Port of Spain on one side of the mountains and Maracas Bay on the other. The trip between the two is about 45 minutes.

View of Maracas Bay.

■ North Central Trinidad

ARIPO is the largest cave system in Trinidad. Reached only after a lengthy, guided hike, the caves are well worth seeing, especially since you will also see flocks of the very rare oilbirds nesting there. See page 101 for hiking trip information.

ASA WRIGHT NATURE CENTRE AND LODGE, Spring Hill Estate, Arima; ☎ 667-4655. Reservations recommended. This 191-acre former cocoa and coffee estate was dedicated as a preserve in 1967. Very professionally managed, Asa Wright is a must-see for all visitors to Trinidad. A morning or afternoon tour is just $6 and includes tea or coffee served on the veranda where, in gracious comfort, you may observe at least 25 varieties of birds. Hummingbirds, toucans, double-toothed kites, and hawk eagles are just some of the possibilities.

Situated at 1,200 feet in the heart of the Northern Range, Asa Wright is home to many of the 400 bird species and over 600 butterfly species found in Trinidad. Although you may have a chance to observe some of the rare species here, the real heart of the place is its dedication to preserving nature in all its forms. Trails vary in length and ease of walking, but the introductory tour will take about 1½ hours and your very-knowledgeable guide will discuss the plants and insects you'll encounter, as well as the wide variety of birds. All trails, whether steep or gently sloped, are well designed to maximize your exposure to the wonders in this rain forest environment.

Nick
6/17/2000

Some of the more exciting birds to see are the bearded bell bird, the white bearded manikin, the golden headed manikin, or the collared trogon. You may also sight a tufted coquette, a hummingbird, a tarantula, or leaf-cutting ants hard at work. Behind the reception desk are two snakes in a terrarium, a yellow rat snake (or *tigre*) and a vine snake, locally known as a "horsewhip." If you have a special interest in snakes, speak with Alan Rodriguez, the grounds supervisor. He may show you his own collection.

Tours are offered at 10:30 AM and 1 PM, but for avid bird watchers the earlier one is probably more fruitful. Two of the better tours are offered only to their hotel guests, one at 8:30 AM and an evening tour at 7 PM on Mondays. On the evening tour, especially during rainy season, you might have the opportunity to see a very rare creature called peripatus. It is the link between soft body worms (annelids) and insects (arthropods). The night tour offers a unique opportunity to explore the nocturnal sounds of the preserve and catch its creatures in action.

A gift shop and library are housed in the main building. Asa Wright is also listed in the *Where To Stay* section, page 68.

> **Special Needs:** *A good insect repellent; a cool T-shirt with long pants and comfortable walking shoes; flashlights and, of course, binoculars and a camera with fast film. Handicap access is limited, but there is much to see and enjoy without leaving the estate house. Call in advance to make arrangements if you have special requirements.*

LOPINOT HISTORIC SITE, Lopinot. A small town with an interesting historic site – the estate of Lopinot. Lopinot came to Trinidad from Santo Domingo. He first owned land closer to Port of Spain but, in financial distress, he set off for the interior and established a cocoa and coffee estate on this site. The small estate house has been restored and contains photographs and artifacts from the estate and some period furnishings. Cocoa is still processed here, and you can see the restored drying shed. Martin Gomez is the estate guide and he'll give you a good rundown of its history. There is no entrance fee, but a tip is in order.

There are also caves in the area; local guides can show you the way. Lopinot is known for its people of Spanish origin and for parang, their unique music, especially popular in Trinidad at Christmas. Locals still make guitars and a wide variety of other stringed instruments, though you will see no evidence of their work in the town.

> **Special Needs:** *For caving you'll need good walking shoes and flashlights.*
>
> **Getting Here:** *From Port of Spain head east on Beetham Highway. Lopinot is between Tunapuna and Arima. Sorry to be so vague, but we got lost and went this way and that way enough, so we don't have a clue how we ended up in Lopinot.*

MARACAS WATERFALL, St. Joseph. The falls are just a half-hour easy walk uphill. Rainy season increases the water flow, but even in dry season it's quite a sight. Water falls from 300 feet, more or less straight off the top of the mountain. At the base of the falls there is no swimming, but if you follow the water down, you'll find very chilly pools lower on the hill. The falls are religious or spiritual places for many people and you will see candles beside the path left as symbols of faith. You'll also see parakeets, cornbirds (black with a split yellow tail), parrots, hummingbirds, and leaf-cutting ants.

Rock climbers can work their way to the top of the falls, but it should not be attempted without a guide as the rock face is very steep. At the top, you can cool off in an icy pool.

There have been reports of robberies on this trail, so it is advisable to have a guide along to handle problems of this sort. We didn't have a guide and no one bothered us, but you can stop in the small town and ask any local fellow if he'd like to go with you. Expect to pay about $5 to $10.

Special Needs: Comfortable walking shoes, binoculars for the birds and butterflies.

Getting Here: Leave Port of Spain on Beetham Highway heading east. Take Uriah Butler Highway north to Eastern Main Rd., where you will turn right. Turn left on Abercromby. Bear right at the only fork. Follow Abercromby to Waterfall Rd., which is the second right after the Catholic church.

← Nick & Davy 6/18/2000 — Missed!

MOUNT ST. BENEDICT BIRD WATCHING, Tunapuna. Just above the Pax Guest House at Mount St. Benedict, by the monastery at the top of the hill, is a gate. Pass through, and head up the trail to the fire lookout far above. It will take about an hour to get there. Stop by the guest house for afternoon tea on your way back between 3 and 6 PM, and ask to see their hummingbird garden. You'll find more information on the guest house under *Where To Stay*, page 73.

Getting Here: From Port of Spain take the highway east. Take a left at the Curepe exit, and at East Main Rd. make a right. Just before the Scotia Bank building take a left onto St. John's Rd. Follow it all the way up; whenever you have doubts about which way to go, stay on the larger road going up and that will get you there.

Beaches

 Beaches are not the main reason to go to Trinidad, but there are some good ones. One of the most popular is Maracas Bay Beach, in a town of the same name, just 45 minutes from downtown Port of Spain. This is the closest to the city and that could explain its popularity, but it is also quite beautiful. Farther up the north coast are other long stretches of beach, like Las Cuevas, but the water can be rough as you get into Blanchisseuse. The coast road ends in Blanchisseuse and limits access to more beautiful beaches like Paria, but you can hike in or have a boat drop you off for the day.

Along the east coast from Manzanilla through Mayaro is a long stretch of beach – miles really – where the water can be tricky for swimming. It is shallow for quite a distance, making it easy to go farther out than you planned. Be careful, or you may find yourself in trouble in these unpredictable waters.

Chaguaramas, in the northwest, was formerly occupied by a large US military installation dating from World War II. The US military left in the '60s, but since then the yachting business developed, so water quality has to be questionable for swimming at most of the easier to find beaches. One ex-

Manzanilla Beach.

ception is the locally popular Macqueripe Beach, and offshore are several islands that have picture-perfect beaches.

Below is a partial list of beaches in Trinidad, mainly ones that have road access. The less-accessible ones are listed in the *Adventures* section, under *Hiking*.

> *There are many opportunities to find yourself on deserted palm-lined beaches. Enjoy yourself, but be especially careful swimming. Watch for undercurrents and riptides before you go out too far or become tired. The waters around Trinidad can be treacherous, and they are often deceptively calm or shallow just before you find yourself in trouble.*

■ North Coast

BLANCHISSEUSE BAY – The waters are rough from December to March; they turn calm in the late spring and summer. Swimming near the mouth of the Marianne River is good, as is surfing in winter, but that is more common on the northeast coast. The calmer the waters, the bluer they get. Beaches along this area are relatively deserted, fringed by palms, and quite beautiful, set as they are against a backdrop of lush, forested hills.

LAS CUEVAS BAY – Between Maracas and Blanchisseuse, in the town of Las Cuevas. The beach facility has changing rooms, bathrooms, and a snack bar. There is a lifeguard on duty in the main swimming area, but you can walk down the long beach and be as isolated as you wish. Palm trees will offer relief from the hot sun. The sand is tan. Sand fleas are sometimes a problem. Nick & Davy 6/19/2000

MARACAS BAY BEACH – This beach is the favorite of Trinis. It has been recently cleaned and all new facilities built. They did a great job. The beach has white sand and is wide with palm trees right up to the water's edge. The new changing rooms, bathrooms and large restaurant make it very convenient, especially for families. Parking is across the street, where you will find small food kiosks selling bake and shark and other beach food. The bake and shark is great and inexpensive at about $1.

PARIA BEACH – Although it's inaccessible by car, by hiking about 1½ hours from Blanchisseuse you'll find yourself on this isolated picture-perfect beach. It's an uphill and downhill walk, but well worth it. Ask for Evette Olivierre in Blanchisseuse; she will be pleased to act as your guide.

Maracas Bay Beach.

■ Northwest Coast

MACQUERIPE BEACH – Chaguaramas. This is a popular beach with people from Port of Spain, both for its accessibility and for its peculiar charm. The area has buildings leftover from the US military occupation and the beach has major decaying cement docking blocks. The beach itself is down a lengthy stairway. Rumors abound that this will be the site of a new tourist resort.

■ East Coast

MANZANILLA BEACH – In the small village of Manzanilla there is a public beach facility with changing rooms and restrooms. The beach is not one of the most picturesque in Trinidad, but it has a wild, windswept, deserted feeling to it that you may find appealing. As you drive south, it will be on your left-hand side for miles. There is just beach and coconut palms, and little else.

MAYARO – It is hard to know where Manzanilla ends and Mayaro begins, except that you'll pass though a few small towns and find the beach becoming a little less wild looking. Other than its tamer look, it's the same as Manzanilla.

■ Toco & The Northeast Coast

Toco and the surrounding areas are densely rain-forested and catch the Atlantic's winds and wildness. The coastline in the northeast is breathtaking with its rocky ledges and crashing waves. There are beaches in **Matura**, **Grande Rivière**, and **Matelot**, but most are better reserved for surfers. If you are planning to spend time in the area, locals will tell you where the good swimming spots are along this coast; most areas are dangerous. This area is a long drive from anywhere, so if you are just looking for a swimming beach there are better alternatives that are easier to reach.

Adventures & Sports

■ On Foot

Hiking

Trinidad offers trails in a wide variety of micro-climates, from dense mangrove swamps to mountainous rain forest, to tropical forest, and just about everything in between. There are easy and difficult hikes and something to please everyone. Many of the easier hikes lead to spectacular waterfalls deep in the forest. The downside is that there are hazards in some areas – both animal and human. Having a local guide with you will ensure that neither is a problem. Another alternative is to plan your hiking adventures with either of the following groups.

SACKETEERS HIKING CLUB, c/o Allied Sewing Supply Co., 49 Saddle Rd., San Juan, Trinidad, or call club leader, Lawrence Pierre, at ☎ 632-9746. Founded in 1979, this group brings people from all backgrounds together to test their skills and stamina about twice a month on hikes into the bush. Hikes vary in difficulty from moderate to rigorous, and cost just under $3. It's a reputable group and you won't be disappointed with the experience. Here is a list of some of the opportunities you may have by joining up with the Sacketeers.

■ **El Tucuche**: Annual hike to the second-highest peak in Trinidad at 3,072 ft. It is favored over the higher mountain, El Cierro del Aripo at 3,085 ft., because of its fabulous views.

■ **Aripo Cave System**: Difficult three-hour hike over rough, wet terrain. The adventurous may also descend by rope 10 feet into the bat guano-filled cave.

■ **Guanapo Gorges and Yarra River**: Difficult terrain and river crossings make this an especially challenging adventure.

- **Salybia Falls:** An easy three-mile trek where you can bring the kids and have a picnic. Those so inclined can climb the falls and take a swim at the top.

- **St. Joseph to Maracas Bay:** Follows the overland colonial plantation route to the coast.

THE CHAGUARAMAS DEVELOPMENT AUTHORITY, in Chaguaramas, ☎ 634-4364. The CDA is responsible for the natural environment of the Chaguaramas area and offers educational programs and tours. You will need to have their permission and be accompanied by one of their guides to explore the many sites in this area. One of the hiking tours offered will take you to an offshore island, Chacachacare, where you can choose between trails to the lighthouse or to the saltwater pond. Tucker Woods/North Post, the Covigne River, and Edith Falls are trails on the mainland, but no less exciting than Chacachacare. The Edith Falls are a remarkable 180 meters (590 feet) high. Economical guides from CDA will cost only $25 during the week, though it's a little more on the weekends.

 Remember to bring water on any hike. Tropical environments drain your reserves more quickly than you think.

Golf

St. Andrew's Golf Club, Moka, Maraval; ☎/fax 629-2314. Open at 6 AM, this 18-hole, par 72 course is hilly, has lots of trees, and is well-maintained. A 9-hole game is about $30 and 18 holes is about $40. Caddies are available and you can rent clubs, but not carts. There is a pro shop on the grounds.

Chaguaramas Public Golf Course, Chaguaramas; ☎ 634-4349, ext. 129 or 145. This is a 9-hole course taking the average player about an hour and a half. The fee for 9 holes is under $10; for 18 holes it's $15. Open 6:30 AM to 7:30 PM, they have golf club rentals and caddie services, which cost $3 for 9 holes and $5 for 18. Shoe rentals are not available. This course was built for the American military when there was a base in Chaguaramas. Rumor has it that there will be a new, more upscale course developed here in the next few years. The entrance to the course is along a pretty, very narrow, country road.

Getting Here: When heading into Chaguaramas, watch for Tucker Valley Rd. on the right, just after a small bridge and before a big block building. Turn right on Tucker Valley Rd. and up ahead watch for a small sign on your left at Bellerand Road, where you will turn left.

Soccer

This sport is very popular in Trinidad. Check local papers for games scheduled during your visit.

Squash

One squash court is available at the **Pelican Squash Club** at the Pelican Inn and Bar in Cascade. Call ☎ 637-4888 for court availability or see the bartender at the Pelican Bar next door; he has the keys. The court is full-size and has a good suspended floor. You can play for about $5/hour.

Tennis

Courts are available at the more upscale hotels, and there are public courts as well, costing only 50¢ per hour during the day and $1 at night. They are located at the **Princess Building Grounds** on Frederick St. in Port of Spain (☎ 623-1121), but you must purchase tickets in advance at City Hall. There are two all-weather courts at the **Holiday Inn** (☎ 625-3366) and two lighted courts at the **Hilton** (☎ 624-3211 or 624-3111). Call to reserve court time.

Health & Fitness Clubs

These facilities are now quite common in Port of Spain. Check at your hotel for the club closest to you.

■ On Water

Kayaking

 Kayak Centre, Williams Bay, Chaguaramas; ☎ 632-2355, fax 633-0292, e-mail kayak@wow.net. Weekday kayak rentals are under $4 per hour, rising to $4.50 on the weekends. Daily rentals are $15.50 weekdays and $21 weekends. Double kayaks are about 50% extra, and basic instruction is $10.50/hour. Rescues and recoveries and rolling and surfing instruction courses are available. Owner/instructor Merryl See Tai offers rates for groups, children, and for high-level kayaking trips as well. The Kayak Centre seems a little worse for wear in the last few years. Call in advance to be sure Merryl will be there when you arrive.

Caribbean Discovery Tours Limited, 98 Fondes Amandes Rd., St. Ann's, Port of Spain; ☎ 624-7281, fax 624-8596, Web site tradepoint.tidco.co.tt/cdt. Guide Steven Broadbridge specializes in personally guided explorations of rivers and wetlands. He loves his work and enjoys a fine local reputation. Steven is multi-talented and a fine bet for the best kayaking experiences in Trinidad.

Surfing

Surfing is good at **Toco Point** in the northeast or along the northeast coast in the winter months.

Windsurfing

Chaguaramas Bay is the best area.

Deep-Sea Fishing

In **Blanchisseuse**, you can fish from the pirogues for between $52 and $90 per day. Ask at the fishing center across from the police station. Fishing is also good in **Chaguaramas**, in the northwest part of Trinidad. The Bocas Islands off the coast provide abundant opportunities.

■ Spectator Sports

The Great Speedboat Race – This is a mid-summer powerboat race between Trinidad and Tobago. Though the islands are only 21 miles apart, this rugged course is over 80 miles long. The direction of the race, toward Tobago, makes it extremely tricky because of winds and currents between the two islands.

Horse Racing – Racing is very popular in Trinidad. Contact the **Arima Race Club** at ☎ 646-2450 (fax 642-1974) to check the schedule. They do not race year-round.

Touring

Renting a car and hitting the road is a great way to explore Trinidad. If you've never done it before, left-hand driving will take your attention in congested areas, but away from Port of Spain it won't bother you too much. The roads in some areas are pretty good; in others potholes will take a bit of care, but we can think of no better way to explore and get to know this surprising country. As they say, "good things come in small packages," and it certainly holds true here.

One of the things that we found surprising was how clean the roadsides were. With very few exceptions, they were immaculate. Another surprise is the wide variety of road kills you might encounter. Our most unusual ever, in any country, was a six-foot crocodile (probably a caiman) that we passed just outside of Port of Spain.

Traffic signs along your way will amuse you more often than give you needed information. One of the funnier road signs is a big exclamation mark. With nothing else to go by, we finally figured out that it means there's a dip in the road ahead or a small hill coming up. Another was a skull and crossbones to indicate a dangerous curve. Much rarer are signs letting you know what road you're on. With relatively few roads to choose from, however, it's not much of a problem. If you get lost, stop and ask directions or, better yet, if you're in the country, find someone who's going where you're headed and take him or her with you.

■ Suggested Driving Tours

Most of these driving routes can be done very comfortably in a day.

Avoid Eastern Main Rd. if you possibly can. It passes through heavily congested towns. The highway follows the same route, is in good condition, and is much easier going. There is a major traffic jam around Port of Spain in the morning, between 7 and 9 AM, and in the evening from 3 to 6 PM. Avoid it if at all possible.

Port of Spain to Arima, Blanchisseuse & Maracas

Leaving the city on Beetham Highway, head east and exit when you see the sign for Arima. We would give you directions through Arima to Blanchisseuse Road, but in Arima we got lost, hopelessly, as always. A maxi-taxi driver with all his passengers took the time to lead us out of town. He drove up and down, and around, and left and right and got us to the right road. He was an absolute angel – we gave him TT$15 to have a beer on us when the day was done.

AUTHOR TIP

You never know whether or not to pay someone for a service like the one described above, but we've found that tips are appreciated when you say something like "have a beer with a friend on us," rather than just handing over money and saying thanks. That can sometimes be insulting when somebody's done something nice for you with no expectation of payment.

The Blanchisseuse Road, where you'll find **Asa Wright**, runs between Arima and Blanchisseuse. It is a marvelous drive, crossing the mountainous area called the **Northern Range**, which separates busy, commercially developed **Arima** and the tiny, quiet, village of **Blanchisseuse** on the northern coast. The road itself is very narrow, a winding mountain trail that takes you through luxuriant, seemingly impenetrable, rain forest. It is a feast for the eyes and for the spirit, dense green vegetation and almost complete isolation. We found ourselves in awe of nature's great abundance.

Along the way you'll see nothing but the spectacular rain forest foliage, wildflowers, birds, and butterflies. If we could choose only one day's drive in Trinidad, this would be it. It has stiff competition from the drive to Toco, but the Blanchisseuse road wins for several reasons. The road surface is in better condition, the vegetation is spectacular without being overpowering, and it's deserted. You might see five cars along the way, but no more. It's very easy driving, but you'll get lots of arm and wrist exercise on the steering wheel. The road is one of the most twisted we've been on.

As you near the coast there is a newly built, quite fancy intersection. If you bear right, you'll find yourself in **Upper Blanchisseuse**, a very small village. Keep your eyes open for **Surf's Country Inn and Restaurant**, **Second Spring** and **Bougan Villa** guest houses. Follow the road along the coast through the village and you'll see the **Marianne River**, the **Blanchisseuse Beach Resort** and **Coco's Hut Restaurant**. Some rivers in this part of Trinidad have caiman, but the Marianne is said to be safe for swimming. Over the river there's an old bridge with a sign that warns of its deteriorating condition. You can cross it in a car, but the road doesn't go very far before ending and there are only a few homes on the other side. From Blanchisseuse, hiking trails lead back up into the mountains and to **Paria Waterfall**. It's best to have a guide. Ask for Evette Olivierre at the Marianne Camping/Car Park when you get to Blanchisseuse; she knows the hills well.

Turning around, follow the road through town once again and turn right at the fancy intersection. Following that road all the way will take you right back into Port of Spain, and there's lots to see along the way. The road between Blanchisseuse and the next town leads through a bit of jungle with a few houses here and there. It's pretty quiet. Heliconia grow wild beside the road. The plant looks much like a young banana plant, but with narrower leaves and heavy hanging flowers with red with yellow edges. The heliconia is prolific in the rain forest.

Continuing along this road you'll come to **Las Cuevas**, another small coastal village. There's a public beach facility here, but the beach goes on almost forever if you want to take a walk to a more deserted section. Even right next to the public buildings there are few people on the beach during the week. There's one very basic hotel in town for the young and not too fastidious.

Back on your way, a little farther down the road and over a hill you'll spot **Maracas Bay**. This is the most popular beach in Trinidad and it is quite beautiful. Fringed with palms, the beach has recently had an overhaul with new facilities and a general sprucing up. Stop here and have a bake and shark for lunch at one of the food stands on both sides of the road – try **Natalie's** or **Richard's**. There's a small fishing village adjacent to the beach. As of this writing, there is one hotel in Maracas, but we think you'll find those in Blanchisseuse much nicer. Two new hotels are planned for this beach area, but they have not yet broken ground.

AUTHOR TIP

This is a very full day's drive from Port of Spain if you do it all at once. Consider staying over in Blanchisseuse, one of the few really delightful places that also has lovely guest accommodations. See the listings for Blanchisseuse in the Where To Stay *and* Where To Eat *sections.*

The road from Maracas begins climbing as you prepare to cross the Northern Range returning to Port of Spain. Following the road up, you'll pass the aptly named **Bay View Restaurant** on your right (and they aren't kidding about the view). Stop for a bite or soft drink. Farther ahead there's a wide overlook area with a telephone booth from which you can see Venezuela on a clear day. Right there is an almost invisible road down to what used to be the Timberline Restaurant. Unfortunately, it is no longer in business, but we heard there are plans to develop something here in the future. Take a look, because things can spring up pretty quickly. Check your brakes before descending. It is extremely steep; once on your way you will not be able to back up or turn around.

Fishing boats at Maracas Bay.

Not too far past the overlook, you will be near the top of the mountain and you'll come to what is locally called "**the saddle**," though there's nothing special about it. Turn right to descend into Port of Spain about a half-hour away.

DID YOU KNOW?

The road from Port of Spain to Maracas was built for strategic reasons by the American military when they had a base in Trinidad in the 1940s. Trinidad later extended the road to Blanchisseuse.

East Coast: Port of Spain to Manzanilla & Mayaro

Leave Port of Spain on the Beetham Highway heading east. Follow the highway to **Valencia** and turn southward on Eastern Main Rd. You'll pass through Sangre Grande following Eastern Main Rd. and be on your way south to upper **Manzanilla** and then lower Manzanilla. Together they make one small village, quaint, but run-down looking. We picked up a few people on their way to the beach who were carrying buckets to collect chip chip – the tiny shellfish native to this coast. As you first near the water, you'll see the official Manzanilla Public Beach. The facility is not as new as at other beaches, but it does have changing rooms. The east coast is relatively flat and the ocean on your left, driving southward, appears as if the waves could wash over the road with just a little more wind.

Along this road there are many abandoned beach homes. It has the appearance of an area that experienced a severe storm and, with all the damage, everyone decided not to rebuild or make repairs. That did not occur. It is simply one of those areas that apparently went out of fashion. People went elsewhere and neglect spread one to the other. A few houses are still maintained, but most have fallen to ruin. Other than these houses, there are coconut palm trees and the unending beach, and not much else.

To take a swim just pull off to the left on any of the tracks and you'll be on your own private miles-long beach. As you drive on, the incredible number of coconut palms that you've seen begin to make sense – there's a coconut factory where they are harvested. Along with the factory, there are some small, unattractive houses built for workers, and coconut husks everywhere. There are also more falling-down, abandoned buildings.

Continuing on, you'll arrive in **Mayaro**. This is a sprawling town with a few restaurants and hotels. We thought **Azee's Hotel and Restaurant** was probably the best of the bunch. This stretch of coast is quite beautiful though, so don't be surprised if you find some new, quite wonderful hotel. The windswept beach dominates the whole coastline and Mayaro is no different. The only resort-style development on this entire coast is owned by the oil industry and operated for their workers, complete with pretty bungalows on the beach and tennis courts.

From Mayaro you can continue southward following the coast on your left the whole way. You'll eventually get to Galeota Point, which we thought might be something special. It might have been once, but it isn't now. It is completely occupied by the oil industry.

Following the road you'll eventually end up at an oil industry facility, where this road ends. There used to be a connecting route to Rio Claro, but the road has not been maintained and there are now impassable areas. From here you simply turn around and repeat your steps in reverse to get back to Port of Spain. This is a comfortable drive to do in a day from a home base in the city.

Port of Spain to Toco & The Northeast

Leaving the city on Beetham Highway, head east. Follow the highway all the way until it devolves into a two-lane road. Pass Waller Field on your right and take the next significant road left. The roads are not marked, but you can comfortably follow traffic because just about everyone will be turning left here. Having turned left, you will come to a T, where you will turn right on Eastern Main Rd. toward Valencia. **Valencia**, which looks like a sizeable town on the map, is really very small. The turnoff toward Toco is right in the middle of town and easy to miss. Watch for the small sign that says "To Toco." You will bear left as the main road goes south. You'll pass through some small towns and you'll see lots of road signs saying "1 km to Matura." After another 10 km you'll see another "1 km to Matura" sign. It can be a little confusing, but there's only one road so it's hard to go wrong. Eventually you will get to **Matura**, which has a police station, houses, a health center, tire service, and a school. Matura Beach is one of the protected turtle nesting areas.

On the road out of Matura, you'll see a sign for **Belandra Beach**. Turn right toward the beach and follow the road. It is short, but taxing; you've got a rental car, so don't worry. The beach is gorgeous with reasonably significant surf. Fishermen here catch shark, kingfish and snapper. Resort construction is beginning in this area so there may be tourist facilities in the near future.

DID YOU KNOW?

Shark oil is advertised for sale on a variety of handmade signs along the roadside in this part of Trinidad. The oil is used as a liniment, massage oil, and as an all-purpose "rejuvenator."

Continue on you'll arrive in **Toco** and see a sign for the **lighthouse**. It's not a splendid adventure, but worth taking a look. The lighthouse windows are tiny and the steps get pretty narrow as you ascend. The lighthouse point is a good place to see the coastline in both directions.

AUTHOR TIP

*In Toco there's a Trinidadian institution – **Antoinette** (Nettie) **Sylvester's ice cream**. She works out of a small place by the side of the road at the nine-mile mark. There's no sign, but anyone there will point it out.*

A typical country bridge.

Leaving Toco you'll pass through **L'Anse Noir**, on a road with lots to catch your eye. It follows the edge of the ocean, which is good for surfing but not for swimming. You'll arrive in **San Souci** and continue as the road leaves the coast and ascends through an enormous jungle. With its towering trees, its hungry green could overgrow you in a careless moment. True jungle, it is remarkably beautiful.

Descending once again to the coast brings you to **Grand Rivière** with rain forest at its back and seacoast at its feet. Here you'll find the **Mt. Plaisir Estate Hotel** (see *Where To Stay*). The small towns you'll pass are not as memorable as the natural environment in this part of Trinidad, which is stunningly beautiful.

Not much farther down the road, in **Matelot**, you'll see a sign that says "end of the road" and the road really does come to an end. You might consider staying in this area if you are willing to rough it a bit. Ask around and you will certainly find a family with an extra room. Grand Rivière currently has the only tourist-quality hotel on this coast.

Turn around, and reverse your route back to Port of Spain. (This is beginning to sound like *Hansel and Gretel*, minus the bread crumbs!) On the road back, you'll come to a small town with a brand-new elaborate concrete bridge over a river with the ocean on your left. Cross over the bridge and take the dirt road beside it to get to yet one more beautiful deserted beach. There's a Rasta selling his wood carvings here and a woman offering roasted corn for sale. Hot off the grill, the corn is delicious.

AUTHOR TIP

The trip from Port of Spain to Toco will take about two hours, making it a comfortable round-trip drive in a day. You might consider bringing food along. As you might guess, there are not a lot of places to stop for a bite.

Port of Spain to The Northwest Coast

Taking the Beetham Highway west out of Port of Spain, the ocean will be on your left. Stay on the highway all the way and whenever you've a choice, bear left. Past the flour milling company, you'll see **the Spectrum**, a stadium used for big productions of steel band and calypso. Next is the **West Mall** on your left, where you'll find **Moon over Bourbon St**. (Also called "MOBS"; see *Nightlife*, page 113.)

The highway soon ends and you'll be on a two-lane, secondary road passing through a small residential area. Just up ahead is the **Kayak Centre**. After the huge Cargo Transfer and Storage Facility, there's a small local beach, but swimming is not recommended because of pollution. **Pier One** (see *Nightlife*) is just around the corner. Down the road is the **Trinidad & Tobago Yacht Club**, where you can stop for a quick, inexpensive and good lunch. Dozens of sailboats from around the world find safe haven here. A restaurant/bar, dancing place called the **Anchorage** is right around the corner to entertain you as well as the yachties. Every weekend there's music and dancing till the wee hours.

Just a little farther on, you'll pass some large green buildings on your right and behind them is the **Chaguaramas Development Authority**. Farther down the road are several yacht anchorage and repair facilities. The more upscale of the group is the **CrewsInn**, where you'll find a good restaurant and stylish hotel along with all the shops and services normally associated with the yachting crowd. **Peake Yacht Services** also has a small hotel and popular restaurant called the **Bight**. Air-conditioned (and very cool) inside, with a lovely outside dining deck, the Bight is a perfect stop for lunch or dinner. (See the *Yacht Services* chapter for more information.) Traveling a short distance farther, just before the road ends, you'll find the **Homeowner's Association**, where you can rent a boat to take you to any of the outlying **Bocas Islands** – one of the more interesting is **Gasparee** with its caves (see page 92).

AUTHOR TIP

This is a pretty quick trip, just about a half-hour to get there. We found ourselves going this way more than once, to visit offshore islands and to have dinner by the bay.

Port of Spain to The West Coast

Leaving Port of Spain heading east on Beetham Highway, turn right onto Uriah Butler Highway going south. Uriah Butler is a divided highway in good condition. Just after getting on this highway you'll see the exit for **Caroni Swamp** off to the right. You'll pass acres of rolling sugarcane fields and eventually see the Couva/Preysal exit, which you take to see the **BC Sugar Factory** (see page 90). If you are in Trinidad in January through March, you'll be sharing the road with a multitude of trucks carrying harvested sugarcane to BC. Just before San Fernando, there's an exit for the Trintoc Oil Refinery and **Pointe-à-Pierre Wildfowl Trust**. Take this exit, turning left, to head toward Piparo and the **mud volcanoes**. (see page 84).

As you get closer to **San Fernando**, stay with the major road past the traffic circles (roundabouts) to Southern Main Rd., also called Trunk Rd. This will avoid the congestion of roads in San Fernando. Driving just a little farther, you'll find signs leading you to **La Brea** and the **pitch lake** (see page 88). You can travel farther south, but it does not get much more interesting. Return to Port of Spain by reversing your steps.

AUTHOR TIP

The drive to La Brea will take just under two hours. It is recommended only for the sights along the way – Caroni, the BC Sugar Factory, the Pointe-à-Pierre Wildfowl Trust, and the pitch lake. The drive itself is not memorable.

Nightlife

THE ANCHORAGE, West Main Rd. at Point Gourde Rd., Chaguaramas; ☎ 634-4334. This large restaurant and bar sits right on the water in Point Gourde. Friday and Saturday nights the place is hopping with live bands and dancing into the wee hours. See its other listing under *Where To Eat.*

Getting Here: Take Beetham Highway west out of Port of Spain. Follow that all the way along the coast, always bearing left when there's a choice. As soon as you see a harbor full of sailboats, watch for The Anchorage on the left.

CALYPSO REVUE, SWWTU Hall, 10 Wrightson Rd., Port of Spain.

CLUB FLAG'S, 141 Long Circular Rd., Maraval, Port of Spain; ☎ 628-3000. A lively spot at night for dining with live entertainment and an after-dinner bit of gambling.

Getting Here: Ask anyone how to get to Maraval. Flag's is right on the main road.

MAS CAMP PUB, French St. at Ariapita Ave., Port of Spain; ☎ 623-3745. Opened more than 10 years ago by three brothers, this is the place where it's Carnival all year long. The small club is open seven days a week, with live music – Latin on Tuesday, calypso on Wednesday, steel band on Thursday, calypso or a band on Friday, a DJ band on Saturday and ballroom dancing on Sunday. Popular with visitors and Trinis alike, the music begins around 9 PM and goes on and on.... Drinks are not expensive and there's good bar food.

Getting Here: Heading west on Tragarete, just after Hong Kong City take a left on French St. Travel a few blocks to Ariapita and you'll see it ahead on the right just across the street.

MAU PAU, Ariapita Ave., next to Mas Camp Pub, Woodbrook, Port of Spain; ☎ 624-3331. Open from 6 PM to 4 AM, Mau Pau is a private gambling club with complimentary memberships available to tourists. There are two club branches, D'Cabin in San Fernando, and the soon-to-reopen Crystal Palace in Scarborough, Tobago. The clubs are not large and all have a bit of the 1920s speakeasy flavor, though new management is promising renovations. Games include Caribbean stud, Caribbean poker, American roulette, baccarat, and blackjack. The latter has the player-favored feature of being able to double down on any combination of cards. Minimum bets are about $4 and upper limits vary by game and table. Higher limits can be granted to high rollers. Safety deposit boxes are available, credit cards are accepted, there's food and drink, and taxi service can be arranged. They even have slot machines; not what you're used to, maybe, but they're inexpensive to play.

Getting Here: See Mas Camp Pub, above.

MOON OVER BOURBON STREET (MOBS) – West Mall rear upper level, West Moorings, Port of Spain; ☎ 637-3448. MOBS offers live music ranging from jazz to reggae to hiphop in an informal outside setting on the second floor of the mall. A good selection of bar foods, like chicken wings, is available. Mobs draws a mix of tourists and sophisticated Trinis. Open from 7 PM to at least 2 AM. The mall is fenced and very secure, so leaving the bar at a late hour is quite safe.

Getting Here: Leave Port of Spain on Beetham Highway heading west, until you reach West Mall. You'll be there in about 10 minutes.

NORMANDIE HOTEL, 10 Nook Ave., St. Ann's, Port of Spain; ☎ 624-1181, e-mail normandie@wow.net. They offer a variety of interesting musical and theatrical performances in an outdoor setting under the trees. Contact them to see what they might have scheduled during your time in Trinidad.

Trinidad

PIER ONE, West Main Rd., Chaguaramas; ☎ 634-4472. A private club open to foreigners. Pier One is on the water and a popular spot for drinks and liming on the weekends.

> *Getting Here: Leave Port of Spain on Beetham Highway heading west. Bear to the left whenever there's a choice. Just past the Kayak Centre on your left you'll find Pier One.*

SPEKTAKULA FORUM, 111-117 Henry St., downtown Port of Spain; ☎ 623-2870/0125. This is a large hall for calypso performances. It has seating for about 3,000, with an inside bar. Sit yourself down for some very amusing and stimulating entertainment. Calypso has its own musical form and structure, but most important is its point of view – lighthearted and acerbic, with political and social commentaries on everything. No one is safe, not even members of the audience. Good fun will be poked at everything and everyone. It makes a great evening and costs about $5 per person. You can also take advantage of "ladies night," when accompanied "ladies" will get in free. Lots of street food vendors set up outside for intermission. Spektakula is open for calypso shows only from the first week of the new year through Carnival.

AUTHOR TIP

> *There's no AC at Spektakula Forum, so wear something light. Parking can be a problem, too, but if you go early there will be space available at the nearby bank parking lot.*

Shopping

For the shop-till-you-drop crowd, Trinidad will probably be disappointing, but with a little luck you may find something interesting. Here a few recommendations to get you started.

■ Clothing, Footwear & Crafts

■ **Handmade sandals** can be found for sale on Independence Square in Port of Spain, or you can visit the place they are made on Piccadilly St.

■ **Zoom Caribbean** has attractive, casual, tropical clothing available at stores in several of the city's malls and in Pigeon Point, Tobago.

■ **African Trophies**, as their name implies, offers a collection of clothing and crafts from African countries. Located at 39 Tragarete Rd. in Port of Spain, it's open Monday to Friday, 9 to 5, and 9 to 1 on Saturday.

- **Bambú**, at the Kapok Hotel in St. Clair and at the Crown Point Hotel in Tobago, has a good selection of high-quality crafts and clothing.

■ Shopping Areas

- The **duty-free shops** at Piarco International Airport offer limited brands of liquor and perfume.

- **Ellerslie Plaza**, Boissiere Village, Maraval, is an upscale shopping center where you'll find better-quality stores.

- **Frederick Street** in downtown Port of Spain is the central shopping area. Here you'll find lots of fabric stores with East Indian materials, and crafts and souvenir shops. If you are looking for a mosquito net you can buy one at Excellent Trading for about $15.

- **Grand Bazaar Mall**, Uriah Butler Highway. When opened in 1996, this was a great place for upscale shopping. Sadly, its location did not turn out to be attractive to shoppers, so many of the better stores have moved on.

- **Long Circular Mall**, St. James, Port of Spain, has shops carrying good quality, locally produced crafts, as well as imports from elsewhere in the Caribbean.

- **True Value Mall**, Circular Rd., Port of Spain, has a food court downstairs with all sorts of local foods at reasonable prices.

- **West Mall**, West Moorings, has small shops with inexpensive souvenirs and T-shirts, and there's a food court where Johnny's looks like your best bet. On the second level at the rear of the mall is Moon Over Bourbon Street, a popular club. Right next door is Restaurant Indigo. The mall itself is a bit dreary.

□ Trin City Mall

Trinidad

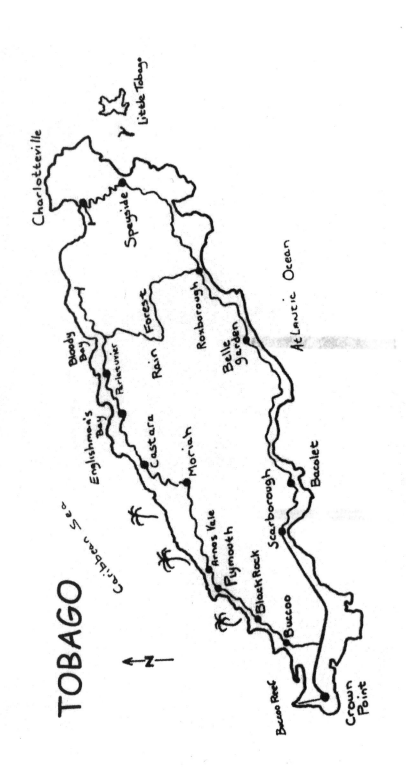

TOBAGO

N

Caribbean Sea

Charlotteville

Speyside

Little Tobago

Bloody Bay

Parlatuvier

Rain Forest

Roxborough

Englishman's Bay

Castara

Moriah

Belle Garden

Atlantic Ocean

Arnos Vale

Plymouth

Scarborough

Bacolet

Black Rock

Buccoo

Buccoo Reef

Crown Point

Tobago

Orientation

Tobago is small, but geographically diverse. No doubt, you'll find an area that is especially appealing to you. Oval-shaped and just 26 miles long by nine miles wide, Tobago runs from Crown Point in the southwest to Charlotteville in the northeast on the Caribbean side. On the Atlantic side it runs from Scarborough in the southwest to Speyside in the northeast. Most of the island's development is on the western end. Down the middle of the island there's a mountain ridge with the hemisphere's oldest forest preserve and very little settlement.

Getting Here & Getting Around

■ Airport Facilities

Although recently expanded, **Crown Point Airport** is still wonderfully small and easy to manage. On leaving the terminal you'll probably be besieged by taxi drivers. Apparently, there's no queue system and it can be chaotic. Pick one of them, actively ignore the others, and they'll drift off. They're not aggressive, but the crush can be annoying after a long flight.

■ Car Rentals

Although we originally planned to rent a car, we ended up with a four-wheel-drive vehicle, and it turned out to be a much better choice for the roads in Tobago. Road improvements are ongoing, but there's a lot left to do. For under $40 a day, you can rent a car or a Suzuki soft top four-wheel-drive vehicle and, if you rent for a week, you can negotiate a better rate. Usually you will save a full day's rental if you pay for a week at a time.

AUTHOR TIP

Remember to keep your rental contract in the car. It has the rental agency phone number if you run into trouble or want to keep the car additional days.

Renting a car here seemed easier and quicker to us than in other countries, with no questions or cumbersome paperwork. If you have a problem with a car, bring it back and they'll give you another with a smile. If you should get a flat tire, there are lots of small places on the road that will fix it for you in 15 minutes or so. When you're done with the vehicle, drop it off and you'll get a ride back to your hotel, also with a smile.

Twisted and narrow, the roads in Tobago are perfect for four-wheel-drive vehicles. It takes about 1½ hours to get from one end of the island to the other with no stops along the way. Although it's a small island, travel is extremely slow going once you get away from the developed western end, so don't underestimate travel time.

CAR RENTAL AGENCIES

■ **Alfred's Auto Rentals**, Crown Point (at the airport next to the police station); ☎/fax 639-7448, evenings ☎ 639-0902. In business for eight years, owners Joseph and Thora have 13 well-maintained cars, including manual and automatic Jeeps, for a negotiable rate of about $35/day. They'll go anywhere to deliver a car or provide service if you need it.

■ **Rattan's Car Rentals Ltd.**, Crown Point; ☎ 639-8271. The location is a ways from the airport, but give them a call and they'll make arrangements for transportation. Their vehicles are very clean and well-kept.

■ **Rollocks Car Rental Service**, Crown Point (next to the airport); ☎ 639-0328, e-mail rovanels@trinidad.net. This company has a large fleet of rental cars and Jeeps, all new and in good condition. Service is available 24 hours a day. Jeeps are about $40/day; cars a little less.

■ **Ted's Sunshine Enterprises**, Store Bay Local Rd., Crown Point; ☎ 639-0547, fax 639-9906, e-mail sunshine@trinidad.net. Ted has good reliable cars and four-wheel-drives for rent at competitive rates, all with one of his big smiles. Recently they've expanded their activities to include tours.

■ **Yvonne Roach Rentals**, Crown Point; ☎ 639-3618, or page her at 625-lisa. Yvonne is a lovely woman who works with her two sons in this new rental service. They are beginning with two small cars. Give her a call and she'll have one delivered to you.

■ Across the street from the Crown Point airport on the left side is a small building with a car rental service. They also rent bikes for about $7. Motorscooters and motorbikes are available there as well, but a car or four-wheel-drive vehicle seems a better idea because of the road conditions and longer distances on the island.

■ Buses

Bus service in Tobago is on the decline, though they do still run. A ride from Crown Point to Scarborough takes about a half-hour and costs around 50¢, but you have to buy your bus pass prior to boarding. Sales points for the tickets vary regularly, but as of this writing you can buy them inside the airport. Ask Tobagoins where to get them and you may find a location closer to where you happen to be. Buy a few extras while you're there, because you can't ride without them. Buses leave every half-hour or so in each direction. Leaving from the airport area in Crown Point, you will arrive at the bus station in Scarborough, where you can make connections on buses plying their routes all over the island. The bus station in Scarborough is just behind the shopping mall.

■ Taxis

Taxi service on Tobago, whether private or shared, takes a while to figure out. Taxi stands exist at most of the larger hotels and, while it is convenient to hop in and go, it can get expensive if you use them frequently. Cars with license plates that begin with an "H" are taxis, private or shared. Plates beginning with a "P" are private cars.

As an alternative to hotel taxis, consider using **route taxis**, which will pick you up if you stand by the side of the road and flag them. The same trip that cost us a few dollars by private taxi was less than a dollar by route taxi. Most of the taxis you'll see are shared route taxis, and they are very economical. For instance, a ride from the airport at Crown Point to Scarborough will cost only $1 per person.

Shared taxis are the most common way for islanders to get around. They are inexpensive and they'll drop you off where you want, if it's on the route or even a little out of the way. These taxis are not in bad shape and they don't overcrowd as they do in some countries. We found them a great alternative when we didn't feel like driving ourselves.

Tobago

RIDING WITH LOCALS

Locals will also stop to give you a ride and you can settle on a price before setting off. We would never dream of getting into a stranger's car in the States, but it is quite safe to do so in Tobago. It reminds us of our first summer on Martha's Vineyard off the coast of Massachusetts. There was no way to get around the island except through the "kindness of strangers." It was a great opportunity to meet folks you wouldn't otherwise get to know and it was very safe. Don't hesitate to stand by the side of the road and flag down passersby. It won't be free, but it will be inexpensive and you'll have a chance to chat along the way.

■ Areas of the Island

Its hard to make a suggestion of where you might choose to stay in Tobago, since almost every visitor we've met is extremely partial to one place or another. On the whole, Tobago is quiet, with its main attractions being its people and its natural environment. Regardless of where you stay, plan to rent a car and explore.

Crown Point

Home to the airport, Crown Point has lots of inexpensive small hotels and guest houses. Most of these places have fewer than 40 rooms, but there is one new full-service resort style hotel with over a 100 units, The Coco Reef. There are lots of open fields in this area, with grazing cows, sheep, and goats, so it has a very relaxed feel to it. From the porch of our hotel we saw a calf born, which was a marvelous experience for us both.

Unlike many parts of the island, Crown Point developed primarily for visitors – vacationers from abroad and from Trinidad. There is a holiday feel to the area with lots of opportunities to meet locals, have a meal out, enjoy Store Bay or Pigeon Point Beaches, and all without getting in a car. A few years ago, the government invested in rebuilding the Store Bay Beach facilities, creating a whole new look to the place while leaving unchanged its delightfully informal and friendly character.

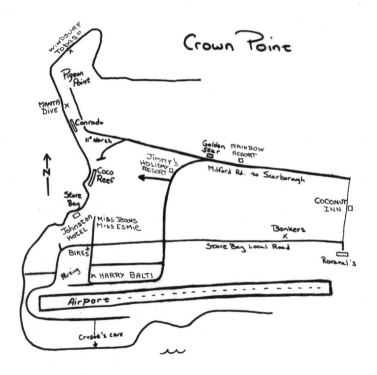

Opposite: "Savannah Stars," Carnival '99

Above: Crosby Sounds, Carnival '99, Trinidad

Opposite: "Carnival in Red," Trinidad

Below: Mt. Irvine Watersports, Mt. Irvine, Tobago

Above: Fishing nets at Parlatuvier, Tobago

Opposite: Store Bay Beach, Crown Point, Tobago

Below: An old-style house in Plymouth, Tobago

Store Bay crafts shops, Crown Point.

Mid-Caribbean Coast

Towns along the Mid-Caribbean Coast include **Buccoo**, **Mt. Irvine**, **Black Rock**, **Plymouth**, and **Arnos Vale**. These towns are home to the island's resort hotels, upscale vacation homes, and local residential areas. It is rural in character now, but there is a lot of development going on and more planned for the future. As you would expect, some of the best beaches on the island are in this area. We didn't find many mid-range hotels and there is almost nothing reasonably priced or inexpensive on the water. There are a few independent (non-hotel) restaurants and more in the works. Arnos Vale is especially attractive with its rolling hills and peaceful environment.

North Caribbean Coast

CASTARA & PARLATUVIER: If you are looking for an extremely quiet spot, either of these will do. Parlatuvier was our favorite because the bay is perfectly shaped and beautiful. Unfortunately, a few years ago a concrete fishing wharf was constructed in the middle of the bay, marring its near-perfect beauty. Parlatuvier has a small budget hotel and a popular restaurant. Castara, larger than Parlatuvier, is a fishing village. Though still very quiet, it has more choices of accommodations and restaurants than Parlatuvier. It's becoming a popular spot for those seeking quiet getaways in a village environment.

Opposite: Trinidad's Northeast Coast

Scarborough

This is the small, bustling, commercial capital of the island and there's not much reason to visit, except on Saturday morning for the lively food market. There are a few other sights to see in Scarborough, but the town itself doesn't offer much. Just outside of Scarborough you'll find the lovely Bacolet.

TOBAGO'S PUBLIC LIBRARY

Scarborough's public library is located between the bus station and the mall in Scarborough (☎ 639-3635). There you'll find books on local architecture and culture. They have an interesting system for loaning books to tourists to assure replacement of lost books. You purchase "pockets," the card that goes in the back of the book to tell you the return date, for just under $2 each. As a temporary member of the library you are allowed two books at a time.

The library is always looking for book donations. The librarian, Miss Johnson, expressed their special need for books in the following areas: environment, sexual harassment, child abuse, teenage coping skills, health (relative to AIDS), handcrafts (basketry, weaving, flower arranging, tailoring), Caribbean history and popular novels. Donations of new or used books will be greatly appreciated.

Bacolet

Just to the east of Scarborough, on the Atlantic coast, Bacolet was *the* place to go on the island in times past and it looks like it will again be the in-place very soon. There is a lovely coast road where views are spectacular and along the way you'll see a few of the old-style gingerbread houses. There's a nice beach (where The Beatles once frolicked), some of the island's better restaurants, and one of our favorite hotels – The Old Donkey Cart.

Atlantic Coast

RICHMOND, ROXBOROUGH, DELAFORD – These towns are not as yet developed for tourism, but progress is on the way. There are basic accommodations and private homes where you probably could find a room, but with the exception of the idyllic Richmond Great House, there's not much else available. It's an interesting part of the island to explore, though. It's along this coast that you'll find the Argyle Waterfall and the Hillsborough Reservoir. If you are a bird watcher, the outskirts of Roxborough are a treasure trove. King's Bay Beach is certainly worth a stop, though with a vacation home development now under construction in this area, the character of King's Bay will certainly be changing.

Northeastern Tobago

SPEYSIDE & CHARLOTTEVILLE – These towns at the northeastern end of the island have a remote charm. Both are very quiet, with Speyside the livelier of the two. Charlotteville is more like a village, while Speyside has good hotels and inexpensive rooms in private homes. The places to stay will easily meet the needs of resort folks or those on a budget and more small guest houses and restaurants are opening. Speyside is certainly the best destination on the island for experienced divers, though more remote Charlotteville also has dive facilities. Charlotteville has a few accommodations, with some near perfect beaches.

Where To Stay

obago is geographically diverse and you'll find the character of villages and towns differing too. Once you've decided where you'd like to stay, plan to spend time exploring the rest of the island. Tobago is a very relaxed place with warm and generous people and it would be a shame to stay at a resort and not experience all the island has to offer. While other Caribbean islands have problems with crime and race relations, Tobago does not, and it's a joy to discover.

Until very recently, Tobago was relatively unknown as an American vacation destination. Those who ventured there grew to love it as we do, for its wonderful people as much as for its Caribbean environment. Flights to Tobago were always expensive but, once on the island, you could find an inexpensive, friendly place to stay and be a part of a very unique and genuine island culture – all while bathing in Caribbean waters and escaping the cold back home.

Tobago now finds itself moving onto the "A" list of Caribbean destinations. It will have multiple golf courses, marinas, and chic hotels and restaurants like all well-known Caribbean islands. What it will also have, at least for the near future, is its friendly people and the same wonderful small hotels and "mom and pop" places to eat that it has had for years. For those of us lucky ones who have known the island for a while, changes are not always warmly anticipated. But change is a part of our world, and it is coming to Tobago. The question now is whether increased tourism will bring good jobs and a hopeful future for the island's youth. As visitors in Tobago, we have a role to play in its future and with care we can all enjoy this wonderful island for years to come.

■ Practical Information

Now rapidly developing for tourism, Tobago offers an increasingly wide variety of accommodations – from the small, economical, weekend-getaway hotels frequented by Trini families and foreigners for years, to the newer mid-priced tourist hotels, and now to the full-service resorts you will find in every Caribbean country.

Airport Transfers

Transportation from the airport is a service offered by many of the hotels listed, but not usually by guest houses. Hotels will either send someone to pick you up or will pay your taxi fare when you arrive, so check on this when you make your reservations. If you are not making reservations ahead of time, upon arriving at the airport call the hotel or guest house you have in mind and see if they'll pick you up. Many will, if you'll be staying at least a few nights.

The existing small airport welcomes five wide-body jets weekly, two from Germany and three from Britain. There are also once-daily American Airline commuter jet flights from Puerto Rico, along with commuter traffic from Trinidad. That will be changing as flights increase and jets grow larger. Crown Point, home to the airport, will certainly feel the difference. We learned that the Tobago House of Assembly is actively working toward increasing the size of the existing airport terminal facility.

Reservations

Reservations at larger hotels during peak times of the year are recommended. At smaller hotels and guest houses, you may not need to make formal reservations with advance payment, but you might want to call ahead and find out if it's likely they'll have room. Right now Tobago seems to have more rooms than it needs to meet demand, and I would say this is true even during peak times. While I can't imagine you won't be able to find a comfortable place on the spur of the moment, you may not get the hotel you want if you don't plan ahead.

Meal Plans

We have listed all hotels under European Plan (EP), which means no meals are included in the room price. Many hotels offer a variety of meal plans, but we have listed only the Modified American Plan (MAP), which is breakfast and dinner, and Full American Plan (FAP), which is all meals. When making reservations, ask about the combination that will suit your needs best.

Car Rentals

Though you might spend your entire vacation in Tobago without renting a car, most people find them essential. Unless you are staying in a more developed area where everything is within walking distance, like Crown Point, you'll be at a disadvantage without a car. Most hotels will arrange car rentals for you. See *Areas of the Island*, page 120, for help in deciding where to locate.

Major New Developments

Tobago Plantations, Ltd., Lowlands, ☎ 639-8000 in Tobago or 637-1025/1030 in Trinidad; e-mail info@tobagoplantations.com, Web site www.tobagoplantations.com. Still in the construction stage during our last visit, plans for this 750-acre resort development include a 200-room Hilton Hotel and two other resort hotels with an additional 350 rooms. The Hilton plans to open in 2000; for information, call 800-HILTONS in the US. Also on the site will be more than 200 two- and three-bedroom condos, selling for $190,000 and $225,000, respectively, and more than 200 villas, each set on a half-acre, which will sell for $300,000-$500,000. Rounding out the accommodation options, bungalows with shared grounds will sell for $200,000-$300,000.

Hilton Hotel underway at Lowlands, Tobago.

Amenities will include an 18-hole, par 72, Nicklaus/PGA golf course. This small island already has a high quality under-utilized golf course, but the new course will offer golfers more variety. Also carved into the landscape will be a two-thirds-mile, 80-foot-wide marina channel to accommodate visiting yachts.

This project is a joint venture between two Trinidadian investors: Angostura, Ltd., and an insurance company, Guardian Life of the Caribbean, Ltd. Ecological concerns have been addressed with a closed-loop waste treatment facility, gray water is used to water golf course greens, and rainwater is saved for use in flushing toilets. Unfortunately, there are no current plans for the use of solar energy.

This is the first of the big tourist developments in Tobago and it will no doubt affect the island in many ways. So far, affluent Trinis are the major group purchasing these vacation properties, though Europeans are also investing. If Tobago's people can retain their wonderful character alongside this and other developments of its kind, we will all be very grateful.

Stone Haven Villas, which was under construction during our last visit, will provide a cluster of luxury villas set on a hill overlooking Stone Haven Bay. Currently planned as a gated community, services and facilities will be set inside the grounds and cooperative relationships with nearby hotels will provide access to golf courses, gyms, and tennis courts. You may contact them at ☎ 639-0102/9887, or by e-mail at stonehav@tstt.net.tt for more information.

On the hill overlooking **King's Bay Beach**, a development of very upscale private homes is underway, and part of the hill overlooking **Englishman's Bay Beach** is owned by a developer with plans for the site. Owners of substantial acreage in **No Man's Land** in **Bon Accord** are in negotiations with the local government to obtain approval for their plans to build a resort, golf course, and private villas.

Check with your travel agent on the status of these properties, as some may be now be open.

Hotels, Guest Houses & Houses

What follows is a list of hotels, ranging from expensive full-service resorts to attractive and less expensive guest houses, as well as houses to rent. There are even a few budget accommodations that we thought were okay when we visited. All are places we would find acceptable for ourselves or for friends with different needs. Acceptable at a minimum means clean, reasonably comfortable, and safe.

We prefer small hotels with spacious rooms facing the ocean and we like having a kitchen. If there's a bit of charm or romance, we like that even better. Some of our friends lead very stressful lives and are looking for luxury and relaxation, and we've found some great resort hotels they would like. Others we know are traveling with children, and we have also found good places for families. If you are handicapped, please see the special notations for places that may accommodate your special needs.

■ Crown Point & Bon Accord

COCO REEF RESORT, Milford Rd., Crown Point; ☎ 639-8571, 800-221-1294 (US and Canada), e-mail cocoreef-tobago@trinidad.net, Web site www.cocoreef.com. Formerly the Crown Reef, this 135-room hotel was renovated and reopened under the name Coco Reef a few years ago. A variety of room styles, suites, and villas are available, and we found the most appealing to be the deluxe rooms. Each has a small balcony and a view of the ocean. Listed rates for deluxe rooms are $250 in high season and $218 in low season. Taxes will add 20% to your bill. Taxes and service charges totaling 25% will be added in their restaurants and bars.

The Coco Reef management was very ambitious in attempting to create a five-star facility. What they achieved is a more modest resort, so you will be able to negotiate better rates for rooms than their listed prices. There are tennis courts across the street and complimentary kayaks, sailboats, pedaloes (paddleboats), and windsurfers are available at their small man-made beach.

> **Amenities:** *Quiet AC, TV, phone, modest pool, beachfront, restaurants and bars, a spa, two lighted tennis courts, and complimentary water sports equipment.*
>
> **Handicap:** *Good access.*
>
> **Good for:** *Couples, families.*
>
> **Comment:** *Its location in Crown Point gives you easy access to the many restaurants and night spots in that area.*

Coco Reef Resort, Crown Point, Tobago.

CONRADO BEACH RESORT, Ltd., Milford Extension Rd., Pigeon Point; ☎ 639-0145/6, fax 639-0755. This 31-room, friendly, older hotel is on the water and close to Pigeon Point. Its second floor, seafront superior rooms are the best, with balconies overlooking the water. These rooms cost $60 double or single, while ocean-view rooms with no balconies cost $45 double or $40 single. Prices do not include 10% room tax, 10% service charge, and 15% VAT, which added together make the rooms here relatively expensive. Meal plans are offered.

Amenities: AC, TV, oceanfront, restaurant/terrace bar.

Good for: Informal couples and friends.

Comment: The Conrado's appeal is its low-key atmosphere and its proximity to Pigeon Point.

HOTEL COCONUT INN, LTD., Store Bay Local Rd., Bon Accord; ☎ 639-8493, fax 639-0512, e-mail coconut@tstt.net.tt. This small hotel is a little off the beaten track, but well worth finding for an economical alternative. There are 16 air-conditioned units with kitchens (a two-burner counter stove and fridge) and spacious private balconies at $60 double/$55 single, plus tax. There are plans to build 16 more on the very ample grounds. A few rooms with shared kitchen facilities cost $32 double/$28 single. Also on the grounds you'll find a car/bike rental office and a restaurant/bar called the Copra Tray (see *Nightlife*, page 184). One of the two owners, Ricarda Solomon, is a transplanted German who arrived in Tobago 22 years ago and never left, so she is a treasure trove of information about the island. Besides personally running the hotel with her partner, Claudia, Ricarda arranges some of the best tours on the island. See her listing in the *Guide Services* chapter, page 219.

Amenities: Pool, AC, phones, restaurant/bar with pool tables and entertainment, car and motorbike rentals, great tours.

Handicap: Not perfect access, but Ricarda is very accommodating to anyone needing special services. Talk with her about what you need.

Good for: Young people on a budget.

Comment: Ricarda has created a home-away-from-home atmosphere for all her guests. She is an avid "biker."

JIMMY'S HOLIDAY RESORT, Store Bay Rd., Crown Point; ☎ 639-8292, fax 639-3100, e-mail ajmal@tstt.net.tt. With 15 two-bedroom and two three-bedroom simply furnished apartments, Jimmy's caters especially to families and groups. Accommodations for four to six cost $60; for eight to 10, $100. The apartments are spacious, with the kitchen and sitting area cooled by a ceiling fan, while bedrooms have air conditioning. Right now they have a grocery store and restaurant and there are plans for a pool. Lila Mustapha, the owner, is down to earth and has a healthy sense of humor. Jimmy's is close to everything in Crown Point, and they will arrange car rentals and tours.

Amenities: AC, cable TV, grocery store, restaurant, kitchens.

Good for: Families and groups on a budget.

Comment: This is a very good value for the money. Its location is great – close to beaches and restaurants.

THE JOHNSTON APARTMENTS, Store Bay Rd., Crown Point; ☎/fax 639-8915/627-1927, e-mail johnapt@tstt.net.tt. Sharing the same location and facilities as the Crown Point Beach Hotel, the separately owned Johnston Apartments are less expensive and very spacious. There are 32 simply furnished units, all with a kitchen/living room and separate bedroom. The apartments are $75 double, $10 for an extra person, and prices are negotiable for an extended stay. Improvements are continually being made at this small hotel. They will soon have cable TV, room phones, e-mail service, and a small store.

Newly renovated and attractively furnished, their huge two-bedroom second-floor apartment has about the best views possible of Store Bay and Pigeon Point. That apartment and a similar one on the first floor cost $200 per day, including tax, and can accommodate a family of up to eight.

Johnston's is located right on the well-known and favorite local beach, Store Bay, and everything in Crown Point is within easy walking distance. Although it may not be as spiffy as some of the newer hotels in the area, Johnston's gets our vote as one of the best. The views are great, the staff down-to-earth and friendly, and the feeling very relaxed. If you are in Tobago and want to inquire about an apartment, call ☎ 639-8915 to see if anything's available. Guests at the Johnston come from all over the world, and Trinis find it a home away from home. It is usually fully booked in July and August and during Easter, Christmas, and Carnival, so reserve well in advance for those time periods.

> *Amenities: AC, beachfront, full kitchen, shared access to pool, restaurant/bar, and aging tennis courts.*
>
> *Good For: Down-to-earth couples, friends, and families on a budget who want to be right on the water.*
>
> *Comment: For a large, comfortable, friendly place on the beach that's in the middle of everything, this can't be beat.*

KARIWAK VILLAGE, Crown Point; ☎ 639-9442/8545, fax 639-8441, e-mail kariwak@tstt.net.tt, Web site www.kariwak.co.tt. This hotel targets guests interested in a holistic, personal growth environment, and has 24 comfortable rooms with ceiling fans, phones, and quiet AC. Single or double rooms are $125 plus 10% tax and 10% service. Though not within comfortable walking distance of the beach (because of the sun and heat), there are lovely gardens and a pool. Activities and services such as Hatha yoga, Qigong, shiatsu, and massage are offered. There is a restaurant with entertainment on the weekends and a shuttle bus will take you to nearby Pigeon Point Beach. Meal plans cost $8-$10 for breakfast, $15-$20 for lunch, and $20-$25 for dinner per person, plus 25% tax and service. Tours and car rentals can be arranged.

> *Amenities: AC, phone, restaurant, personal growth activities.*
>
> *Good For: Those seeking a California lifestyle in the Caribbean.*

Tobago

Comment: Kariwak is quite expensive for its location, but if the activities and services offered are your priority, this is where you'll find them in Tobago.

LAGOON LODGE, Bon Accord; ☎ 639-8555, fax 639-0957, e-mail lagoon@tstt.net.tt, Web site www.trinidad.net/lagoonlodge. Avoiding the usual whenever possible, Norman Sabeeney built his own home and two cabins on his four acres of landscaped grounds. Peacocks roam freely, Herbie the macaw spies on you from the trees, and a striking ostrich parades for your admiration. Every attention will be paid to making your visit here easy and comfortable, and there are many nice surprises – a complimentary dinner with wine on your arrival, your own four-wheel-drive vehicle waiting, all taxes included in the price of $225/day, and a full wine rack in your kitchen, to name a few.

Lagoon Lodge,
Bon Accord, Tobago.

The short bridge to your cottage leads you over a koi pond, where you'll find a porch with Norman's own beautifully handcrafted furniture. Inside is a sitting area with full kitchen should you wish to cook, but you can also arrange to have meals prepared for you on the grounds. Upstairs is the loft with your king-size bed and, of course, you'll have quiet AC, ceiling fans, a phone, and cable TV.

At the back of the property is a mangrove swamp, where a wooden walkway leads you to Bon Accord Lagoon, now a protected National Marine Park. There you may while away the hours in a hammock under the palapa, or set off in one of the kayaks left there for you. For more energetic days there are mountain bikes and scooters, and a pool with jacuzzi to revive you upon your return.

Amenities: Privacy, AC, cable TV, phone, pool, Jacuzzi, cars, kayaks, mountain bikes, and TLC.

Good For: Anyone wanting to avoid tried-and-true resort-style pampering, but still seeking the perfect getaway.

Comment: Very stylishly offbeat.

RAINBOW RESORTS, Crown Point; ☎ 639-8271. Each of the 12 one-bedroom and two three-bedroom apartments here is beautifully maintained. The rate for a one-bedroom apartment is $60, for the larger ones, $125, not including 10% tax. The separate kitchens are well equipped with full-size stove and refrigerator and a microwave. All apartments are nicely furnished and each has a private patio overlooking the immaculate garden pool. Maid service, TVs, plants, and good ventilation make the apartments very amenable. The affable owner, Mr. Rattan, is on site and will arrange tours and discounted car rentals for guests.

Amenities: AC, TV, full kitchen, pool, car rental.

Good For: Couples, friends, families.

Comment: About the only thing lacking here is the beach, but it's close by. We think this is a very good choice for an economical apartment hotel.

ROVANEL'S RESORT, Store Bay Local Rd., Crown Point; ☎ 639-9666, fax 639-0328, e-mail rovanels@trinidad.net, Web site www.trinidad.net/rovanel's. Opened in 1996, this 32-room hotel is set on spacious and well-landscaped grounds. It is immaculate and service is terrific – fast and friendly. The spacious rooms have kitchens and terraces and are attractively furnished with locally made teak furniture. Rates are $130/single and $140/double, inclusive of all taxes and service charges. With meal plans for breakfast and dinner, rates are $165/single and $200 double. Rovanel's is not on the water, but you do have a view of it across green lawns and the airport runway from all second-floor rooms. Shuttles will take you to beaches several minutes away. The downside to Rovanel's is its proximity to the airport runway. Right now, there are few large planes arriving in Tobago, at most one a day, but that will be changing.

Owner Sylvan Rollocks started out on the island as a farmer and hasn't lost his green thumb. The grounds are beautiful. One remarkable feature of this hotel is its elaborate water-saving system. Rainwater is collected in a huge cistern for use during the dry season. This forward-thinking design is unusual and laudable. They are also using solar water heaters and drip irrigation.

The pool is one of the largest and best-maintained on the island. The restaurant specializes in local food and steak; a meal averages $20 per person, tax and service included. Car rentals and tours can be arranged and airport transfers are included.

Amenities: Quiet AC, TV, phone, full kitchens, large pool, restaurant / bar, beach shuttle.

Handicap: Access is not all it might be. Give them a call and discuss your needs before reserving.

Good for: Couples, families, friends.

Comment: The gardens are beautiful and everything is perfectly maintained. Airport noise can be a problem.

Tobago

■ Mid-Caribbean Coast

ARNOS VALE HOTEL RESORT, Arnos Vale Rd., Arnos Vale; ☎ 639-2881/82, fax 639-4629, e-mail avhotel@opus.co.tt. Arnos Vale Hotel is one of the oldest on the island and, in the first edition of this book, we thought it was one of the best resorts in Tobago. Times change, and so has Arnos Vale. Just recently it has come under new management, and we are hopeful that it will again be what it was. Check with your travel agent to get an update. While we can't give a glowing report on the hotel right now, we can say that the new Italian manager, Antonio La Fera, is a delight. We wish him well.

Situated on 400 acres and surrounded by hills, Arnos Vale feels very isolated and is known all over the island as a great place for snorkeling. The beach is surrounded by rocky cliffs that create a small horseshoe-shaped bay. It has a very exclusive and private feel. Do stop by for an afternoon of snorkeling.

Arnos Vale Hotel beach.

BLUE HORIZON, Jacamar Dr., Mt. Irvine; ☎/fax 639-0432/33. Set above the Mt. Irvine Golf Course and overlooking Buccoo Reef in the distance, all rooms have well-appointed kitchens and patio areas. This guest house was designed to make the best use of sea breezes, so air conditioning isn't necessary on a continual basis. The setting is high on a hill overlooking Mt. Irvine Bay, and you can see all the way to Pigeon Point. This is a very pleasant place with lots of opportunities to interact with other guests. It is a little out of the way, so plan to have a car.

Their 12 units include seven rooms at $50 single or $75 double. A deluxe apartment is $60 single or $90 double; their spacious two-bedroom apartment with a large loft runs $150. Prices do not include 10% tax and 10% service. They also offer a barbecue terrace, grocery shop, and free ground transfers. Kameal Ali is one of the managers and he's a very nice fellow. They've been open for a few years now and have kept everything looking brand new. The gardens are wonderfully healthy and well settled in. There is no restaurant on the grounds as yet, but the small Rolita Restaurant nearby serves pizza and other simple meals.

Amenities: AC, phones, pool, full kitchens, laundry service, view of Buccoo in the distance.

Good For: Families, couples, friends.

Comment: For folks traveling with children and wanting a mid-priced hotel, this might be it. The views are great and the hotel is very small and pretty.

THE GINGERBREAD VILLA, Plymouth (Mailing address: Box 391, Scarborough); ☎ 639-4461. With just one self-contained studio room, this is a small guest house indeed. Sitting right by the beach in Plymouth, the house was designed and built to resemble the old-style gingerbread houses on the island, as its name implies. The studio has a private bath, kitchen area, and patio overlooking the lawn and beach. There are a couple of mountain bikes for guests to use. Owner Eve Mendes has created a very special place at $45 per night, and she'll even pick you up at the airport.

Amenities: Kitchen, beachfront, mountain bikes.

Good For: Independent couples wanting peace and privacy.

Comment: This delightful, private little place is right on the water, but you'll need a car.

GRAFTON BEACH RESORT, Black Rock; ☎ 639-0191, fax 639-0030, e-mail grafton@trinidad.net, Web site www.grandehotels.com. Situated on a steep hill, the Grafton is a long-established resort overlooking Stone Haven Bay. As island hotels go, it is large, with 104 rooms and four suites. Rooms cost $168/person, including three meals, afternoon tea, local brand drinks, and all taxes. Children over 12 count as an extra person at a charge of $70/day. Rental cars are available and there is a taxi stand. One of their several restaurants, The Buccaneer, is right on the beach below the hotel. All rooms have balconies and are nicely furnished, but they are not large. Squash courts are on the premises and tennis courts, golfing, and a complete weight training gym are available at neighboring hotels.

Amenities: AC, phone, TV, mini-fridge, pool (swim-up bar), several restaurants and bars, squash courts with AC, gymnasium, hair salon, dive shop, beachfront.

Good For: Couples and families looking for a holiday vacation experience with all services provided.

Tobago

Comment: This is a mid-level resort hotel for people who like to have everything taken care of in one package. You can leave home and still have all the comforts. Most guests are from Britain.

LE GRAND COURLAN, Black Rock; ☎ 639-9667, fax 639-9292, 800-223-6510 (US), Canada 800-424-5500 (Canada), e-mail legrand@trinidad.net, Web site www.legrandcourlan-resort.com. On a steep hill overlooking Stone Haven Bay, the 78-room Grand Courlan is right next door to and owned by the same company as the Grafton. It was designed to be a more luxurious resort than the Grafton with every available amenity. Their 60 deluxe rooms are spacious with balconies overlooking the beach. Furnished with locally produced teak, rooms have quiet, remote-controlled AC and large bathrooms equipped with everything, even a scale. Deluxe rooms are $275. Rooms with an enclosed patio jacuzzi are $295, and one-bedroom suites are $475. All prices are plus 20% tax and service charges. Children five to 12 are an extra $30/day. Meal plans are available with MAP at $57.

There is a long pool, perfect for laps, and it also has a swim-up bar. The spa with sauna, hot tub, and massage will soothe you after a visit to their large, fully-equipped gym, which has all the weight training and aerobics options you could want. You may use the squash courts at the hotel next door and the Mt. Irvine Hotel golf course down the road. Two restaurants are on the premises: the open-air Pinnacle offers local and international dishes, and the informal Leandros serves Mediterranean cuisine. Business travelers have access to computer, fax, and secretarial services. Conference facilities are available as well.

Amenities: Quiet AC, TV, phone, in-room safe, mini-bar, pool, two restaurants, swim-up bar, lighted tennis courts, fully-equipped gym and spa, beach access, business services, handicap access, non-smoking rooms.

Handicap: Access is good and on-site wheelchairs are provided.

Good For: Couples, friends, business people.

Comment: This hotel was clearly designed with every attention to detail. Unfortunately, it priced itself out of the market in Tobago. That will change but, in the meantime, you might take advantage of this by negotiating a better room rate than their listed prices. Be aware that upkeep of the facilities is not all it might be.

MT. IRVINE BAY HOTEL & GOLF CLUB, Mt. Irvine; ☎ 639-8871, ☎ 800-74-CHARMS (in the US), fax 639-8800, e-mail mtirvine@tstt.net.tt, Web site www.sputnik.com/mtirvine/. Built on the site of an old sugar mill estate, this is an impressive 105-room hotel with 16 acres of well-maintained grounds. The hotel is large by island standards, with rooms, suites, and cottages. Its most unique feature is its 18-hole golf course on an additional 127 acres, and there are lighted tennis courts, too. Taxis and car rentals are available. Their premier restaurant is the Beau

Rivage, located in a separate stone building with a good view of the bay. When first opened, the Beau Rivage was not up to its high prices. They've since lowered the prices and improved the quality. We've heard good reports about the other restaurant, too, the Sugar Mill.

Standard rooms run $220 in high season and $165 in low. Cottage rooms are $350/high and $320/low, while one-bedroom suites are $550 in high season and $510 in summer. Children under four stay free; ages five to 12 are charged an additional $25 per day. All of the above rates are subject to 10% service charge plus 15% VAT. Meal plans are available; MAP is $40 and FAP is $60, which are also subject to 10% service and 15% VAT.

Although it is not directly on the beach, this lovely, gracious hotel is more luxurious than other resorts of its kind on the island. The hotel's beach restaurant and facilities are just a walk down the grounds and across the road onto the very pretty Mt. Irvine Beach.

The hotel has recently undergone renovations and restyling so there are now upscale shops, a seated check-in area, and tile flooring in all rooms. Most of their guests are British or European, but they do have American visitors too.

> **Amenities:** *AC, TV, phone, nice pool, golf course, restaurants, bar, beach bar/restaurant, tennis courts.*
>
> **Good For:** *Golfing couples, people who like understated luxury.*
>
> **Comment:** *This is a hotel where service and luxury are what it's all about. It's perfect for golfers as well as small business conferences.*

KP RESORTS, Shirvan Rd., Buccoo; ☎/fax 639-9481, e-mail kpatino@ tstt.net.tt, Web site kpresorts.com. Don't let the name put you off; this is nice. Though it is not on the water, KP's is a very pretty guest house. The rooms are thoughtfully designed – thre is good ventilation and AC when you want it, and the kitchen and dining area are on the large patio, separate from the sleeping quarters. The tastefully decorated rooms have phones and cable TV. With the nice pool, garden area, cascading water wall, and good restaurant, KP's offers most of what you'll want, and at a very reasonable price.

Studios with kitchens are $75 double and the honeymoon suite with Jacuzzi is $95. This is a very lovely room with all the right touches, including a fruit basket and bottle of wine to set the mood. Prices include transfers from the airport, but not the 10% tax and 10% service charges. Please see their restaurant listing, Patino's, under *Where To Eat*.

> **Amenities:** *Kitchen, AC, cable TV, pool, restaurant/bar.*
>
> **Good for:** *Couples, friends, families.*
>
> **Comment:** *This is a lovely place. Although not on the beach, it is close by and, for the price, it is one of the better choices.*

Tobago

SANCTUARY VILLA RESORT, Grafton Estate (Mailing Address: PO Box 424, Scarborough); ☎ 639-9556, fax 639-0019, e-mail sanctuary@ tstt.net.tt, Web site www.sanctuaryvillas.com. This is a new resort combining a variety of accommodation options, including hotel rooms, semi-detached small homes, and private villas. Development of Sanctuary Villas has been underway for a few years now, but they will have everything ready for millennium year travelers. Contact them directly or ask your travel agent for details on the accommodations and activities. Also see Sanctuary's listing under *Houses to Rent*, page ###. The homes are especially attractive and each has an ample pool.

Amenities: Full-scale resort – restaurants, sports, pools, etc., with a variety of accommodation options.

Good for: *Couples, friends, families.*

Comment: *Not on the water, but with nice views. This is a good choice, especially for families.*

TOP O' TOBAGO, Arnos Vale; ☎ 639-3166, fax 660-7181, e-mail topo-tob@istar.ca. Newly built, this combination of three cabanas and one house sits on six acres of landscaped grounds at the top of a hill in Arnos Vale. In high season, the main house is $125; cabanas run $75. In low season prices fall to $100 and $60. The setting is spectacular, overlooking the hills and ocean in the distance. Each cabana has an open plan with sitting area, kitchen, and king-size bed, and a small, private, shaded patio. There is a shared pool where, while swimming, you overlook the ocean down below. A management couple live on site and your rooms will be cleaned every other day. It is beautifully situated and much attention has been paid to the architecture and gardens to create a space that is both elegant and casual. More details about the house are below under *Houses to Rent*.

Amenities: Pool, private patio, kitchen.

Good For: *Couples, friends, groups.*

Comment: *This is a lovely slice of Caribbean life. Gather your favorite people together and spend a week or more.*

TURTLE BEACH HOTEL, Courland Bay; ☎ 639-2851, fax 639-1495, e-mail turtle@tstt.net.tt. This hotel is right on the water, and all rooms face the beach. Including taxes, rates are $195 single or double in high season. An extra person brings the cost to $255, inclusive of taxes. Children under 12 may stay with you free. Over 12 they are counted as an extra person. Their most popular meal plan includes seven breakfasts and three dinners for about $180/person. Discounts may apply, so be sure to ask.

Right by the beach, the grounds are wonderful. They are planted with orchids and flowering tropicals and all of them are identified, so it's a gardener's delight. The rooms are more spacious than at many island hotels, and the second-floor rooms have steeply pitched wooden ceilings that give an even more spacious feel. There are 125 rooms, but the hotel appears deceptively much smaller. Scuba diving and deep-sea fishing are available at an additional charge. Their children's club is open Monday through Friday, offering supervised activities for children ages four to 12. The Turtle Beach, as you might have guessed, is a site for leatherback turtle nesting on the island. Hotel staff keep watch and will notify guests when a turtle is arriving. This is a great hotel for families. Some rooms have small separate sleeping quarters for a child at no extra charge. The air conditioners can be noisy. If you're looking for a low-key resort hotel on the island, this would be one of our picks.

Amenities: AC, phone, TV rentals available with satellite, restaurants, bar, nightly entertainment, beachfront, windsurfing, Sunfish sailing, snorkeling, tennis, volleyball, free children's club. Tours and car rentals can be arranged.

Handicap: Specially adapted rooms with rail bars and wheelchair access.

Good For: Couples, families, just about anyone.

Comment: This is one of my favorites for location and appearance. The garden is beautiful and the beach is right there. The Turtle Beach staff are very gracious, especially Esther Dumas, Reception Supervisor.

■ Atlantic Coast

HILTON HOTEL AT TOBAGO PLANTATIONS LTD. For information, call toll-free in the US, ☎ 800-HILTONS. Currently under construction, this Hilton will have 200 rooms and will be only a small part of a very large resort development called Tobago Plantations, set on 750 acres.

OLD DONKEY CART HOUSE INN AND RESTAURANT, 73 Bacolet St., Scarborough; ☎ 639-3551, fax 639-6124, e-mail olddonk@opus.co.tt. Located on a hill overlooking Bacolet Point on Rockly Bay, the Donkey Cart has two small guest buildings with a total of 10 units and a pool set in between. A quaint colonial home serves as quarters for the office and restaurant. It is not right on the water, but is well worth considering as Bacolet Beach is just a few minutes away. Owned by Tobagonian Gloria and her German husband Reinhold Knapp, the hotel blends each of their influences beautifully. You'll see the mix reflected in the restaurant menu. Superior Blue Rooms are $90 double, and the Penthouse Suite is $240, including continental breakfast, taxes, service charges, and airport transfers. Prices fall about 30% in the off-season.

Although the rooms are lovely and spacious, I fell in love with the Penthouse Suite. Wonderfully Caribbean and very romantic, the suite takes up the top floor in one of their two small buildings. It is the only room on the island that I'd love to take home. It's done in beautiful mahogany with a pitched ceiling and wooden louvers all around to let in the constant breeze. It is not air conditioned, which should not be a problem in any but the hottest weather. The space reminded me of a Caribbean version of an artist's loft with very modern touches. Doors are all center-hinged and swivel artfully. The bed has white mosquito netting and a crocheted lace covering. There is a small refrigerator, a large shower big enough for two, and a lovely bath. From the room-sized, comfortably furnished porch you'll have a fantastic view of Scarborough and Bacolet Bay. The pool is small, but unique, and there is satellite TV. You can discuss a meal plan with the owners when making reservations. A plan for full breakfast and dinner will be about $46/person, plus service and taxes.

Their restaurant offers a combination of local and international foods and is set in a lovely garden. At night small lights in the trees make it very romantic. See *Where To Eat*, page 154, for more information on their restaurant.

Make reservations two months in advance for November through February; other times of the year are more flexible. The Old Donkey Cart is environmentally aware, with water recycling facilities and non-smoking rooms. Car rentals are available and are discounted to guests.

> *Amenities:* Mini-bar, phones, TV, pool, restaurant/bar, water views, car rentals, non-smoking rooms.
>
> *Good For:* Romance.
>
> *Comment:* I love this place, as you can tell. For romantic couples it's perfect, and Bacolet Beach is just two minutes away.

RESTRITE SEA GARDENS GUEST HOUSE, Delaford; ☎ 660-4220. On the Atlantic coast, just off Windward Rd., this three-unit guest house is owned by the very gentle Mistress Buntin Or. Each unit has a stove and refrigerator (now decorated with wallpaper), bath, and sleeping accommodations all in one room. This setting is probably best for folks on a budget or those who like rustic accommodations. The units are only about 12 feet from the water, depending on the tide. At $10 per person, you might guess it's not fancy, but Mistress Or has been improving them each year since they were listed in our first guide.

Gauguin probably would have liked it here and you might, too, but you may want to stop by before committing yourself. The Restrite is for the more adventurous traveler who wants the beach and a taste of village life. The quality of the rooms is still a bit primitive, but the beach is lovely.

> *Amenities:* Kitchenette, beachfront.
>
> *Good for:* Couples or friends on a tight budget.
>
> *Comment:* This is for adventurous, budget-minded romantics.

RICHMOND GREAT HOUSE INN, Belle Garden; ☎/fax 660-4467. This old home was an estate residence carefully restored by Tobagonian Hollis Lynch, retired Professor of History at Columbia University. The inn sits on six acres in the hills 45 minutes from the airport in Crown Point and has a lovely remote feeling about it. It is just what one would dream up when imagining the perfect Caribbean guest house. Filled with splendid African art and textiles, chess games, an eclectic library, and a great variety of walking sticks, the character of the place will charm and delight you. With a little luck, Hollis will be in residence; he's thoroughly disarming.

The deluxe double at $120, the suite for two at $145, and the two-bedroom suite for two at $170 are the best rooms in the house; rates include breakfast. These rooms are in the older part of the house and have a unique charm and fabulous views from oversized windows. Newer doubles are very nice for $95. A tax of 10% and service charge of 10% is added to all room rates. You may also ask for prices quoted with meal plans, including both breakfast and dinner. Summer season prices fall about 10 to 15%. We didn't arrive in time for lunch, but the food looked great. There is a small pool just down from the reception area and a tennis court has just been completed. Also ask about renting their recently completed bungalow.

> *Amenities: Fabulous views, antiques, pool, restaurant, tennis court.*
>
> *Good for: Couples, singles, people who want a taste of the more gentle past, bird watchers.*
>
> *Comment: The Richmond is an ideal place to stop for a night on your way to or from visiting Speyside and Charlotteville. It's also a peaceful and graceful environment from which to hike in the hills or wend your way down the hillside to the very quiet beach. If you don't stay here, make it a must for lunch or dinner.*

TARA BEACH HOUSE, Milford Rd., Scarborough (no phone yet). This small hotel was under construction as we passed by and it looked good enough that we stopped in. It sits right on the water and will have 12 rooms and a couple of very spacious terraces both in the sun and under the trees. There aren't many good choices in this area, but with this little gem, that might be changing. We didn't meet the owners and there was no phone or rate information available when we stopped by.

■ North Caribbean Coast

THE NATURALIST BEACH RESORT, Castara; ☎ 639-5901, fax 660-5357, e-mail natural@trinidad.net, Web site seetobago.com. This small guest house sits just by the beach in Castara. All of the five simply and comfortably furnished rooms have kitchenettes and TVs and cost between $25 and $35 (the more expensive unit has air conditioning). Though it is not done "resort style," it has its own charm. We spoke with the lovely Tobagonian owner, Gemma, who joked with us that some people assume the name of the hotel means nudity. Not so! It is a sweet little place, and you'll have to keep your clothes on. They will arrange rental cars and tours on request.

> *Amenities: Beach, kitchenette, AC, TV.*
>
> *Good For: Young friends or romantics.*
>
> *Comment: This is certainly the best choice in Castara and one of the best low-cost choices in Tobago.*

Tobago

PARLATUVIER TOURIST RESORT, Parlatuvier; ☎ 639-5629. Just one minute from the beach, this small basic hotel has five units, with a variety of options: bath/shared bath, kitchen/shared kitchen. Owned by Duran Chance and his wife Islin, the hotel's rooms are $25, all-inclusive. There's no maid service, but the building is relatively new and well maintained. It is located on one of the more beautiful bays on the island – Parlatuvier. There is absolutely nothing to do in this tiny town except enjoy the sun, sand, and water. It is very quiet, and was the most beautiful bay we'd ever seen until they constructed a concrete fishing pier a few years ago, but it is still gorgeous. The Chances also own the general store in town, which is next door to the apartments. You can people-watch from your balcony and pick up groceries just down the stairs. Regrettably, sometime in the last few years they acquired a small monkey, which they have chained up in front of the store.

> **Amenities:** *Some AC rooms, kitchenettes, grocery store.*
>
> **Good for:** *Couples, friends on a budget.*
>
> **Comment:** *For a taste of village life in the Caribbean this is just fine for the price.*

■ Speyside

BLUE WATERS INN, Batteaux Bay, Speyside; ☎ 660-4077/4341, fax 660-5195, e-mail bwi@bluewatersinn.com, Web site www.bluewatersinn. com. The setting for this hotel is spectacular, but is isolated down a steep road that gave me the willies. Blue Waters is owned by a couple of transplanted German ladies, but under the new manager service may not be as friendly as it once was. It is wonderfully situated on its own private bay and lies sheltered by high hills on all sides. All guest rooms face the beach and there is excellent diving and snorkeling. Winter rates for standard rooms are $140 single, $160 double. A one bedroom suite/bungalow with kitchen, dining room, and porch is $330. Prices include tax and service. Meal plans are available: breakfast at $10, breakfast and dinner at $33, and all three for $40 per person. Most of the rooms are not air conditioned, but it is available for an extra charge. Book accommodations well in advance for high season. Be sure to ask for applicable discounts if you're staying a week or more.

> **Amenities:** *Beachfront, restaurant, bar, tennis, kayaking, windsurfing, snorkeling, and scuba diving.*
>
> **Good for:** *Families, couples, scuba divers.*
>
> **Comment:** *For divers this was the only choice for many years. It is still lovely, but there are now other options.*

MANTA LODGE, Windward Rd., Speyside; ☎ 660-5268, 800-544-7631 in the US, fax 660-5030, e-mail dive-manta@trinidad.net, Web site www. trinidad.net/tobagodive. Opened in 1995, it still has all the spit and polish of a new hotel. It is small, with only 22 rooms, and offers personal service and a professional dive shop. In fact, owner Sean Robinson is himself a dive master. Standard rooms are $95 single in winter and $75 in summer; doubles are $115 in winter and $95 in summer. Make sure to ask for one with a view of the ocean and a balcony. Superior rooms are $115 single in winter and $90 in summer; doubles are $135 and $110. Prices do not include 10% tax and 10% service charge. We think the standard rooms, which have ceiling fans but not AC, or the superior rooms, which do have AC, are the best bet. The loft rooms aren't great. Meals plans are available. All guests are entitled to a complimentary scuba experience, although many guests are already serious divers. Those new to diving often sign up for further training.

Amenities: *Quiet AC, phone, pool, restaurant/bar, dive shop.*

Good For: *Couples, friends, scuba divers.*

Comment: *Manta is a very appealing small hotel, one of three in Speyside. For anyone with a serious interest in diving it is perfect. For those who don't yet know how to dive, you might just be seduced.*

SPEYSIDE INN, Windward Rd., Speyside; ☎ 660-4852; e-mail yawching@trinidad.net, Web site www.caribinfo.com/speysideinn/. This pretty hotel overlooks Tyrell's Bay, where you will have a view across the water to Little Tobago Island. There are nine rooms and three cabins; room rates include breakfast, but the cabin rates do not. The inn is popular with German scuba divers. There is not much action in Speyside that does not involve the ocean, though the area is developing quickly. It is considered the best area for diving and snorkeling in Tobago, and there are lots of full-time fishermen in the small town of Charlotteville just over the hill. Singles/doubles here are $90/$105 in high season and $70/$85 in low season. Prices do not include a 10% tax. If you are not a guest of the hotel, breakfast is $7.50 and dinner will be about $20, not including tax and service. All rooms face the ocean and each has a balcony.

Amenities: *Beachfront, restaurant, good views.*

Good For: *Couples, friends, scuba divers.*

Comment: *This is a very pretty small hotel.*

TOP RANKING HILLVIEW GUEST HOUSE, Top Hill St., Speyside; ☎ 660-4904. Ann Davidson runs this small guest house on a hill in Speyside. A room will cost $40 and comes with good kitchen facilities and a terrace. We spoke at length to one of their guests, a fellow from Maine; he was extremely pleased with his three-week stay. It is a good alternative to the much more expensive hotels closer to the water. Ask for a discount if you'll be staying a while.

Amenities: *Kitchen and terrace.*

Good For: *Divers on a budget.*

Comment: *If the name is any indication of the quality of service, you're sure to be pleased.*

■ Charlotteville

CHOLSON CHALETS, Charlotteville; ☎/fax 639-8553. These nine sim-ple apartments are economical at $20, $30, or $60. Prices depend on apart-ment size and location (first or second floor). At the extreme northeastern tip of the island, Charlotteville is a small, sleepy, fishing village with, as yet, no upscale tourist accommodations. These cottage apartments are fine for the relaxed tourist who wants a Caribbean getaway and an oppor-tunity to get to know village life on this small island. The apartments are managed by Miss Rosa, a very sweet and charming older lady. Her grand-son seems to keep the details straight, but she does the cleaning and offi-cial renting. Check ahead and make reservations if you're interested, because there's quite a waiting list. When we were there recently, all the other cottages were occupied by Danish families. For swimming, the lovely Pirate's Cove is just a walk over a steep hill. The whole town is pretty re-laxed. It's a good spot for people who like to fish or scuba dive. Otherwise, good books, swimming, and snorkeling top the short list of things to do.

Amenities: *Waterfront, kitchenette.*

Good For: *Relaxed couples, friends, families.*

Comment: *Unfortunately, on Saturday nights noise from the bar next door continues into the wee hours. The look of the cottages is improving year to year.*

MAN-O-WAR BAY COTTAGES, Charlotteville; ☎ 660-4327, fax 660-4328. These several cottages are grouped among the trees at the edge of the beach, just outside the small village of Charlotteville. Each has a com-fortable veranda, living/dining area, a separate fully equipped kitchen, and from one to four bedrooms. They are equipped with ceiling and mov-able fans, but are not air conditioned. A single is $55 and doubles are $60. A two-bedroom cottage for two is $70; for four, $80. A three-bedroom is $95 and a four-bedroom is $130. These prices do not include 15% tax. Arrange-ments can be made for maid service, starting at $8/day for one or two per-sons and increasing with the size of the group. Cooks can be arranged for an additional fee. Charlotteville is about 36 miles from the airport and, surprisingly, this is one of the few places on the island that does not make arrangements for car rentals. Get a rental car before leaving the airport in Crown Point. Man-O-War Bay Cottages have been in existence long enough to have many repeat customers, so you should reserve well in ad-vance. However, don't hesitate to give them a call on the spur of the mo-ment. Sometimes they have a cancellation.

Amenities: *Beachfront, fully equipped kitchens.*

Good for: *Relaxed couples, families, friends, singles.*

Comment: *If you are going to stay in Charlotteville, Man-O-War Bay Cottages is the best of what we found.*

■ Houses To Rent

MOTMOT RIDGE AND THE OBSERVATORY, in Arnos Vale, just a short way up a dirt road from the Arnos Vale Hotel. Contact David Montgomery at D. Montgomery & Co., Port of Spain, Trinidad; ☎ 623-4573, fax 623-6610, e-mail monty@wow.net. You may also call him at home in the evening, ☎ 624-5445. The lovely MotMot Ridge rents for $2,100 weekly in high season and $1,125 in low. Be sure to ask for a 15% discount if you do not rent through an agent. Owners David and Hilary Montgomery are gracious Trinis. They spent an afternoon showing us their two rental homes and explaining what went into selecting the land and building plans. MotMot sits very high on a hill, overlooking the ocean on one side and grassy hills on the other. They spared no time, effort, or expense building this colonial Caribbean-style residence. The house is wonderfully open and carefully furnished to create casual, comfortable, elegant spaces.

MotMot house for rent.

Upstairs you'll find three air-conditioned bedrooms and two baths. All rooms have spectacular views and access to the second floor porch. Downstairs there's a living/dining room, a cook's dream kitchen, and laundry room. Beside the house is a small, immaculate pool. A maid cleans twice weekly, and the caretaker lives in a small cottage on the grounds. A 10-minute walk down the path in front of the house will lead you to a very private beach, which has no access by road. The walk up will take a bit more time, but there is always a price for privacy.

The Observatory, a smaller house on the property, was built with David's fascination with astronomy in mind. On the roof, but not accessible to renters, is his 14" telescope. The design of the house is based on that of an old sugar mill, so the the central part of the house is rounded and sloped. Because Tobago is at 11° north latitude, the slope is 11°. Esoteric, yes, but interesting. On the second floor, there are two large bedrooms with equally large and delightful baths. Between the bedrooms, there is a large sitting area. The first floor has a foyer leading to a tiled kitchen/dining/sitting area. The kitchen is wonderfully outfitted with everything you could want in modern appliances, including an island cooking surface. Outside there are morning and afternoon landscaped terraces and a large plunge pool. The owners have a young son, so the house has been constructed to provide safety for children. This house rents for $1,250 a week in high season, less at other times.

PLANTATION BEACH VILLAS, Grafton; ☎ 639-9377, fax 639-0455, e-mail villas@wow.net, Web site www. wow.net/villas. These six Caribbean-

Plantation Beach Villas.

style gingerbread houses are situated on a lushly planted hill overlooking Stone Haven Bay. Each has three air-conditioned bedrooms with bath; two are on the second floor. Downstairs is a comfortable and attractive living/dining area and a complete kitchen. All rooms open onto spacious, covered verandas with deck-style furniture. There's a barbecue grill, wall safe, and laundry room, and daily maid and laundry service are included. Cooks and babysitters are available for an additional charge. Rental during the high season is $495 per day for four persons; $560 for six. Long-term and group rates are negotiable. Low season rates fall to $300/$390. Prices do not include a 10% tax, but repeat visitors receive a 10% discount. Although each of the houses is independent, there are opportunities for socializing at the shared pool and bar. Management will arrange rental cars and tours of the island.

SANCTUARY VILLA RESORT, Grafton Estate; ☎ 639-9556, fax 639-0019, e-mail info@sanctuaryvillas.com, Web site sanctuaryvillas.com. Sanctuary Villas offers an alternative to renting a privately owned home. The owners of this soon-to-be-completed resort have constructed several very appealing individual homes in or near their complex in Grafton. Each of these houses has a 32x16-foot private pool and is well appointed with everything you'll need, from towels to toasters. Furnishings are attractive and comfortable; much of the furniture was designed and built of teak, mahogany, or cypress right in Trinidad and Tobago. Housekeeping services are included, as are airport transfers. Rates begin at about $2,200 a week for up to four people.

TOP O' TOBAGO, Arnos Vale; ☎ 639-3166, fax 660-7181, e-mail topo-tob@istar.ca. This very pretty house shares its six acres of grounds on the top of a hill with three two-person cabanas, making it less isolated and more social than most privately owned rental houses on the island. Costing just $125/day in high season, the house is a special bargain in off-season at just $100/day. With an open floor plan making a pleasant kitchen/living area, this home has one large master bedroom with a small attached children's room. The pool and terraces provide wonderful views across the hills to the ocean below. Use of the pool is shared with the cabanas and there is an outside shower and bath. The resident managers, Mr. and Mrs. Dow, are grandparents of the owner and are there to assist you. Cleaning service is provided every other day. This is a perfect place for four couples to find a little bit of paradise. We liked it so much we were trying to decide whom to invite.

Camping

Camping is not common on the island, but a few years ago we met a young couple camping at Englishman's Bay. Avid snorkelers, they were catching their dinners and having a wonderful time. Local police checked on them each afternoon to make sure they were okay. Though this may seem idyllic, camping might not be a great choice for everyone. With the rapid development now taking place in Tobago, there are few accessible areas where you can pitch your tent and settle in without a lot of company. **Canoe Bay Beach Park** was a good choice for camping in the past, but now serves only groups of 15 or more. Still, they might be worth a call in case things change. Check with Ashton or Carol-Ann Birchwood James; ☎ 639-4055 days, 639-0540 evenings. See page 163 for more information.

The Tobago House of Assembly has plans to develop camping facilities in the Bloody Bay area at the end of the road on the Caribbean side of the island. Nothing is in place yet, but may be soon. To get a progress report, contact the Tobago Tourism Information Office in Scarborough, ☎ 639-2125.

Where To Eat

Unlike many Caribbean islands, Tobago has fruit and vegetable farms and ranches raising cows, sheep, and goats. Fresh fish, lobster, and conch are also readily available from the surrounding sea, so there is an abundance of wonderful food of all kinds.

LOCAL FOODS

■ **Breadfruit:** This wonderful food grows on huge, very beautiful trees. Their large, shiny leaves are deep green and shaped like frilly fingers. Harvested from the trees by hand, the large fruit is cooked for a short time and cubed in salads or cooked for a longer time and used like potato. It is known as a "belly full" in Tobago, because you don't have to eat very much. It is very satisfying and nutritious.

■ **Callaloo:** A favorite in both Tobago and Trinidad, this green soup is made with dasheen and ochroes (the local word for okra).

■ **Curried crab and dumplings:** Crabs are seasoned with herbs and coconut milk and served with dumplings to sop up the juices. It's filling and messy, but traditional food. Try it at Miss Jean's or Miss Esmie's at Store Bay Beach in Crown Point.

■ **Dasheen:** This plant produces large, deep green leaves that are used in making **callaloo soup** and roots that are used like potatoes. The roots are purplish gray-white, very dry, and relatively tasteless on their own, but make a great vehicle for various sauces. The blue dasheen root is considered very nutritious.

■ **Dumplings:** A boiled, biscuit-like preparation, usually made with flour, though sometimes cornmeal or another flavoring is added. Crab and dumplings is a staple in Tobago, and should not be missed.

■ **Ground provisions:** These include sweet potatoes, dasheen, breadfruit, yams, green bananas, and plantain. Usually cooked with their skins on and peeled when done, ground provisions will be served with all of the wonderful local stews.

■ **Macaroni pie:** A staple accompaniment to stews with chicken, beef, or goat.

■ **Pelau:** Rice, pigeon peas, and meat – your ideal one-pot meal in Tobago.

■ **Pigeon peas:** Tall bushes bear pigeon pea pods from December to February. You'll see pigeon peas sold everywhere in the market. They are almost always served in rice.

■ **Tanya:** A plant similar in appearance to the dasheen, but larger. The large, brown, and hairy root is used in cooking like a potato.

■ About The Food

Seafood

In Crown Point, fishermen come in with their catch by the Conrado Hotel in Pigeon Point. You can show up there by the fishing shacks at about 5 PM and see what's available. The catch will vary by season, but you may find flying fish, dolphin, red snapper, tuna, or grouper. You may also enjoy seeing a seine being pulled at Mt. Irvine, Black Rock, Turtle Beach, Bloody Bay, Man-O-War Bay or Castara, and you can purchase some of the catch. On King's Bay Beach from about 1 to 4 in the afternoon you can buy the catch of the morning, which might be yellowfin or blackfin tuna, kingfish, dolphin, snapper or grouper. The young fishermen will filet it for you right there. If you are staying at the eastern end of the island, Charlotteville is the place to go for the widest variety of fresh fish.

If you want lobsters, the best person to see is **Renwick Thom** (☎ 639-9425), who is at Pigeon Point by the Conrado Hotel around 10:30 AM (but give him a call the day before to set a time). If you

Our friend, Cuthbert Williams, with lobsters for dinner.

are at all inclined to cook, don't miss the lobster and dolphin. Surprisingly, we met up with Renwick this time at our hotel. Someone on the lawn was busy at the old steel drum barbecue and we went nosing around to see who was there and what they were cooking. There was Renwick, barbecuing chicken and fish for a group of his friends here at the hotel. He and his brother Seldon regularly prepare a beach barbecue at No Man's Land after the Buccoo reef tour, but will come to your hotel or your favorite beach and cook up a storm whenever you like. For about $25 US per person, they'll do a grand barbecue of Caribbean lobster for you. Fish or chicken barbecue dinners cost a little less. Also included in the price is a variety of prepared vegetables and salad, so gather a few new friends together and enjoy.

Sweet Treats

Sesame candy sweets are available at the airport from a number of friendly ladies. The sweets come in all sorts of shapes and combinations and they're pretty good. Candy bar lovers will find a good supply at Penny Savers.

Beer & Rum

Local beers are **Carib** and **Stag**, and either one might become the next Red Stripe. You may also get a chance to try **bush rum**, a local brew that's as good as it is powerful. Rum is made in Trinidad, so you'll be offered lots of rum and Coke and rum punch.

For Vegetarians

Tobago has fruits and vegetables galore, and restaurant offerings are expanding greatly. If you eat fish, there's no problem. If you don't, the Turtle Beach Hotel (see page 136) specializes in vegetarian fare, but it's not inexpensive. An average dinner will cost about $30 per person, including tax. Lots of small local food stalls serve non-meat rotis that our vegetarian friends thought were very good and, in Scarborough, there are a few vegetarian shops in the mall. None has extensive menus or many basic foods that you can cook yourself, and none of them had prepared meals that we thought were appealing. **E & F Health Foods** there is probably the best for herbs. **Penny Savers** carries various forms of vegetable protein and soy products.

■ Grocery Shopping

Many smaller guest houses and hotels on the island provide cooking facilities. If you want to cook while on vacation, here are some places to shop.

Penny Savers Supermarket in Canaan, just outside of Crown Point, has all the basics – food staples like coffee and sugar, but also wonderful New Zealand cheese, Irish powdered milk (which rivals the taste of fresh milk, no matter where you're from), terrific Indian spices, a wide selection of beers, liquors and wines, and a few fresh fruits and vegetables. They also have lots of candy bars and some other home-away-from-home foods.

Smaller markets, more like neighborhood grocery stores, are common on the island. They won't have a full selection like Penny Savers and they are more expensive, but they are very convenient.

Fresh fruits and vegetables are available all over the island at small **roadside stalls**. There are tomatoes and lettuce and peppers and onions and plantains and papayas and mangoes and pineapples and watermelons and bananas and lemons and limes... One of our favorite stalls is in Crown Point where the road splits toward Pigeon Point. They have a very good selection of local and Trinidadian produce. Owned by Lenor Archer and Ann James, this small shop provides onions, tomatoes, peppers, potatoes and all kinds of local fruits, along with terrific fresh Tobago lettuce. Do try it , as it is some of the best we've ever had, and a big salad makes a great meal in this warm climate. We looked for seeds to take home with us, but didn't find any.

*Lenor Archer and Ann James sell wonderful fruits
and vegetables in Crown Point.*

Tobago

The **Golden Grove Farm** in Canaan raises livestock and ages their meat. It's disappointing that most of it is for sale frozen, but they'll sell you fresh if they have it. Frozen meats and seafood, fancy groceries, fresh heavy cream, and a wide selection of imported cheeses are available at **R.T. Morshead's** (☎ 639-8855), just off Shirvan Rd. If you are planning a dinner party, this is a must-stop for those special treats you won't find elsewhere. Morshead's is open 8 to 4 PM Monday through Friday, closing from 12 to 1 PM for lunch, and from 8 to 1 PM on Saturday.

A food fancier's highlight is the **weekly market in Scarborough**, beginning at 6 AM on Friday and Saturday mornings. There you can buy very fresh and wonderful foods of all kinds. The meat market is inside the main building, and offers beef, lamb, pork, goat, and sometimes animal parts you'd rather not see. Free-range eggs and chickens are also available. Outside in the market, fruitarians and vegetarians will have a field day. Everything looks and tastes great. You won't find any of those US supermarket mystery foods, such as big, bright red strawberries that taste like air. Beans, salt, oils, crabs, herbs, vegetables and fruits are in abundance. It's a celebration not to be missed.

AUTHOR TIP

*For the very freshest and most tender beef for a special barbecue, see **Lloyd Ottley** in stall #28 at the Scarborough Market. He's there on Friday, from 5 AM to 6 PM, and Saturday from 5 AM to 3 PM. We have bought T-bone steaks from Lloyd on many occasions and they have always been fabulous. One of the funny things in this market is that they don't use knives. All meat is cut with machetes, which makes quite a sight. If you miss seeing Lloyd, see **Cornell Battis**, just across the aisle.*

Restaurants

While we can't give rave reviews to restaurants on the island in general, there are some that are doing a very good job. In most cases, the lower down on the restaurant food chain you go, the better the fare gets. Local food is delicious. There are wonderful stews with chicken, beef, or fish and all cooked with light touches of herbs and served with a variety of fresh vegetables. If you select local dishes on any menu, you can't go wrong.

Because Tobago is becoming more of a tourist destination, new restaurants are opening all the time. We've listed some of the better places we found, but there seems to be a new one every week. They are all well worth trying.

You'll see many restaurant advertisements requesting reservations. It's rare for a place to be full but, especially in the case of smaller restaurants, reservations are necessary so they'll have an idea of how many people are coming and how much to prepare. In many of the restaurants we tried for lunch we were the only ones there, so don't hesitate to stop by even if you haven't called ahead.

■ Crown Point & Bon Accord

BACKYARD BATIK SHOP & CAFE, Crown Point; ☎ 639-8765. This little place has outdoor seating with light meals and sandwiches. They carry Eve Mendes' fruit juices, which is a plus in anyone's book. Stop by have a fresh juice drink and see their selection of batiks.

CAFE CALLALOO, on the road to Pigeon Point, Crown Point; ☎ 639-9020. Reservations are recommended for this newcomer to the restaurant scene. The menu offers lobster creations and USA beef, and the decor is light and appealing.

ELEVEN DEGREES NORTH, Store Bay Rd. off Pigeon Point Rd., Crown Point; ☎ 639-0996. This popular spot, on the way to Pigeon Point, was opened only a few years ago by husband and wife team Barry Treau and Bechna Seereeram. Tragically, Bechna died in the spring of 1999. If Barry continues with the restaurant, you will find the comfortable, well-designed open-air place. The wood ceiling, delicate pastels, individually painted tables, and revolving exhibitions of local art make it a sophisticated setting. It opens for dinner at 6:30 PM, Tuesday through Saturday, and offers entertainment by The Old Time Jammers on Tuesday and Thursday. Barry joins in with his guitar, and even the most reserved people get up and dance. You'll find an eclectic mix of Caribbean, Cajun, and Mexican dishes on the menu, under the umbrella description of "new world cuisine." A lobster crêpe appetizer, followed by an entrée of home-made carrot and spinach pasta with a chicken or lobster sauce, should leave you too full for a slice of guava cheesecake, but do your best. Dinner with wine will be about $80 for two, though you can spend less. We recommend you dine after 8:30, when the mosquito coils have done their job and the odor has dissipated. **Note:** Just before press time we heard through the grapevine that Barry will be selling the restaurant, but we were unable to confirm the rumor. Stop by and let us know what you find.

HARRY BALTI, Storebay Rd., Crown Point. Just across from the airport, this informal open-air restaurant serves interesting appetizers, seafood pastas, steaks, and fish. One specialty is pizza, and it is very good. Prices are reasonable compared to other restaurants in Tobago.

MARCIA'S DINER, Bon Accord; ☎ 639-0359/1762. For genuine local fare served in a pleasant air-conditioned restaurant, this is the place. They have drinks and good local food, with entertainment on Thursday evenings and happy hour from 7-8 PM. Marcia's has been around for awhile, so you know they are doing something just right.

MISS JEAN'S, MISS ESMIE'S, MISS TRIM'S, MISS JOYCIE'S, ALMA'S AND SILVIA'S, Store Bay Beach, Crown Point. Very popular folksy places to eat delicious and filling food on the cheap, these small kiosks across from Store Bay Beach are run by island ladies who make Tobago "mom's food." We especially recommend the roti at Miss Esmie's. More filling crab and dumplings are great too. There's also a bar/restaurant where they make a passable hamburger with fries. It's not what you'd get in the States, but it's pretty good. Two people can eat their fill for under $10.

TOUCAN INN AND BONKERS, Store Bay Local Rd., Crown Point; ☎ 639-7173, fax 639-8933, e-mail bonkers@trinidad.net, Web site www.tou-can-inn.com. British owners Chris James and James Vaughan opened this teak extravaganza in 1995. Constructed as an open-air bar/restaurant/inn, the heavy teak lends it a substantial feel. Open for breakfast at 7:30, through lunch and dinner until 11 PM. The food is reasonably priced, and they offer good entertainment nightly. Besides appealing to foreigners, Bonkers has developed quite a following of Trinis on holiday in Tobago. It can be warm even in the evening; you'll be more comfortable wearing very light clothes.

Tobago

■ Mid-Caribbean Coast

ARNOS VALE WATERWHEEL RESTAURANT & BAR, Franklyn Rd., Arnos Vale Estate, Arnos Vale; ☎ 660-0814/0815. Set in the exquisite Arnos Vale Waterwheel Nature Park, the restaurant was carefully constructed around the remains of an 18th-century sugar mill. It is open every day from 8:30 AM to 10:30 PM. You can enjoy a light lunch of ceviche of kingfish or crab meat with papaya salad, but don't miss having dinner in this very romantic setting. Friday is probably best, when entertainment is provided on the stage set off from the dining area in lush tropical foliage. Perhaps you'll meet chef Philip Bronte, who is creating a new style of cooking called "modern Caribbean cuisine." The menu offerings begin with a wide selection of wonderful appetizers, including the not-to-be-missed prawns grilled in tamarind sauce and anchar, served on yam puree. I could have made a meal of this alone. Entrées are equally sophisticated and delicious. Try the parcel-baked mahi mahi with lemon ginger, or toasted scallops and lobster. If you still have room, which is doubtful, you must try Auntie Katy's cheesecake. We hope you'll get to meet Catherine Bronte Tinkew, who was introduced as Auntie Katy. She is delightful, and her cheesecake irresistible. The wonderful food, combined with warm, friendly service and the elegant place settings, make you feel very special indeed. Dinner with wine will be about $100 for two. More information on the park is in the *Sightseeing* section on page 160.

BLACK ROCK CAFE, Main Rd., Black Rock; ☎ 639-7625. This is a place for open-air dining with linens, lots of breezy air, and ceiling fans to keep it moving. The restaurant is owned by a BWIA pilot, who also owns the Peacock Mill Restaurant. The varied menu is described on a large chalkboard, and food is appealingly presented. It's open from noon until 3 PM for lunch and from 6 PM until whenever for dinner. Two of us had lunch and drinks for under $20.

PAPILLON RESTAURANT, Buccoo Junction, Mt. Irvine; ☎ 639-0275. Aside from their menu featuring lobster, conch, and fish, they have a three-course special each day priced between $20 and $42 for two. They are open for lunch from 11:30 AM to 1:30 PM, and for dinner from 6:30 PM to 10 PM. You may dine on the outside patio or inside in air-conditioned comfort. Along with the restaurant, the owner, Jacob, operates the Grange Hotel. Papillon was under major renovation while we were there, so we haven't seen the end result. The restaurant, however, has years of experience behind it. Many years ago, Jacob's father opened the first restaurant in Tobago, called "Voodoo."

PATINO'S, Shirvan Rd., Buccoo; ☎ 639-9481. Open for breakfast at 8 AM, and serving through lunch and dinner until 10 PM, Patino's focuses on fish, but offers beef and chicken alternatives. Two daily dinner specials are offered at about $30 per person, and include soup, entrée, and dessert. The menu is more ambitious than some, with Thai-style seafood and chicken. It's owned by Trinis Marcia and Kenneth Patino. One of the chefs is their son Roger and the other chef is Eddy Baynes. Thursday dinners are accompanied by live steel band music.

SHIRVAN WATERMILL RESTAURANT, Shirvan Rd., Mt. Pleasant; ☎ 639-0000, fax 639-0534, e-mail swmill@tstt.net.tt. Serving cocktails at the bar at 5 with dining from 6 PM, casual elegance is the watchword at Shirvan's. Their menu board features a changing selection of entrées, such as Shirvan honey-style duck, grilled fish with shallot vinaigrette, shrimp tempura, and Tobago river lobster, a larger variety of the American crawfish. Beginning dinner with a light salad topped off with freshly ground pepper from any one of their great collection of pepper mills, you can't help but be pleased when your main course arrives on a warmed plate. I'm a great fan of duck, and I ate every bit of that deliciously prepared and beautifully presented entrée. Stassi had the river lobster, which can be messy to eat, but with the finger bowl for cleaning up served after dinner, it's worth every sticky finger. If you can manage dessert, try the crème caramel or banana mousse.

When asked why he likes having a restaurant, Managing Director David Ford said with his great smile, "I like food and good company." And indeed he does. Dining here is a lovely experience and much more reasonably priced than comparably elegant restaurants on the island. Dinner for two will be about $70. The setting is a roofed open-air building with stylish and comfortable wood furnishings, surrounded by lovely tropical gardens. The service is professional, and you can't help but leave with plans to return.

LA TARTARUGA RESTAURANT, Buccoo Bay; ☎ 639-0940. Owned by Gabriel de Gaetano and his wife Andrea, this small bistro-style Italian restaurant has a fixed-price menu that includes a sampling of appetizers, a choice of pastas, and dessert. Gabriel makes fresh pasta daily and orchestrates your dining experience, while Andrea supervises the kitchen and specializes in desserts. Try her wonderful almond chocolate cake, luxuriously served with chocolate ice cream. They also have a good wine list and a variety of authentic Italian grappas. Everyone on the island thinks highly of La Tartaruga. It's on the expensive side – dinner for two will be about $100 with wine. Open evenings; closed Sunday and Monday.

■ Lowlands, Scarborough & Bacolet

BLUE CRAB, Robinson St., Scarborough; ☎ 639-2737. Known for its creole cuisine with chicken, fish, or vegetarian options, the Blue Crab offers an attractive setting with great views. Lunch will be about $16 for two and dinner is about $35. This is a good stop on your way back from Fort St. George. Reservations are required for dinner.

DOUBLE D'S DELIGHT, Lowlands, across from the guest house called Viola's place. No phone yet. Open for lunch and dinner, this little place is cute and the food is good and inexpensive. It was recently opened by trained chef Derrick McLetchie, who has experience at one of the large hotel restaurants in Tobago. He summed up his thoughts on that job for us,

Tobago

Double D's Delight restaurant, in Lowlands.

"You can have a hotel job, or you can have a life." No doubt he's working harder now than ever, but on his own terms. Friday is barbecue night and Saturday night he dedicates to preparing Chinese-style fish with fried rice. A la carte entrées range from angelic shrimp with cashews to stuffed pork chops with apples in a coconut sauce. Dinner will be under $30 for two. They don't have a liquor license, but do serve a wide variety of special local juices, and you can always BYOB. We stopped for lunch and had one of the best rotis we've tasted, along with a delicious fruit punch.

OLD DONKEY CART HOUSE RESTAURANT AND WINE BISTRO, "La Locanda," Bacolet St. #73, Scarborough; ☎ 639-3551. Local and international cuisine is served outside a French colonial-style house. The owners specialize in a selection of German wines. With candlelight on the table and twinkling lights strung in the trees overhead, it makes a lovely, romantic setting. We dined there on our anniversary and were very happy with our meal, the service, and the setting. Dinner for two with cocktails will run about $70, including tax and service.

THE PEACOCK MILL, Friendship Estate, Canaan; ☎ 639-0503. This interesting, out-of-the-way place opened several years ago, but recently changed hands and wasn't fully open the last time we visited. The pretty inside dining room has been closed, and a barbecue pit, pool table, and dining area are now outside under a palapa. Peacocks still live under the huge tree in front. You'll see the sign on the main road from Scarborough to Crown Point, quite near to the Shirvan Rd. turnoff. You'll also see this listed under *Nightlife*, page 185. It's a good place to spend an evening liming.

ROUSELLES, Old Windward Rd., Bacolet; ☎ 639-4738. Casual but sophisticated, Rouselles is open for dinner only, though you can stop by for cocktails from 3 to 11 PM. This delightful and well-regarded restaurant is owned by Bobbie Evans and Charlene Goodman. With a lovely view, wood floors, teak tables, and lots of plants, the outside porch has the best seating. It is also pleasant inside, with a teak bar and casual but elegant ambiance. They offer four beautifully prepared entrées – lobster, seafood, pork chops, and chicken. Meals range from $15 to $30, plus drinks. The porch overlooks a pretty garden, if you tire of the sea view, and the music is very pleasant. Reservations for a table on the porch are necessary during the high season.

▪ Atlantic Coast

FIRST HISTORICAL CAFE & BAR, Windward Rd., Studley Park; ☎ 660-2248. On the Atlantic side of the island where there is very little development for travelers, this is a wonderful little treasure. Opened by Tobagoin Kenneth Washington about four years ago, the café serves a light menu of sandwiches, burgers, hot dogs, salads, and local meals, along with fresh juices, beer, and rum. The setting and decor are terrific. They've decorated all of the walls with tidbits of Tobago history, local language, homilies, and other bits of fascinating local lore, like "Trinidad is bright and loud and Tobago is calm and whispers. Trinidad is cosmopolitan, Tobago is natural and unspoiled. However, citizens of both islands are hospitable and dignified." Sitting right over the water, the views are great. Locals and visitors are equally at home here. They are open from 9 AM to 7 PM.

First Historical Café & Bar, Studley Park, Tobago.

RICHMOND GREAT HOUSE INN, Belle Garden; ☎ 660-4467. This is your very best choice for a special lunch or dinner in Belle Garden, a small village on the road from Scarborough to Speyside. The inn is a lovely old estate house and the food is delicious and freshly prepared. Situated on a hill, the inn has spectacular views all the way to the ocean in the distance. You must call ahead and make reservations for dinner, a four-course meal served from 6:30 to 8 PM and costing about $50 for two. Dinner is always served in the main house dining room, but lunch may also be served in the small bar below the main house. A full lunch with dessert runs about $20 for two.

■ Charlotteville, Speyside, Parlatuvier

GAIL'S CAFE, Charlotteville (no phone). This is a good place in town for a breakfast of pancakes or omelettes with fresh local juices and homemade bread. They're also open for dinner, and for $6 you can enjoy their curried crab and dumplings or other local specialties. They have a few outside tables where you can dine while enjoying the cool of the evening.

JEMMA'S TREE HOUSE RESTAURANT, Speyside; ☎ 660-4066. As the name implies, this restaurant sits in a tree over the water. There are many new restaurant choices in Speyside, but Jemma's unique charm holds up nicely against the competition. You won't find a printed menu, but chicken, fish, or shrimp dishes are served with rice, fried plantains, vegetables and salad. They do not serve any alcoholic beverages, but you are quite welcome to bring your own. Three of us ate lunch at this island institution for $32, including tip. It looks like Jemma's is getting more expensive, but eating in a tree house seems worth it. The food is not fancy, but it is nicely presented and the servings are plentiful.

RIVERSIDE RESTAURANT & LOCAL DISHES, Parlatuvier; ☎ 639-4935. Serving Tobago-style food, the Riverside is one of the better locally owned restaurants to come on the scene in the last few years. The menu of fish, chicken, and lobster dishes will please almost everyone, especially at prices between $10 and $12. This open-air restaurant, set on the hill over Parlatuvier Bay, will take you back to the "good ole days" in Tobago before it was discovered. The people are very nice and the food is good. Open from 8:30 AM to 10 PM, it is owned by the delightful Gloria and Joseph and run with pride by all the family.

READER'S COMMENT *"We are in the catering business and found their standards very high – the food was all freshly cooked on both of the occasions we called, a very ample helping and very reasonably priced... "* The Wrights, Devon, England.

Sightseeing

■ Bird Watching

While Tobago does not offer the variety of birds found in Trinidad, it balances fewer species with easier observation. **Roxborough** in the afternoon is a great place to see whole flocks of parrots flying from tree to tree. **Little Tobago** is a favorite; **Arnos Vale Waterwheel Park**, the **Grafton Estate Bird Sanctuary**, **Hillsborough Dam**, the **Adventure Farm and Nature Reserve**, **French Fort**, **St. Giles Island**, and the **Main Ridge Forest Reserve** are good, too. Tobago has lots of trails, so feel free to explore. For a truly able guide whose knowledge of and fascination with birds is wonderful, see the listing for Simon McLetchie Tours in the *Guide Services* chapter, page 219.

AUTHOR TIP *For any of the hikes or bird watching trails, you'll need sneakers or good walking shoes. Binoculars are also a must and the ubiquitous camera should always be with you. Bring a bottle of water, too. Other than that, there is nothing special you'll need while exploring Tobago. It has a tamer environment than Trinidad.*

■ Atlantic Coast

ARGYLE WATERFALL, Roxborough. Open from 8 AM to 3 PM. This is a lovely site and very popular, but it is also one of the few areas where there have been problems with troublemakers, so it is best to go in a group or with your own guide. Entrance and parking fees seem to vary with the avarice of the staff, and for some reason the Tourist Board seems unable or unwilling to straighten out the situation. Ask about it at your hotel in case things have changed since we were there.

You'll pay from $1 per person or up to $5, if you've got a car, to enter the site. As you're walking to this beautiful waterfall, you'll pass by a swampy area on your right and, if you're lucky, you'll be there when the white and pale blue water lilies are in bloom. There are even some ramshackle picnic tables for you to rest and enjoy the sight. Birds and butterflies abound even if nothing's blooming, and it's not a long walk. Along the way are banana plants and orange-flowered flamboyant trees. Flamboyants are often home to birds called the king of the woods, whose nests are the long burlap-sack-like bags that you'll see hanging from the trees.

You'll be getting close to the falls when you first come upon a creek. Follow it along the rocks and you'll arrive in a few minutes. Though the falls run year-round, they are more spectacular in the rainy season. Have a swim or climb to the top for a water massage, though I'd recommend this only for those who like climbing. I stayed below and entertained myself with swimming, admiring the falls, and chit-chatting with the fellow selling handcrafted leather and beadwork.

COCOA ESTATE, Roxborough. Chocolate lovers will find this interesting – we did. You'll drive right through old cocoa estates if you are heading to Argyle Waterfall from Roxborough. You'll see acres of 20- to 30-foot trees with six-inch pods, ranging in color from purple to yellow to red, hanging off woody parts of the trees. The yellow cocoa pods are harvested and opened and the contents dried and ground into chocolate. If you get a pod that's bright yellow, crack it open and eat the white gooey stuff inside (you'll have to spit out the seeds). It doesn't taste like chocolate, but has a delicate, sweet flavor. When picking pods, watch for the snakes that live in

Tobago

the trees, called "cocoa police" by the locals. They aren't poisonous, but you may be startled. As you enter the estate, note the ruined stone building where slaves worked. The building is slowly being restored.

HILLSBOROUGH DAM – Take a left from Windward Rd., at the sign between Mt. St. George and Granby Point onto Mt. St. George Back Road. This is an interesting stop for nature lovers and bird watchers. Follow the not-great road to the dam. You are supposed to purchase entrance tickets in Scarborough, but nobody does. If questioned, just pay your minimal ticket price right there. Caiman up to six feet long are commonly sighted, along with a variety of birds. The dam is relatively small and in dry season (beginning in May), you may walk along its left side to an area for nesting birds. The best times to go are very early in the morning or just before sunset. Do not wander off on the right side of the dam or the creepy crawlies will get you. This is well worth a visit, especially if you continue on the cross-island road. Miraculously, even in a car, bird sightings are an every-other-minute occurrence.

Be careful. Although the caiman look tame and sleepy, they are not. They move like lightning when prey is near.

KING'S BAY WATERFALL, Delaford. Here's one more reason to explore this part of the island. The fall is 100 feet high and runs well in the rainy season. As with all waterfall sites, it is recommended that you do not go alone. Bring a friend or a guide with you. Don't miss King's Bay Beach while you're in the area.

RICHMOND GREAT HOUSE, Belle Garden; ☎ 660-4467. This is a restored 18th-century plantation house set in the hills on the Atlantic Coast. It is now an inn with a good restaurant and, with its wonderful views and marvelous antiques, it is an ideal spot for a gracious lunch. Call ahead and make a reservation the day before you go. Hiking on any one of the trails through the hills nearby will help you work off lunch.

■ Crown Point

BUCCOO REEF – This once pristine reef lies off Pigeon Point. Tragically, major parts of it have suffered from a combination of pollution, boat anchors, and unmindful tourism. The best way to see the reef is by scuba diving or snorkeling, though most often visitors take one of the much-touted reef tours. Arrangements for seeing the reef without adding to the damage can be made with any of the dive shops in the area, especially those near Pigeon Point.

Glass-bottom boats ply their way to Buccoo Reef on a daily basis from various spots on the island. The round-trip to the reef takes about 2½ hours and costs $10 per person. The ride out is pleasant enough, but on arrival at the reef an anchor is thrown overboard and dragged until it catches on the coral. Protective shoes are passed out so that passengers may walk on the reef, which at this point is only three or four feet under the boat. We stayed on board and looked through the glass at the mostly dead coral below.

Once everyone is back on board, the anchor is hauled up and the boat motors over what is called the coral garden. This area is too deep for walking so everyone stays on board. It was fantastic and well worth seeing. The next stop is called the nylon pool. This area of the reef is very shallow, with a coral sand bottom, and it warms up in the sun and feels like a bath. They say if you swim in the nylon pool you'll feel 10 years younger. With the rum and Cokes and beers that have been consumed on board a boat with no bathroom, I'm sure this stop at the nylon pool truly does make a lot of people feel 10 years younger. Buccoo Reef is stunning where it is still alive.

ECO-TOURISM AT BUCCOO REEF

In the interests of encouraging eco-tourism, Buccoo Reef is now called a "protected marine park," but there is no evident protection. Please take a snorkeling or scuba diving trip here rather than one of the glass-bottom boat tours. If you can't swim, take a glass-bottom boat tour and simply stay on the boat; decline use of the reef-walking shoes and don't use the nylon pool for anything but wading.

Tobago

CRUSOE'S CAVE, Crown Point. Tobago has the honor of being the island chosen most likely to have provided a safe haven for the fictional Robinson Crusoe. There is a small cave where he is said to have lived; you can see it by paying a fee of about $1 to a lovely woman named Alison, or her mother, Mrs. Crooks. They own the right-of-way to the shore where the cave is found and maintain the rough stairs leading to it.

We decided to bike over to the cave one day and found it disappointing. However, the ride was nice and the view was great, so we felt we'd gotten our $1 worth. You won't find much in the Caribbean so reasonably priced. The cave is located on the shore side of the airport. At the end of the airport where planes land there's a road that goes by the edge of the sea. Follow that to the second dirt road off to the right. Go down that road and you'll find a small-painted sign saying Crusoe's Cave. When you see the house, just give a shout and Mrs. Crooks or her daughter will collect your $1 and point you in the right direction.

PIGEON POINT – see *Beaches*, page 168.

■ Mid-Caribbean Coast

Arnos Vale, Black Rock, Plymouth

ADVENTURE FARM AND NATURE RESERVE, Arnos Vale Rd., Plymouth; ☎ 639-2839, fax 639-4157, e-mail adventur@tstt.net.tt. This is a tropical 12-acre organic farm with many varieties of fruit trees, including mangoes, bananas, papayas, guavas, West Indian cherries and several kinds of citrus. They also raise sheep and racing goats. The owner, Ean Mackay, has a very special regard for the environment and has dedicated his land to the maintenance of native birds and plants. Trails throughout the property provide opportunities for you to see such bird species as king of the woods, chachalaca, woodpeckers, herons, egrets, parakeets, blue tanagers, hummingbirds, bare-eyed thrush, jacamar, and the barred antshrike. Guide Simon McLetchie is a special treat (see his listing under Simon McLetchie Tours in the *Guide Services* chapter). I think he knows every bird on the island personally. The farm is open Monday through Friday, 7 AM to 5:45 PM, and there is a minimal admission fee.

> ***Getting Here:*** *Head toward Plymouth and turn right onto Arnos Vale Road. It's just ahead on the right.*

ARNOS VALE WATERWHEEL NATURE PARK, Franklyn Road, Arnos Vale Estate, Arnos Vale; ☎ 660-0814/0815. On this old sugar plantation estate is a small shop with nice quality gifts, a room where artifacts found on the property are displayed, a wonderful restaurant and bar, and guided or independent walking trails to the old master's house, the dam, and an Amerindian village site. They are open every day, with restaurant hours from 8:30 AM to 10:30 PM. We stopped by one day and were very fortunate to meet Philip, the owner's son, who is one of the chefs. He generously spent a few hours with us, relating what he knows of the history of this remarkably beautiful place. The interesting story follows.

Tobago was colonized by the British just after the mid-18th century as a base for sugar plantations and, within a few years, Arnos Vale and other estates were well established. On the present site of the Arnos Vale Hotel was a port area from which processed sugar was shipped to another port in Tobago, called Barbados Bay, where it was reloaded on a boat sailing first to Barbados and then on to England.

The Arnos Vale sugar factory opened in 1768, first powered by the type of waterwheel still in place. The huge wheel was fed with water flowing from a dam on the stream that still runs through the property. An aqueduct, which is also still there, brought water along the hillside. From there it flowed to a point just above the new bar; the water would then flow across a chute turning the wheel clockwise. Eventually rollers would push the sugarcane through crushers and the juice was collected below.

Three boiling basins of the original five remain in place. These were called "coppers," and this method of refining sugar was called the "Jamaica trade." Juice was boiled in consecutive coppers until it reached the hottest one, called a "strike pan," where the juice immediately got very thick. That liquid was put in barrels that were stored in a huge, three-story building called the "drying rack." There the barrels would sit until the molasses settled to the bottom, leaving the rest to form sugar crystals.

"Coppers," or sugar boiling pots, at Arnos Vale Waterwheel Park.

When it was ready, workers punctured the bottoms of the barrels, collected all the molasses, and made rum by the side of a huge old tree that is still there. Rum-making at that time involved using something called a "worm tank"; you can see the remains of the tank. Once the rum was made (I like their priorities), the sugar was sent to the port for shipping.

Fires used in the process, whether for boiling the cane juice or making rum, were fueled with "bagus," which is the remains of the cane after it has been crushed, making these early factories were very efficient. If you tour the wonderful sugar factory in Trinidad, you'll see this same efficiency. Bagus is still used as fuel, and the ash remains are carried back to the sugarcane fields for use as fertilizer.

The Victorian age brought the steam engine to the estate, replacing flowing water as the source of power. This very decorative engine is still in place today. Though it was able to turn the wheel much faster than flowing water, it was not as reliable, and water remained a backup system. Later, a steam pump pushed the water from above much faster than it would have flowed from the dam. Laughingly, with great appreciation for all that had been accomplished there, Philip said, "It was quite high-tech for its day."

Arnos Vale is the only estate in Tobago that had two sources of power. They produced 70,000 tons of sugar annually, along with quantities of rum. Slaves, numbering over 100, worked the cane and lived in a village opposite the property, and you can see the area where they had their huts. Overseers lived there, too, and straight through the valley there's the master's house on top of the hill. One of the trails leads to the old estate house site, where there's a spectacular view.

The existing wheel that dominates the bar and restaurant area was made in Scotland in 1857. Philip thinks it was probably the third wheel installed here, as wheels did not normally last long under the constant pressure of the flowing water. Because it was in operation a relatively short time, this wheel is in good condition. The combination of abolition and mechanization of the sugar industry in other parts of the world made the business in

The waterwheel at Arnos Vale Waterwheel Nature Park.

Tobago uneconomical, though they continued for some years to produce sugar for local consumption.

Mr. Bronte, Philip's father, who restored and designed this wonderful place, has an avid interest in maintaining the historic remains of the sugar industry and in communicating its history to locals and to foreigners alike. You may have seen some of the estate if you watched the 1999 Miss Universe contest in Trinidad. Some of the filming was done right here.

DID YOU KNOW?

If you snorkel at the Arnos Vale Hotel beach, you can see a channel in the reef. This passageway was dynamited to allow passage of the boats carrying sugar.

Getting Here: *On Shirvan Rd., turn left over Courland Bridge just past the Turtle Beach Hotel. Take the right-hand turn toward Arnos Vale and, just when you see the Arnos Vale Hotel, turn right on Franklin Rd. (the only right turn that's paved) and drive about a half-mile. On the right you'll see the entrance to this unique place, which opened in 1997. Park your car and prepare to deal with the old fellow at the gate. In his own style, he'll collect about $1.50 from each person entering the property, but don't let his grumpiness dampen your spirits. He's been with the owner's family for years and he just won't change. Your $1.50 will be returned with any purchase you make, either in the bar, restaurant, or shop. While it doesn't seem like much to charge as an entrance fee, it does help with the cost of grounds maintenance.*

FORT JAMES, Plymouth. While in Plymouth stop at this pretty overlook. It's a lovely, quiet place for a picnic. There's an old building and a cannon, and the view of the coast is beautiful.

GRAFTON ESTATE BIRD SANCTUARY, Black Rock, across from Le Grand Courlan hotel. This is a small bird sanctuary on private land. The trails are not maintained, but are easily walkable. In the early morning or late afternoon you may spot many of the local bird species. We would recommend going in a small group. There is a bathroom at the site, but watch out for spiders. Don't forget to sign the guest book. Nearby is the private Grafton Estate house.

MYSTERY TOMBSTONE, Plymouth. If you are passing through Plymouth, do stop and take a look at this historical oddity. You'll find a small gravestone with the following inscription: "She was a mother without knowing it and a wife without letting her husband know it except by her kind indulgences to him." Betty Stiven was buried here in 1783.

■ North Caribbean Coast

PARLATUVIER BAY, Parlatuvier. This small, exquisite bay was our very favorite on the island until a concrete fishing pier was constructed in the middle of it. There is a tiny, quiet village by the beach, which is shaded by palms and lapped with gentle waves.

■ Scarborough & Vicinity

TOWN OF SCARBOROUGH – Scarborough is a friendly, ramshackle market and commercial port town. Be wary of taxi fares here; always confirm the price before setting off. Fridays and Saturdays are market days in Scarborough; don't miss it! Upper Scarborough, referred to as "up-town" is the part of the town on the hill where you'll find quaint pubs and tourist shopping developing in response to cruise ship visits. If you don't have a car, there's a route taxi stand in the parking lot behind the KFC.

BOTANICAL GARDENS, Scarborough. Worth a visit if you are in Scarborough. No entrance fee.

CANOE BAY BEACH PARK, Friendship Estate, entrance off Claude Noel Highway on the right just past Shirvan Rd. heading toward Scarborough. A beach, group camping, and picnic area, the privately owned Canoe Bay provides large, grassy lawns and palapas for island getaways and parties. They also have modest camping facilities, which are open to groups of 15 or more. You'll have your choice of where to pitch your tent, clean tile bathrooms, and outdoor shower facilities. It is a pleasant, quiet place with a wide, sandy beach. The water is blue-green, calm, and shallow for quite a distance, so it's a great place to bring young children to swim in safety.

Tobago

There's a bar open daily and they promised us there will soon be a restaurant serving inexpensive creole food and sandwiches for lunch. This is the perfect place for a country getaway. The cost of a campsite is $15 per person; if you have a group of 15, ask for a discount. Winston Baptiste is the manager and he's delightful. He'll answer all your questions with a smile. The owners are Tobagoins. Used mainly for parties and weddings, Canoe Bay also hosts occasional concerts. There is a cell phone for emergencies and they now have electricity. Make reservations with Ashton or Carol-Ann Birchwood James; ☎ 639-4055 days, 639-0540 evenings. If you're visiting for the day or camping, they'll lock up valuables for you. There is a security guard there at all times.

FORT KING GEORGE, Scarborough. Built by the English in the late 1770s, this old fort is a wonderful site with spectacular views, especially at sunset. There are several colonial buildings, cannons, and two museums. One has memorabilia of the island, both Amerindian and Colonial, and the other has recent island paintings and sculpture. The grounds are beautiful and well maintained. Admission is free except to the artifact museum, where they charge about $1 per person. There are wonderful plants all over the grounds and some magnificent trees covered in epiphytes. The Tobago hospital is right next door. This site is scheduled for extensive restoration.

FRENCH FORT, Windward Rd. Heading toward Speyside, just past the turnoff to Lower Scarborough, watch for Calder Hill Rd. and turn left there, then turn right before the soccer field. Follow this awful road up the hill for some great bird watching, a cashew tree on the right, and fabulous views from the top. Unfortunately, there are no remains of the fort to be seen.

■ Northeast Central & Coastal Areas

CHARLOTTEVILLE – The largest village in Tobago, Charlotteville sits on a small bay surrounded by mountains. It is not yet developed for tourism and is quite beautiful. There are a few rustic places to stay and a couple of quaint restaurants serving local food. The town faces the harbor with its anchored fishing boats, and each evening there's a fabulous sunset. We arrived in Charlotteville in the late afternoon, and found the locals to be reserved. But once we'd settled in at one of the Cholson Cottages on the main road about two hours later, everyone accepted us as part of the village and were very friendly. Don't miss walking over the hill to Pirate's Bay Beach.

SPEYSIDE – This is a pretty village on the eastern end of the island, and just offshore is Little Tobago. Speyside is an advanced diver's heaven, so the village is developing rather quickly. As of now, there are small hotels, from upscale to moderate, and several restaurants.

LITTLE TOBAGO ISLAND PRESERVE, Speyside. Little Tobago is also known as Paradise Island, because in 1909 Sir William Ingram, an estate owner in Tobago, released 24 pairs of the endangered species called the greater bird of paradise on this small island. Lying a mile or so off the coast at Speyside, Little Tobago is now home to a number of species, but the bird of paradise has not been seen there in over a decade. The hurricane that hit Tobago in 1963 was very destructive, and it is assumed that these birds never really recovered after that storm.

Resident birds on Little Tobago include feral chickens and the red-billed tropic bird, and other species like the redfooted and brown boobies make temporary homes on the island. It's not an unpleasant trip, and for avid bird watchers it may be quite exciting. Try to find a legitimate guide service, perhaps Simon McLetchie for a personal guide or David Rooks for a group (see *Guide Services*). Relying on finding someone with a boat in Speyside, as we did, will greatly limit your potential to appreciate the island.

Little Tobago Island and Goat Island.

MAIN RIDGE FOREST RESERVE, Bloody Bay Rd., between Roxborough and Bloody Bay on the eastern end of the island. Protected since 1765, this rain forest lies at the eastern end of the island, at an altitude of 2,000 feet, between Roxborough on the Atlantic coast and Parlatuvier/ Bloody Bay on the Caribbean. A few years ago there was a very good road crossing the island between these two villages, but its condition is now deteriorated. About halfway between the two coasts you'll see signs for the forest. Though it doesn't seem necessary, you are supposed to enter the preserve only when accompanied by a guide. The preserve is large – over 20,000 acres – and it has wonderful trails. At the very least, take the short walk to the gold coin waterfall, so named because the rocks have turned golden where the water rushes over them. From there, you can continue walking for hours, and it's a very pleasant hike.

MURCHISON TRACE, just before Speyside. If you are visiting the eastern end of the island, you might want to take a long leisurely walk through these woods. You'll see lots of birds and plants native to Tobago. To find it, watch for the dirt road off to the left just before the Speyside lookout. Tobago offers many opportunities for hiking through the woods; this is one of the better trails.

ST. GILES ISLAND, off the northeast shore of Tobago. This rocky island, not far from Little Tobago, is known as a seabird nesting site. It has little substantial vegetation, reminiscent of some of the barren islands in the Galapagos where birds nest prolifically in the rocky crags.

■ Pulling a Seine

At Store Bay and Turtle Beaches and a few others, you'll still be able to see this traditional cooperative fishing effort. A huge net is cast offshore early in the morning and later pulled in hand-over-hand by village fishermen and whoever else is there to help. If you pitch in, you'll get a share of the catch.

When we stopped by the Mt. Irvine Watersports shop one afternoon we met Bertrand Bhikarry, the owner. We were talking about our book on Tobago, and he contributed the following lovely essay on pulling seines.

Pulling a seine at Store Bay Beach.

"SEINE TIME, SAME PLACE"

by Bertrand Bhikarry

"Don't stand there when it's coming in," the old man advised, "you never know what could be swimming around in that net." The woman back-pedaled away, her eyes wide with anticipation. She continues to jockey for a position, however, between the villagers hauling in the net and her friends, who are trying to capture the entire event on their video camera. Except for the nationality of the onlookers, this scene has remained remarkably unchanged on Tobago's beaches for close to 150 years.

Each time the fishermen bring in the seine, people congregate at the water's edge, baskets and pails dangling from their hands, while onlookers stare and village dogs dash around, eager to snatch at any dropped morsel.

As the bunt of the net comes in, fishermen, standing by in their pirogues, skim off bait fish and tenderly deposit them in bait wells. These small fish will become the bait for the next day's catch. As the net is drawn in, prized fish like kingfish, dolphin, and tuna begin to appear and are snapped up eagerly by the anxious fishermen. Once the main catch has been retrieved, the net is hauled farther out of the water, just beyond the surf, and the remaining fish are dumped into depressions scooped out in the sand.

Next, the owner, or one of his trusted assistants, allots portions of the catch to awaiting housewives, laborers, and market vendors. Any money collected goes under his hat, hidden high and dry, but not everyone pays in cash.

Onlookers might wonder how this activity remains viable, when most of the time not a lot of fish is caught. What holds such a large group of men together in so consistent a manner? Usually the equipment belongs to one person, a resident of the village who has acquired the lump sum necessary to purchase a net and the boat used to set it out. He or she in turn hires a core group of about six to 10 men. Their job is to set out and haul in the net, and perform any necessary repairs. They are paid weekly, the amount proportionate to sales from the fish they have netted.

Nets are set in the morning, and hauled in immediately afterwards. If a shoal of fish is evident in the bay, the men may repeat the 'shoot' later in the day. On average, they work six days a week, but generally public holidays, village harvest festivals, and fishermen's fetes are considered 'rest' days.

The number of nets used on any one beach is dictated by the size of the bay and the population of the village. The types of fish caught range from bait fish (herring, balao, and jacks) to the

Tobago

larger species, such as bonito, kingfish, salmon and, sometimes, small shark.

At present, beaches that can boast of some seine fishing activity are those at Mount Irvine Bay, Black Rock, Turtle Beach, Castara, Bloody Bay, Man 'O War Bay, and on the windward side of the island, Mount St. George and Goodwood. This little industry provides direct employment for close to 300 people, and creates economic opportunities for 50 fish market vendors and 40 deep-sea fishermen.

The bad news for people dependent on this type of fishery is that the industry's days are numbered. A declining catch rate and a lack of interest from the younger men mean that one of Tobago's signature activities will become a thing of the past, a beautiful memory poignantly recorded by visitors' video cameras.

Beaches

Tobago has a wealth of beaches. Many have public baths, changing rooms, and bar/restaurants. No beach is very crowded and some are romantically isolated and private. Most of the more desirable beaches are on the Caribbean side of the island where the water is calmer and safer for swimming. Beaches on the Atlantic side, with a few exceptions, are windswept and can have tricky currents. The Atlantic side of the island is dotted with small towns and has very little tourist-style development, though that is gradually changing.

■ Crown Point

PIGEON POINT BEACH RESORT – Open from 8 AM to 6 PM, it is the only beach on the island with an entrance fee, and for under $2 per person you get your money's worth – calm, pristine, turquoise waters, palm trees and lawns, and soft white sand. There are changing facilities, bathrooms, small restaurants, beach shops, and a bar. You may hear or read that it's a populated beach, but by US standards it's not crowded and it is very beautiful. This is the sort of place you can settle into for the whole day, day after day. Windsurfing equipment is available for rent, there's a PADI dive shop, and small craft and gift shops. Buccoo Reef tours leave from the dock.

STORE BAY BEACH – This is probably the most popular beach on the island, for a variety of reasons. The water is a lovely blue and the surf varies from calm to very active. Store Bay is a great swimming beach and good for socializing both in and out of the water. You'll see parents and children frolicking after a hot day at work and school, and it's a great place to fit in and talk with locals. Just up from the beach are vendors selling island crafts and several of the tiniest restaurants you'll ever see. These include

Sunset at Pigeon Point.

Miss Jean's and Miss Esmie's, which serve simple but good food. Try the roti.

■ Mid-Caribbean Coast

BACK BAY BEACH, Shirvan Rd. – Accessible across a stretch of bush, this isolated beach lies on the shore beside Shirvan Rd., right in the middle of everything and all but invisible. There are no real landmarks, but when you're driving on Shirvan Rd., look toward the sea side of the road until you see a wooded area with dirt road tracks. Drive in as far as you can and walk the rest of the way. It's quite beautiful and you're unlikely to have company, but it is not a recommended spot for women alone.

BUCCOO BEACH, Buccoo – With very calm water and gray, well-packed sand, this is a narrow beach that curves out to the point of the bay, giving lots of space to wander off on your own for sunning or swimming. Recently there has been serious shore erosion in front of the beach facilities, but farther away there is still a narrow strip of sandy beach to explore.

Though there are changing rooms and a bar, the area seems to be deteriorating and has little charm. On Sunday evening there's a raucous "Sunday School" on the beach, with music, dancing and general revelry. There is no food available at the beach, but there are lots of small mom-and-pop places nearby where you can get some local lunch. La Tartaruga is about 100 feet from the beach as well, if you're looking for finer fare. It's open only in the evenings, and never on Sunday or Monday.

GRAFTON BEACH – see Stone Haven Bay Beach, below.

MT. IRVINE BAY BEACH, Mt. Irvine – Just down the hill and across the road from the Mt. Irvine Hotel, the beach has a small bar/restaurant owned by the hotel and operated for its guests, but it's open to the public. There is a water sports shop that can provide whatever you'll need in the way of equipment while on the island. They also sell wonderful silver jewelry, so it's worth a look. Mt. Irvine beach is on a wide curving bay with hotel facilities at one end and the public facilities at the other. It's a toss-up as to who has the better end.

At the public beach there are changing facilities and baths, a beach-side bar/restaurant, picnic sites, and a delightful local craft cooperative, all nestled under tall palms. The beach itself is long and relatively narrow with tan sand and a comfortable surf. The beach facilities here are very attractive, maybe the best on the island, with the possible exception of Pigeon Point.

Mt. Irvine Bay Beach.

STONE HAVEN BAY BEACH (or Grafton Beach), Grafton – Lined with tall palms, this narrow beach seems to typify the Caribbean. The surf is light so it's excellent for swimming and sunning. The sand is a pretty tan and, although there are some small stones here and there, it's a good beach for walking. Though this beach is used by major resort hotels, such as the Grafton just across the road, you won't find it too crowded. If you're not comfortable with isolated spots, this is perfect. There are no public changing facilities, but there is a bar and beach food restaurant called the Buccaneer, owned and operated by the Grafton Hotel.

TURTLE BEACH, Great Courland Bay – Seasonal nesting site to leatherback turtles, this white sandy beach with its fringe of palms extends for about a mile. The surf is relatively calm and very inviting. The Turtle Beach Hotel occupies only a small portion of this long stretch of beach, while islanders' homes dot the rest.

■ Caribbean Coast

CULLODEN BAY, Culloden – Accessible by a terrible road that is now being repaired. There are better beaches that are easier to reach.

KING PETER'S BAY BEACH – Unfortunately, we haven't seen this beach. The day we were headed there with our laptop and camera equipment, a local fellow advised us that some hooligans had lately been robbing the rare foreigner at the beach. True or not, that day we decided not to go and we've just never gotten back. Some readers of our first guide, though, said it was wonderful. So give it a try, and write and let us know what you think of it.

CASTARA BAY BEACH, Castara – Lying on the Caribbean shoreline, the village of Castara and the beach are inseparable. There are minimal public facilities, but there are a few restaurants and a couple of cute, simple guest houses right on the beach. You'll see the catch of the day as fishermen arrive from sea.

CELERY BAY BEACH, GORDON BAY BEACH and **LITTLE BAY BEACH** – We didn't get to these remote beaches, but are listing them as options for readers who are looking to be absolutely alone. Accessible only by trail or boat, these are as isolated as it gets in Tobago. Hire a boat in Castara.

ENGLISHMAN'S BAY, just northeast of Castara – Formerly one of the prettiest places we've seen anywhere, this wonderful beach is a bit under siege. Scheduled for nearby development in the next few years, right now the beach is still lovely, though the peaceful feeling is marred by the snack and craft shops that have materialized in the last few years. The sand is coarse tan and the waves are just right; swimming and snorkeling are great. Some days there are thousands of tiny fish circling so closely they look like one big rock or coral bed, but if you heave a stone in the water close by, you'll see the "big rock" dissolve and reform itself. There are lots of gommangalala lizards on the trees. You'll find no changing facilities, but there are lots of places to do it comfortably. If you're not a sun worshipper, go in the late afternoon, say, after 4 PM. You may have the beach all to yourself and see a lovely sunset with very romantic possibilities.

■ Charlotteville

MAN-O-WAR BAY – In Charlotteville, one of the more picturesque villages in Tobago, Man-O-War Bay is a sheltered harbor at this end of the is-

Tobago

Englishman's Bay Beach.

land. The water is calm and good for swimming, and the village is right there.

PIRATE'S BAY BEACH – At the end of the road and over the hill from Man-O-War Bay, this is a delightful private setting used by locals and visitors to Charlottesville. There will almost always be a picture-perfect yacht anchored here as well.

■ Atlantic Coast

BACOLET BEACH, Bacolet – Just past an abandoned old hotel on your right, a stairway leads down from the road to this very quiet beach. In the '60s The Beatles are said to have frolicked here, and with all the choices they must have had at the time, they made a good one. Bacolet was also used to film scenes for the movie *Swiss Family Robinson*. The sand is tannish-gray like many of the island beaches, and the surf is pleasant. In the late afternoon you'll sometimes find Tobagoins playing soccer here. There is parking for about three cars, but there are no other facilities.

HILLSBOROUGH BEACH – Just by Hope village, this mile-long stretch of beach may appear inviting. Be very careful, because there is a strong undercurrent.

KING'S BAY BEACH, Delaford – This out-of-the-way beach is surrounded by thick vegetation and has deep-gray sand and a pebbly bottom. It offers lots of privacy and is seldom frequented by tourists. Located in Delaford, King's Bay is an Atlantic Ocean beach, but the water is calm and very pretty. There are changing rooms and picnic tables. If you're there in the afternoon, you can buy fresh-caught fish right on the beach. As with Englishman's Bay Beach, there is a development underway close to King's Bay Beach. We hope its impact will not be too damaging to this wonderful natural site.

Adventures & Sports

Tobago is a quiet island and, with few exceptions, activities are focused on the sea. Above and below the water you'll have every chance to explore this small wonder. Listed below are some of the sports available to you. In almost all cases, experts or novices will fit in somewhere.

■ On Foot

Hiking

Hiking in Tobago is one of the best ways to enjoy the island. Various locations and trails are listed in the *Sightseeing* section of this chapter. One hike that we have not had time for is from **L'Anse Fourmi to Charlotteville**. There is an old road, so to speak, connecting these two villages so there is a trail to follow. The hike is 12 miles long, and it is advisable to have a local along with you, more to deal with other locals than for any other reason. Remember to bring water and sunscreen.

Squash

Courts and equipment are available at the **Grafton Beach Resort** (☎ 639-0191).Court time will be about $10 an hour.

Tennis

Asphalt courts are available at **Mt. Irvine Bay Hotel & Golf Club** (☎ 639-8871); **Coco Reef Resort** (☎ 639-8571); **Turtle Beach Hotel** (☎ 639-2851); and **Richmond Great House Inn** (☎ 660-4467). Hotel guests normally have free access during the day, but pay small fees for lights in the evening. Public courts in **Scarborough** are lit until 11 PM.

Golf

There a is long-established, high-quality golf course at the **Mt. Irvine Bay Hotel & Golf Club** (see *Where To Stay*). To make arrangements, contact them at ☎ 639-8871. Home to a Pro Am Tournament, this 18-hole, par-72, 6,793-yard course designed by the late John D. Harris is set on the grounds of an old coconut-palm estate. Greens fees for 18 holes are $48, golf cart rentals are $36, club rentals $15, and caddie fees $10. All prices, except caddie fees, are subject to a 15% tax. Mt. Irvine Hotel guests receive a 15%

Tobago

discount. A new course is in the beginning stage and will be associated with the new Hilton Hotel, though details on fees and discounts for hotel guests are not yet available.

Health & Fitness Facilities

Le Grand Courlan hotel (☎ 639-9667) in Black Rock (see *Where To Stay*) has the most complete facility in Tobago, with Nautilus equipment, free weights, aerobics, and a full spa.

A variety of healing arts and therapeutic services were introduced at the **Kariwak Village** hotel (☎ 639-9442) in Crown Point (see *Where To Stay*) within the last few years, including yoga classes and the latest massage techniques.

■ On Wheels

Bicycling

Mountain bikes in good condition can be rented for about $7/day from **First Class Bike Rentals** in Crown Point, at the corner by Columbus Restaurant and Bar. If owner James Percy isn't there, page him at ☎ 662-3377 (ask for ext. 1973) and he'll deliver. Bike rental shops are popping up everywhere and the quality of equipment is quite good.

Motorcycling

Before renting, see Ricarda Solomon at the **Hotel Coconut Inn** in Bon Accord (☎ 639-8493). She leads off-road bike tours to historic sugar mills in the "bush" and is an avid biker herself. She can fill you in on the best rental situations and good off-road tracks.

■ On Water

Diving

The best scuba diving in Tobago is for experienced divers, though there are some good sites for novices. Carrying abundant nutrients from Venezuela's Orinoco River, the waters are not as clear as in other areas of the Caribbean, but physically challenging dives and opportunities to see large underwater species are plentiful.

Tobago is well known for its many drift dives that offer divers the chance to ride underwater currents, sometimes for miles. These dives are generally for the most experienced and skillful, though there are a few where novices can experience this underwater thrill. Safety precautions are especially important in drift diving, as you will rise to the surface far away from where you entered.

Riding with Ricarda Solomon.

Most experienced divers spend their time in Speyside, where the reefs are as yet undamaged and larger fish and rays abound. Depths range from 70 to 90 feet in that area and it has dive sites for the most skilled and adventurous diver. For less experienced divers, Buccoo Reef offers an abundance of smaller fish to see and wonderful coral gardens.

Diving is generally taken seriously on the island and its risks respected. Dive masters will want to see your certification papers and dive logs, but will not lend them much credence until they've actually seen you dive; be prepared for a cautious first experience. There are many dive shops but, before signing on with someone, check their dive master's qualifications and the quality of their equipment and boat. Until very recently, all dive groups used the local fishing boat, the pirogue, which is specially adapted to the waters here. Now you will find more sophisticated dive boats, but always pay special attention to maintenance standards and the quality of safety equipment.

Robin, a good friend of ours from England and an avid diver, especially liked **Tobago Dive Masters** in Speyside (see *Guide Services*, page 218). He's a confirmed vegetarian and animal rights advocate, and he loved the fact that Tobago Dive Masters didn't have the traditional caged parrot or tied-up monkey outside their shop. He found the staff very respectful of the dangers of this sport and of the animals and plants they encountered underwater. They are not affiliated with a hotel and no advance arrangements are necessary. Kevin Frank and Ellis John own the shop and are careful that each group of four divers has a separate Dive Master.

With varying depths and visibility in the many dive sites, you can expect to see mantas, nurse sharks, moray eels, a huge variety of small and large fish, uncountable sponges and corals, and especially the giant brain coral, largest in the Caribbean. You might see lobsters nestled in the coral, and conch are everywhere. Below is a list of some of the more interesting dive sites.

DIVE SITES

CHARLOTTEVILLE

■ **Fishbowl:** As the name implies, you will delight in the quantity and variety of fish. Qualifications: Not rated.

■ **London Bridge:** From a depth of 110 feet, a rock bridge grows upward and breaks the surface. Below, on a good day when currents are not too strong, experts can "thread the needle." Qualifications: Intermediate to advanced.

■ **The Sisters:** Coral-covered rocks reach a depth of 130 feet off Bloody Bay coast and larger marine species are commonly sighted. Qualifications: Intermediate to advanced.

SPEYSIDE & NEARBY SITES

■ **Blackjack Hole:** Up to 100 feet in depth, this is a good site for seeing dolphins, sharks, mantas and, of course, blackjacks. Qualifications: Intermediate to advanced.

■ **Bookends:** From 80 feet down, two rocks break the surface and provide a home for tarpon. Underwater, waves aerate the top level of water and, while you laze below marveling at the clouds of trapped air, tarpon emerge almost magically through the clouds. Qualifications: Intermediate to advanced.

■ **Cathedral:** Aside from a chance to interact with manta rays here, the site offers you an opportunity to work with the always present currents in a relatively safe location – currents run from an easy quarter-knot up to four knots. Adding to its appeal, Cathedral is also known for its dense growth of coral and sponges, including brain coral up to eight feet across. Qualifications: Intermediate.

■ **Flying Manta:** This is a fast drift dive; sometimes with mantas for company. Qualifications: Intermediate to advanced.

■ **Japanese Gardens:** As the name implies, this is a lovely sponge-dotted reef dive at a depth of 20 to 80 feet with active currents. Qualifications: Beginner to intermediate.

■ **John Rock:** Canyons and turtles are the thrills at John Rock. Qualifications: Not rated.

- **Kamikaze Cut:** This is the first choice for thrill-seeking experts. Ride the current at break neck speed between two vertical rock faces, hopefully finding yourself in calm waters on the other side. Qualifications: Advanced.

- **Kelliston Drain:** Giant manta rays and huge brain corals make this an always popular dive. Qualifications: Not rated.

- **Sleeper:** For a site with a little of everything, at Sleeper you'll see rock formations, fish, turtles, and lots of invertebrates.

- **Shark Bank**: Near to Bookends, Shark Bank is famous as the site of some of the world's largest brain coral, some reaching 16 ft. across. Soft corals and sponges grow prolifically on the rocky slopes and large fish, mantas, and turtles are not uncommonly sighted. Qualifications: Not rated.

WEST COAST SITES

- **Arnos Vale**: Its 40-foot depth makes this great for novice and intermediate divers. It is known for its moray and snake eels and the occasional sighting of stingrays. Qualifications: Novice to Intermediate.

- **Castara:** 30-80 feet. Qualifications: Novice to intermediate.

- **Culloden Reef:** 30-60 feet. Qualifications: Novice to intermediate.

- **Mt. Irvine Wall:** Best known for night dives and only 60 feet in depth, the nooks and crannies of this coral-encrusted wall make an interesting daytime dive as well. Qualifications: Beginner to intermediate.

- *Scarlet Ibis* **wreck:** Explore a 350-foot ferry deliberately sunk off Mt. Irvine. Qualifications: Not rated.

SOUTHWEST SITES

- **Buccoo Reef:** This dive site has the features most people expect to find in a Caribbean dive. The depth is only 40 feet, the waters are clear, and the coral is fabulous. Qualifications: Beginner.

- **Diver's Dream:** Here is yet one more opportunity to drop in for a fast drift. Qualifications: Intermediate to advanced.

- **Flying Reef:** Appropriately named, this is a fast drift dive with rays and moray eels at 40 to 80 feet and, on the dull side, there is an old anchor but no sign of a boat. Qualifications: Intermediate to advanced.

- **Runway:** On the Atlantic side of Tobago, this fast drift dive offers experienced divers a chance to travel up to a mile on one tank of air. Qualifications: Intermediate to advanced.

Tobago

- **The Shallows:** In the channel between Trinidad and Tobago, experienced divers, at 50 to 100 feet, will find this a good site for encountering large fish, turtles, dolphins, and sharks. Qualifications: Intermediate to advanced.

- **Two Blokes Reef:** Depth doesn't always define the risk, as this 30- to 60-foot dive is not for beginners. Qualifications: Intermediate to advanced.

- **The Merchantman:** 35 feet. Qualifications: Not rated.

- **The Frenchman:** At only 35 feet, this is a good novice dive. Qualifications: Novice.

- **Cove:** In case divers who like to ride the currents haven't gotten quite enough, this is another drift dive at 30-80 feet. Qualifications: Intermediate to advanced.

- **Divers Thirst:** This is yet one more drift dive and, at depths of only 50-60 feet, it is not for the unskilled. Qualifications: Advanced.

Diving is an inherently dangerous sport. If you have not been diving recently, review safety practices before diving in Tobago. Make a good diving plan for your skills and stick to it. We lost a good Tobagoin friend last year in a tragic dive accident at The Shallows. He was young, athletic, and an experienced diver. Accidents do happen.

Snorkeling

Buccoo Reef is fantastic, and other spots can be found all over the island. **Arnos Vale Hotel beach** is especially good. Although the hotel looks very private, you'll have no problem using the beach. You can rent equipment in lots of places, but serious snorkelers should bring their own. If you forget to bring yours or want to purchase rather than renting, visit **Mt. Irvine Watersports Shop** (see *Guide Services*, page 219). They have good equipment for sale.

Boating

Fishing boat charters, sailing, and touring trips are all offered. For responsible visits to reefs, remember you will have to swim in order to avoid damaging these spectacular and very fragile living colonies. Avoid any tour service that offers the use of reef-walking shoes.

Sportfishing

As of now, fishing trips can be arranged with a relatively small number of captains. See listings in the *Guide Services* chapter. The cost runs just under $600/day. You can also talk to fishermen on the beaches; many of them will be happy to take you out in their pirogues, though this may be more of an adventure than you were planning.

Surfing

This popular sport is most often enjoyed on the waters of **Mt. Irvine Bay**, but much of the Atlantic coast looks inviting for surfers as well. Try **Minister Bay** in Bacolet.

Windsurfing

Rentals are by the hour at about $20, but ask for a discount if you'll be renting for more than one hour. **Mt. Irvine Watersports** (☎ 639-9379, caters mostly to individuals and families. **Windsurf Tobago** (☎/fax 639-3846), at Pigeon Point Beach Club in Crown Point, deals mostly with large groups.

Jet Ski Rentals

Unfortunately, there are now a few for rent, but islanders have organized and are working to prohibit any further permits for jet skis.

Kayaking

Rentals are available at the **Grafton Beach Resort** (☎ 639-0191) for about $40 per day, less for a partial day.

■ On Horseback

Though we've never seen anyone on horseback in our travels around the island, you can rent horses at the **Palm Tree Village Hotel** in Lambeau (☎ 639-4347) and ride along Little Rockly Bay Beach. A new stable called **Looking Out** opened in the fall of '99. For current prices and options, contact them at ☎ 639-4008, e-mail tobago@pobox.com.

Touring

 This section is for those of you who, like us, don't have a good sense of direction. It always takes us a lot of time to figure out where we're going and how to get there again.

■ Suggested Driving Tours

Bacolet

If you are on the southeast side of the island near **Scarborough**, make your way to **Bacolet Street**. Turn right off the highway onto Wilson Road. Follow it until you're facing the water, then turn left. Follow that road until you come to a black-and-white-striped building where you turn right, and go up the hill. Straight ahead you'll see the **Blue Crab** restaurant and Bacolet Street, where you turn right. Bacolet is a short drive, but it is a nice one with some of the older homes on the island and views of the ocean. On this road you'll find the **Tobago House of Assembly**, **Rouselle's** restaurant, the **Cotton House** clothing store, and the **Old Donkey Cart Inn and Restaurant**. All of these restaurants are great for dining, but Rouselle's is open only for dinner. Farther on you'll see an old abandoned hotel on the right, and just past that is the stairway down to **Bacolet Beach**. Just before Bacolet Street ends at Windward Road, you'll see an area on your right with a lot of older summer homes that look like they were built by visiting Germans. The homes are very sturdy and substantial and appear to be constructed for a much less hospitable climate. Turning into this area, you'll find long stretches of unoccupied palm-fringed beach.

AUTHOR TIP

Years ago, Bacolet was THE place to stay in Tobago. Its popularity declined for a while when the airport was built in Crown Point, but it is staging a wonderful comeback. It's lovely and worth considering as a base if you are looking for a quiet, more residential setting.

Crown Point toward Scarborough or the Caribbean Coast Turnoff

From Crown Point, follow the signs for Milford Road, Scarborough. This is a straight road, passing through Bon Accord, where you will see **Pottery World** on your right. Farther along, in Canaan, you'll find **Pennysavers** supermarket, the **Golden Girls Bakery**, and the entrance to **Peacock Mill** on the right. Follow this road straight to Scarborough or turn left onto Shirvan Road to see the Caribbean coast.

Crown Point & Caribbean Coast to Scarborough

On Milford Road in Crown Point, which is the only highway, you'll first see **Tobago Fine Art** on your left, and then **Canoe Bay Park** on your right. Not too much farther will be the entrance to a huge new development that includes a Hilton Hotel, golf course, marina, and upscale private houses and apartments. Just ahead is Hampden Lowlands and **Double D's** restaurant on your left, and the road to Little Rockly Bay on your right. If you turn right here, you will pass Palm Tree Village on your left, across from **Little Rockly Bay Beach**, and a new little hotel called the **Tara Beach House** right on the water. Staying on this road, you will pass through **Lambeau** and eventually reach **Scarborough**.

DID YOU KNOW?

Local lore has it that Lambeau was originally named "Flambeau" after the locals who, in the night, would run to Signal Hill with flaming torches when they spotted a ship on the horizon. Ship's captains would follow the lights into what they thought was a safe harbor, but was in fact a reef. Once ships foundered on the reef, locals would board and take what they chose.

If you stay on Milford Road, take a right at the sign for lower Scarborough where it says Wilson Road, which will bring you into the center of town. You'll have to bear left at one point as the road becomes one way. You'll pass the bus station and library on your right and come to the end. Turn right and park anywhere. This is the center of Scarborough, where you will find the delightful fresh **fruits and vegetables market**. Turn right at the KFC to return to the highway.

To Roxborough, Speyside & Charlotteville

Pass through Scarborough on Milford Road. Just ahead on your left is Calder Hill Rd., where you would turn to go to French Fort. Continuing on Milford Road (which changes names to become Windward Road), you'll travel for about 1½ hours until you reach the northeastern end of the island – Speyside and Charlotteville. It's a very narrow and twisted road, but has some great ocean views and will take you through several small villages, most of which lie on deserted Atlantic Ocean beaches. Watch for the entrance to Hillsborough Dam in Mt. St. George.

CROSS ISLAND ROAD #1 – Taking the turnoff to Hillsborough Dam, you'll be on Mt. St. George Back Rd. On your left below the road, you'll pass **Green Hill waterfall**, which flows year-round. A bit farther on you'll see **Hillsborough Dam** on your right. After visiting the dam with its birds and caiman, you may continue on this road across the island. This unpaved road is locally called a "safari road," and a four-wheel-drive vehicle would be best, but we did it just fine in a regular car. Bird life abounds

Tobago

right by the side of this lonely road. Eventually you'll arrive in **Mason Hall**, one of the largest villages on the island. Turning right, you'll drive through **Moriah** and come to the the main road on the Caribbean side of the island. A little farther you'll come to a turnoff that takes you to **Top Hill**, an overlook giving you views up and down this wonderful coast. Back on the road, just past **Castara**, is a little-known entrance to part of the **Main Ridge Forest Reserve**. As you travel along this lovely and very isolated unpaved track, parrots and other birds will fly overhead. Park by the side of the road and walk, as the quiet will allow you to see and hear many more of the birds and small animals here.

CONTINUING TOWARD SPEYSIDE – Staying on Windward Road, you'll come to the **First Historical Café & Bar**, where you just have to stop. Farther on is the village of Delaford, with the **Restrite Sea Gardens Guest House** and the very cute **King's Bay Café** on the hill just before **King's Bay Beach**. Another new development is in the works here, this one with upscale private homes. Just past the beach is **Liz's Café**. Farther along, you'll find the entrance to **Rainbow Waterfall**, **Argyle Waterfall**, the **Richmond Great House**, and Roxborough, a great town for bird watching in the morning or early evening. **Roxborough** is the site of an old cocoa estate, so you may see whole flocks of bright green **parrots** as we did. They love to eat cocoa.

Atlantic coastline, Tobago.

CROSS ISLAND ROAD #2 – In Roxborough, you have the choice of continuing on toward Speyside and Charlotteville or taking the road across the island toward **Bloody Bay** and **Parlatuvier**. If you take the cross island road, about midway you'll find the **Main Ridge Forest Reserve**. Although this was a new road just a few years ago, it is not in great condition now, but there is little or no traffic and it's a lovely, peaceful ride. At the end, turn left to pick up the main road on the other side of the island to head toward Crown Point.

CONTINUING TOWARD SPEYSIDE – If you continue toward Speyside, you'll come to a wonderful overlook just before descending toward town. Offshore you'll see two islands; the smaller one is privately owned **Goat Island** and the larger is **Little Tobago Island**. Follow the road down, passing the **Top Ranking Guest House** off to the left. Speyside is growing by leaps and bounds, so you'll now find new restaurants, including the **Seafood and Pizza House** and the **Bird-watcher's Restaurant and Bar**. **Redmans' Restaurant** is open for local dishes along with the original and well-known **Jemma's Restaurant**, where you will dine in a tree house set over the water. Farther on is the **Speyside Hotel**, **Manta Lodge**, and **Blue Waters Inn**. Once past those hotels, you'll be on your way to Charlotteville. Follow the only road and soon you'll see the beautiful bay of **Charlotteville** down below. The village is large by island standards and was always popular with foreigners who wanted to keep Tobago a secret. There are two long-established places to stay: the **Cholson Chalets** right in town, and the **Man-O-War Bay Cottages** just out of town. Charlotteville has wonderful fishing so, if you stay here, you will eat fresh fish as never before. If you want to stop for lunch, try **Gail's Café**.

The Caribbean Side of Tobago

Coming from Scarborough or Crown Point on Milford Road, turn onto Shirvan Road. Just ahead you'll see the entrance to the popular evening spot, **Lush,** on your right. Not too much farther there's a right-hand turn that will take you to **Moshead's** fancy grocery store. After passing the sign for Mt. Pleasant on the right, take a left at the sign for Buccoo and follow it down to **Buccoo Beach**. Restaurants such as **La Tartaruga** are right by the beach and there are lots of smaller places like the **Teaside Pizzeria**, **Hendrix Sandwich Bar**, and the **Match Box**. You can rent bikes by the beach, or visit on Sunday evenings for **Sunday School**.

Returning to Shirvan Road, turn left. You'll pass **Mt. Irvine Bay Hotel and Golf Course** on the right, **Mt. Irvine Watersports** and **Mt. Irvine Bay Beach** on the left. Take a left at the sign for **Stone Haven Bay** to get to **Stone Haven/Grafton Beach** and the Buccaneers Bar. Going back the way you came and turning left on the main road, you'll pass the **Grafton Estate Bird Sanctuary** on your right, **Le Grand Courlan** and **Grafton** hotels on your left. Take a left at the sign for Black Rock, then an immediate right and follow the road to **Turtle Beach**. Return to the main road and turn left. Continuing on, you'll pass the **Black Rock Café** and the delightful **Under the Mango Tree** restaurant, followed by the **Turtle Beach Hotel**. Just past the Turtle Beach Hotel, turn left over Courland Bridge and follow the road into Plymouth, where you'll find the **mystery tombstone**, **Ft. James**, and the **Gingerbread Guest House**. Plymouth is a quiet residential town where many islanders live. Turn around and head back the way you came.

Turn onto Arnos Vale Road, where you'll pass the **Adventure Farm and Nature Reserve**, a **craft shop**, and then the **Arnos Vale Hotel**, which is a great spot for snorkeling. Arnos Vale is a lovely, very hilly part of the island. Past the hotel is a dirt road leading up a hill. Up ahead on the left you'll see a small wooden house; the views from just in front of it are fantastic. A small paved road to the right of the house leads up to private rental homes, **MotMot Ridge** and the **Observatory**.

Drive back down by the Arnos Vale Hotel and turn left. Just ahead on the right is the driveway that takes you up to **Top O' Tobago**, a new style accommodation combining a private rental house and three cabanas. A short way farther will bring you to the entrance of the **Arnos Vale Waterwheel Restaurant and Nature Preserve**. It is well worth stopping by. You can follow this road through hills and villages to arrive at **Englishman's Bay Beach**. Continuing on toward **Castara**, you'll find a path to the local waterfall, the **Naturalist Beach Resort** guest house, and boats which will take you to **Celery Bay, Gordon,** and **Little Bay beaches**, all relatively inaccessible by land. Past Castara is **Parlatuvier**, a delightful little Caribbean village, where you'll find the **Parlatuvier Tourist Hotel** and the popular **Riverside Restaurant**.

AUTHOR TIP

Tobago's roads are not in great condition and signs are sometimes absent or misleading. Not to worry. There just aren't that many wrong turns you can make, and everyone is friendly and helpful if you get lost.

Nightlife

 ARNOS VALE WATERWHEEL RESTAURANT, Franklyn Rd., Arnos Vale Estate; ☎ 660-0814/0815. Fridays are special at this very romantic restaurant set in the gardens of the Arnos Vale Estate, site of an 18th-century sugar factory. Set off in the lush tropical foliage of this nature reserve, the small stage lights up with entertainment. Though relatively expensive, an evening here is well worth it. Also see their listings on pages 132, 152, and 160.

COPRA TRAY RESTAURANT AND BAR, Store Bay Local Road, Bon Accord; ☎ 639-8493. On the grounds of the Coconut Inn, this is a large, comfortable bar/restaurant recently redecorated with biker posters. With pool tables, lots of entertainment, and its very informal atmosphere, Copra Tray is especially attractive to the younger crowd. Open from 6:30 PM until the wee hours.

CRYSTAL PALACE, Milford Rd., Scarborough; ☎ 639-4829. This is a small casino, reminiscent of the speakeasies of the prohibition era. With blackjack, stud poker, baccarat, and roulette, the Crystal Palace is open from 6 PM till closing Tuesday through Sunday evenings. Men must wear long pants. Table bets are a minimum of $4 up to a limit of $300. For avid blackjack players, they have a favorable rule – you can double down at any time. Note: They're planning a face-lift, and adding a restaurant and sports betting.

GOLDEN STAR, Crown Point; ☎ 639-0873. Although the restaurant is open seven days a week from 7 AM, Golden Star is best known for music and dancing until the wee hours. They usually offer special entertainment on Wednesday nights, but call to confirm. It's next to the Surfside Inn in Crown Point where the road divides to go to Pigeon Point. This is a very popular place for the late night crowd.

LES COTEAUX CULTURAL THEATER. Choreographer Verleen Bobb-Lewis has been working with this troupe of dancers and musicians since February 1988. You can see them perform at the Crown Point Hotel on Sunday, Turtle Beach Hotel on Wednesday, Mt. Irvine Hotel on Thursday, Arnos Vale Waterwheel on Friday, and The Grafton Hotel on Saturday. Call the hotels ahead to verify any changes in the schedule. The troupe offers spectacular, exciting entertainment. If you need to get in touch with them, write to Verleen at Cradley Trace, Government House Rd., Scarborough, Tobago.

OLD DONKEY CART INN, 73 Bacolet St., Bacolet; ☎ 639-3551. This romantic inn has entertainment and dancing under the stars on Friday and Saturday evenings. It's also listed in the sections on *Where To Stay* and *Where To Eat*.

THE PEACOCK MILL, Friendship Estate, Canaan; ☎ 639-0503. Formerly a restaurant, this out-of-the-way place has a group of resident, free-roaming peacocks that live under the giant tree in the front yard. Open in the evenings, it's a pleasant place to play pool with friends or catch up on TV sports and have a drink or two. Watch for special events with entertainment. The long dirt road leading to The Peacock Mill is off the main highway close to the Shirvan Rd. turnoff.

PLEASURE PIRATES. This is a performance group recommended by Verleen Bobb-Lewis, choreographer of the Les Coteaux Cultural Theater. We didn't get a chance to see them, but we were so impressed by Verleen's work we'll take her word for it. Watch for advertisements about their performances.

LUSH, Shirvan Rd., Canaan; ☎ 639-9087. This is a "liming" and "dancing till dawn" sort of place. It's open Tuesday through Saturday from 6 PM until everyone runs out of steam. It's probably not a great place for a woman to go alone.

Tobago

The Sunday evening block party at Buccoo is an institution on the island. Early in the evening, from 7 to 9 PM, there is steel pan music and a fairly calm atmosphere. Later, there is recorded music. Serious drinking, dancing, and socializing starts at about 10 PM and continues until dawn. Hundreds attend, but only a few are tourists. Beers are about $1, and you can bring rum and order Cokes to make your own drinks. It's best to go in groups, and it is definitely not a place for women to go alone. Parking can be a problem, so you might consider using a taxi. It will cost you about $15 to have the taxi drop you there and return for you when you are ready to leave.

Shopping

■ Clothing, Footwear & Crafts

Tobago's handcrafts are improving in design and workmanship. Handmade jewelry, leather sandals, clothes, and decorative pieces are now widely available in small shops and roadside stands all over the island. Along the entrance to Pigeon Point Beach you'll find small craft shops, and across from the airport several ladies sell very good homemade sesame seed and nut candies. Airport and hotel stores are good sources for sun lotions, over-the-counter cure-alls, magazines, etc. Opportunities for parting with a few dollars are improving as more visitors arrive, so keep your eyes open.

Stacy Ferguson, craftsperson at Store Bay.

■ **Store Bay Beach** has had a face-lift and there are now more than a dozen small attractive shops offering island crafts, from **sandals** to **beach wraps**. You can even have your hair braided and beaded.

■ **Hugh Richards**, in Store Bay Shop #12, makes wonderful **leather sandals**. He made some to order for us two years ago and we went back to buy in quantity. Prices are very reasonable, designs are good, the quality is high and they are very comfortable. In Tobago, they call a sandal that has no leather around the heel a "slipper." You can see Hugh almost every day at his shop, where you can place your sandal order on the way to Store Bay Beach. Your new sandals will be ready in just a couple of days. Slippers are under $20 and more substantial sandals cost $20 and up.

∎ **Lorris Duncan**, who lives on Arnos Vale Rd., has opened a small roadside shop where he sells his **wood and bamboo carvings**. Using cedar, mahogany, and teak, Lorris carves birds and animals or an image of your choice. Bamboo work sells for between $10 and $25, wood carvings up to about $60. Lorris does his carving in the heat of the day, using the cooler morning and evening to tend his large garden and care for his sheep, goats, and pigs.

Hugh Richards, sandal maker.

∎ **Bambú** at the Crown Point Hotel carries good quality crafts and lovely hammocks. They have a second store in Trinidad at the Kapok Hotel, St. Clair, Port of Spain.

∎ **The Cotton House** on Old Windward Rd. in Bacolet sells comfortable, colorful, Caribbean-style **clothing** in bright batik colors. The clothes don't have the great feel of cotton I like, though, and prices seem on the high side.

∎ **Mt. Irvine Watersports,** on Mt. Irvine Beach, surprisingly has the best selection of **silver jewelry** in Tobago, along with all the watersports accessories and equipment you might need.

∎ **Things Natural**, at Rovanel's Resort on Store Bay Local Rd. in Crown Point carries nicer **crafts** and **clothing** than we've seen in many other places. It's worth a visit.

∎ **Zoom Caribbean** at Pigeon Point Beach Resort, Crown Point, is the place for wonderful "made in the USA" **cotton knit clothing** for both women and children. The fabric and designs are terrific, but not inexpensive.

∎ Art

∎ **The Art Gallery**, Allfields Crown Trace, Lowlands; ☎ 639-8535, fax 639-0457. Open from 10 AM to 5 PM. Owned by artist couple Martin and Rachael Superville, who exhibit their work and the work of other local artists, this out-of-the-way unpretentious gallery is worth a stop. The prices seemed high to us,

relative to emerging American artists, but you can probably negotiate. The overall quality of work is good, and here and there you'll
find a real gem.

■ **Jason Ned** is a local artist whose work we saw exhibited at
The Art Gallery. If they have none of his work on display when
you're there, you can always call him at home in Lans Fermi,
☎ 660-7771. He does some intriguing paintings of people.

■ **Tobago Fine Art by Hira** is a tiny shop on the highway between Crown Point and Scarborough, exhibiting the works of its
owner, Hira, a retired Trini. The work is of local subjects and,
though it is not sophisticated, it can be charming and is available
for the very reasonable prices of between $12 and $25.

Carnival

From all we'd heard of carnivals in New Orleans and Brazil, neither Stassi nor I were anxious to attend Carnival in Trinidad. Our preconceptions of the types of people drawn to these events and the bacchanalian atmosphere held no appeal; not because we don't love a good time, but we just don't like being in the middle of that many raucous people. Still, we felt obliged to cover this very singular event to give you insight into what to expect.

In anticipation of being there, we read as many books about Carnival in Trinidad as we could find and, in doing so, our attitudes gradually changed. I became fascinated with the idea of Carnival. Somehow, it seemed an almost more than magical event and, in the end, we were both excited to be going to see for ourselves what Carnival is all about.

The historical antecedents of the modern Carnival pageantries and customs, the spectacular costumes, the Kings and Queens competitions, Carnival songs and music, all have a structure and meaning year to year. This is not just a party. All the hours of preparation and the participation of thousands of people in an event so brief has to be worth seeing at least once. We bought lots of film and off we went.

Writing about Carnival in Trinidad is not easy. Yes, there are crowds and there is raucous behavior, but this is a special Carnival where everyone can find a place where they are comfortable. Trying to make sense of it all and to convey to you the excitement and the warmth that make this Carnival unique, leads us to say what everyone told us, "You have to be there to believe it." This is a Carnival for families, for opening your heart, and for jumping to the music with all the joy you can muster.

For the millennium, Trinidad's Minister of Culture and the Carnival Organizers are planning a most spectacular event, inviting bands from around the world. Carnival in Trinidad has been a best-kept secret for years, but the millennium celebration might just change that forever.

■ History

Eighteenth-century Trinidad was owned by the Spanish. It was only sparsely settled until the year 1783, when Spain made an effort to increase the population by providing very attractive tax and land incentives to Catholic immigrants. The French, in particular, responded very favorably and Trinidad finally had the population it needed to grow and prosper. Prior to the arrival of the French, there is no record of Carnival in Trinidad, so it is probably safe to assume this tradition arrived with them. For many years it remained a celebration primarily by the white, landed upper class. Every year just before Ash Wednesday, they held masked balls, wore elaborate costumes, paraded through the streets, and held open houses.

Carnival, even in these early years, was not just a two- or three-day-long party; it had many levels of meaning and tradition. One of these traditions is the cast of costumed characters that is played every year in masquerade. Over time, some of the characters have evolved and some have fallen by the wayside, while others have been added. Some of the newer characters made their way into Carnival in the 19th century with the participation of freed slaves in the revelries after Emancipation. They brought the "moko jumbie," a West African cult figure, more familiarly known as a stilt-walker. Moko jumbies are an important part of Carnival even today; important enough that there is a school in Trinidad entirely devoted to imparting the skill needed to walk on stilts.

Moko jumbies, Carnival '99.

"John Canoe" is a military renegade who engages in mock duels with wooden swords. "Jab-molassi," or molasses devil, is yet another character whose face and body, once blackened with soot and molasses, now is more typically covered in black paint. "Pierrot," another marauder, was known to attack first with words and then with sticks. Masked and elaborately costumed, Pierrot was popular until the later years of the 19th century, when, in an effort to exert more control over Carnival, in 1892 the government required persons playing Pierrot to be licensed. Licensing, unfortunately, eliminated one of the essential characteristics of Carnival – the anonymity of the mask. With licensing, the popularity of playing Pierrot declined.

Also central to Carnival are staged interactions. One of the most traditional is Canboulay. This is a performance where one character acts as a chained slave who is drawn through the streets by his masters while occasionally being struck by the sticks they carry. These performances were torchlit and accompanied by music and songs. Before Emancipation, it was not unusual for whites to imitate the behaviors of blacks, dressing up and performing skits of their perception of the activities of their slaves.

Emancipation in 1834 brought freed slaves into the Carnival celebration and increased participation of the lower classes who, together, added a flavor of rowdiness to the event with street dancing and stick-fighting. Oddly enough, in Trinidad, it was traditional for slaves to carry large sticks. Perhaps they were used in warding off snakes in the fields or used in some way in working or burning the cane. Whatever their original use, they became quite popular as the weapon used in stick-fights. These staged fights were well-attended sporting events long before slaves were freed.

The *calinda*, a dance form likely of African origin, also incorporated the use of sticks. This dance was not restricted to slaves, but was also mastered by the upper classes who prided themselves on its skillful execution. With these two sources of expertise, stick-fighting continued and expanded after Emancipation, with organized groups fighting each other while singers egged everyone on with outrageous lyrics and barbed comments directed at participants. The singers who accompanied the stick-fighters are considered by some to be one of the many historical antecedents to modern calypso. Unfortunately, clashes between revelers and the police eventually brought prohibitions against group stick-fighting.

In the 19th century, after Emancipation, Christmas and the Lenten season were perceived as more risky for the ruling class as a time for revolt, so martial law was routinely instituted in British colonies during this time of year. Rather than dampening Carnival spirits, though, the increased presence of the military led to their participation in Carnival as well. An 1820s newspaper account described the parade of troops as a major social occasion with tents erected for spectators of the mock battles. Even back then, it seems, no one was immune to the magnetism of Carnival.

August 1, 1834 was Emancipation Day, and it was celebrated in style on that day for some years. There is evidence that its celebration later became a part of the existing traditions of Carnival. After Emancipation, the entire character of Carnival was markedly changed from an elitist, social entertainment to a populist event and costumes and performances took on more of the character of satire. Originally celebrated the Sunday, Monday, and Tuesday before Ash Wednesday, after Emancipation Carnival celebrations were restricted to Monday and Tuesday. With the transition from an elitist to a populist event, the celebration took on some of the character of a freedom festival and its importance grew. Governmental and moralist efforts to restrict Carnival during the 19th and early 20th centuries were not infrequent, but they were entirely unsuccessful.

With all of the musical groups, military bands, and costume bands becoming a part of Carnival, large numbers of people came together each year to provide these entertainments. With the need for preparation, the tradition of "tents" as rehearsal sites developed. Rehearsal eventually took on the character of performance and small admission fees were charged the public. The two days of actual Carnival evolved into a season of performances and competitions were instituted for costume designs and musical performances.

Because post-Emancipation Carnival was so changed, the landed upper classes, its originators, no longer participated in the street masquerades. They turned instead to celebrating with elaborate costumed balls and pageantries, which evolved into today's Carnival King and Queen shows, two of the spectacular events of today's *Dimanche Gras*, Sunday evening's opening of Carnival on the Savannah.

Though the middle and upper classes began to return to the streets during Carnival at the end of the 19th century, it would not be until the mid-20th century that they did so with heart and soul again. Today, Carnival is a wonderful mix of all classes, races and cultures. Words in the Trinidad and Tobago National Anthem say it best, "Every creed and race find an equal place."

■ Carnival Today

While the French brought Carnival and the pre-Lenten party spirit to Trinidad, the British brought their strong tradition of Christmas festivities. These two cultural influences have merged into a season of celebrations. The season begins before Christmas with traditional performances of Parang music and continues through New Year's. With New Year's resolutions hardly yet broken, pre-Carnival events take the stage, continuing until Ash Wednesday.

Though not a public holiday, Carnival officially takes place only on the Monday and Tuesday preceding Ash Wednesday. Those two days are the grand finale to a season of competitions and performances where the pace has been ever quickening as pan yards and mas camps prepare and perform. In the weeks before the final event you can feel it in the air, and certainly it's what everyone's talking about – Carnival. This is not just a huge street fair or parade; it is a procession of traditional figures, it is street theater, it is music and dancing, and it is spectacular costumes.

Carnival is more than an event; it is a state of mind. Thousands of Trinis and Tobagoins work together in preparation and thousands more are involved in its events. In all, about 10% of the country's population participates, a staggering 125,000 people. Old and young, thin and chubby, plain and beautiful, rich and poor – all are involved side by side, whether in the streets or on the Savannah stage. And, whether local or foreign, you are quite welcome to jump in.

The most heartening quality of Carnival is that it is real; it is not something staged for visitors. No matter how Carnival will be marketed for tourism, it will remain a part of the soul of every Trini. Children are included in the celebration and even have their own fabulous masquerade competition; when they are grown, Carnival will be second nature to them. Because Trinidad's Carnival involves so many of its own people, it has remained a celebration for family and friends. While raucous and outrageous sometimes, it is also an event where a lot of very nice people have a very good time.

■ Fêtes

Public parties, called fêtes, are also part of Carnival and, for a small entrance fee, you too can join in. The noise will be astonishing – often with live music. Sometimes these parties are cleverly named, such as "Soca Flowing Like Water," a fete located at the water company. Some fêtes provide food and an open bar, as well as dance music, for a set fee. These are usually smaller and tamer, and often are vehicles for fund-raising. Tickets can be hard to find, so ask at your hotel; someone there may know who's selling them and where.

■ Masquerade

Masquerade, the impulses of the inner self hidden behind the mask, is the very heart of Carnival. In Trinidad, it has been taken to the nth degree and then a little further. In most places in the States we celebrate Halloween, a bit of the mask, but it is only for an evening and primarily for children. In Trinidad, the celebration is days long and it is for everyone, young and old.

Each year, costume designers, called band leaders, develop new themes for their bands. Themes can be almost anything – historical, social, artistic, or fanciful – and, based on the theme, costumes are designed and music is selected. The group is called a **mas band** and the place where costumes are produced or available is called a **mas camp**. Depending on the size of the mas band, members may be divided into sections, each portraying some part of the overall theme, and each distinctively costumed.

Each year mas camps have their costume designs ready by mid-Autumn for the public to see and choose from. Prices for the most elaborate costumes and band fees can be over $100, but many are more reasonable. Choosing your band each year is part of the excitement, whether the costumes, the theme, or the music wins your heart. **"Playing in a band"** means "chipping" through the streets and dancing in costume with the band during Carnival. **Chipping** is a rhythmic strut; it is arrogant, provocative, and somehow perfect for Carnival processions.

Internationally renowned Peter Minshall has a very popular mas camp and his costumes are always surprising. His reputation for creativity earned him a place in the Barcelona and Atlanta Olympics, designing both opening ceremonies. More expensive to join than most, and maybe more commercial, Minshall, along with Poison, Wayne Berkeley, Barbarossa, Hart's Carnival, and Legends, each year produce truly spectacular and very popular mas bands.

Carnival

Less expensive, but no less wonderful, are the bands that forego elaborate costumes in favor of paint. Water-soluble colored dust is sold in pharmacies and hardware stores. Once mixed, sometimes with oil to make it shiny, you pick your colors and apply the paint – head to toe. Bryan "Tico" Skinner is a band leader long known for this type of mas, called Devil Bands, and he's terrific. We loved his "Some Love Ends in Hell" mas band for 1999. It was especially appropriate for Valentine's Day, which may have been all but forgotten as Carnival fell on February 14th.

One peculiarity we noticed, in both individuals and bands, is the popularity of American Indian costumes, which are for some reason a tradition in Trinidad. Though we asked about it, no one gave us any good answers. If you know anything or find any information, we'd love to hear from you.

While in Trinidad, we talked about Carnival with Lambert Julien and Cecil Alfred, a Trini living in Canada, but still actively involved in Carnival. The uncle of a friend of ours in Tobago, Lambert is a retired professional who plays in a mud mas band for J'Ouvert and chips with Tico Skinner's band in Monday and Tuesday's masquerade. Lambert is a quiet and gentle man, who, when asked "Why are you so involved in Carnival?" responded, "Because it is fun." He then went on to describe masquerade in the most placid of voices, "You don't have to have a big headpiece with the feathers and so on. You may have a headpiece, but just two horns if you wish. And you have the normal tail and you have short pants or tights and the handmade cape. The band has a name, like 'Love Ends in Hell,' and you have the devils because it's only in hell that you have the devil." This is the soul of Carnival, a suspension of day-to-day realities, a time for engaging your imagination. As someone told us, "Carnival is a full contact sport."

JOIN A MASQUERADE BAND

Here is a partial list of **Mas Camps** where you may purchase a costume and "jump in."

■ **Barbarossa Associates**, 26 Taylor St., Woodbrook, Port of Spain. Web site www.barbarossaintl.com.

■ **Funtasia**, 26 Maraval Rd., Newtown, Port of Spain, Web site www.funtasiainc.com.

■ **Harts Ltd.**, 5 Alcazar St., Woodbrook, Port of Spain, Web site www.hartscarnival.com.

■ **Ivan Kallicharan**, 17 Harris St., San Fernando.

■ **Legends**, 88 Roberts St., Woodbrook, Port of Spain, Web site www.legendscarnival.com.

■ **Masquerade**, online at www.masquerade.co.tt.

■ **Peter Minshall**, Building C, Western Main Rd., Chaguaramas.

- **Poison**, 1 Harroden Pl., Petit Valley, Web site www.poison.co.tt.
- **B. Skinner & Assn.**, Sportsflex, Barataria, Presenter is Brian "Tico" Skinner (known for devil bands).
- **Wayne Berkeley**, 49-51 Cipriani Blvd., Port of Spain.

■ The Main Events

Most of the events you will attend are held at the Savannah, where a 40-foot wide, city-block-long stage sits between two open-air, stadium-style seating areas. One is the Grand Stand, for the more posh and reserved audience; the other is the North Stand, where dancing in the aisles is not uncommon. Food and beverages are served in a variety of small kiosks.

Saturday Evening, Steel Band Panorama

This is the night for the best steel bands to shine and for one to win and, even without a program, you will be caught up in the energy. When we were there, the first band was wheeled on stage almost right on time. Dozens of people pushed lovingly decorated but sometimes rickety metal carts carrying the hundreds of pans onto the stage. The pushers left, and the musicians quickly took their places. Banners waved, the lights came up, and the music began. The energy and excitement were fantastic. The music was stunning. The lights went off and the musicians clambered over the carts to push them off the stage while the next band was wheeled on by dozens of supporters from the Savannah Park outside. The pushers left, sometimes on request from the loudspeakers, the lights shined, and the next band began to play. We had our favorites, but could not imagine having to choose one best band. It was a fabulous evening, and didn't end until 3 AM.

Devil, Carnival '99.

One thing we found incredible was that there was no written music anywhere to be seen. Yet each band had up to 100 musicians playing elaborate music on a variety of instruments, with notes and rhythms and crescendos all perfectly played. We found out later that, in most bands, up to 90% of the musicians do not read music. They play by ear and can learn a selection of the band's songs in only two weeks, with no formal training. The music is in their heads and hearts and hands.

Sunday Evening, Dimanche Gras

This is the evening when Carnival hosts the Calypso Monarch finals and crowns the King and Queen of Carnival. If you go, rest up well on Sunday, because this seven- to eight-hour show leads straight into *J'Ouvert*, the official opening of Carnival, at 4 AM Monday morning.

Held at the Savannah, the show opened with a mélange of characters and skits on stage celebrating the history of Carnival and the changes over time – stick-fighting, stilt-walking, and canboulay. Next came the winners of the **Children's Mas Camp**. If you had not seen the Junior Mas Parade

on Saturday, you might think all of the children's bands were on stage. Hundreds of children of all ages pranced on stage in fabulous costumes. Children are fully involved in Carnival competitions, with Kings and Queens, Band of the Year, and Junior Calypso finals. There is even a steel band competition just for them.

Next came the finals of the **Queen of Carnival** competition. The first woman rushed on stage in a costume we could barely believe. It extended about 15 feet in all directions and was absolutely incredible. She danced around and around, carrying all of the costume with her, making it shimmer and shake. One after another, the finalists came on stage in costumes whose size is limited only by the size of the stage. Incredibly, in these unwieldy costumes, they danced. Queens were followed by Kings

Queen Sheba, from the band "Jewels of the Nile," Carnival '99.

who, not to be outdone by the Queens, put on an equally unbelievable show. They appear again on Tuesday during the day, but performing at night allows them to show off the pyrotechnics of their astounding costumes.

The **Calypso Monarch** competition was disappointing, because the sound system, combined with the differing accents, made the words almost unintelligible. Calypsonians are true entertainers, though, and many put on very theatrical shows. Competitors for the title all have three or four backup singers and some have actors carrying out the theme of their song. One sang of "receiving a letter," as an Airborne Express truck drove right onto stage with, what else? A letter. They seem unendingly able to pull off this sort of kitsch and the crowd loves it.

If you are interested in hearing the words of the calypsos, which are great, go to a smaller venue, because at the Savannah you will have trouble understanding the words. This problem may be solved in the future, since we saw articles in the local papers after Carnival criticizing the sound system. Maybe next year they'll have a new one.

Sugar Aloes, winner of 1998's Monarch Title, came on stage in '99 with a particularly fantastic presentation. There were about 50 children in costume, winners of the Band of the Year mas camp, who let fly their balloons at the end of his performance. Wearing a white satin double-breasted suit, he obviously had showmanship on his side.

"Singing Sandra," Sandra des Vignes, won 1999's Calypso Monarch title with her songs of ghetto life and race relations. Players dramatized the hatreds of racism and the waste of the human spirit it represents. Her title was well deserved, especially since the only other woman to win Calypso Monarch did so in 1978.

Monday Morning, J'Ouvert

Monday's Carnival events begin with *J'Ouvert* (pronounced JOO-vay, and also spelled *Jouvay*). This is the time for "**mud mas**," a masquerade of col-

ored mud, and for the more outrageous portrayals in a competition now being formalized. *J'Ouvert* may be evolving into a "people's carnival," as mas band memberships have grown in cost and some of the traditions of mas have faded in favor of more lavish costuming. *J'Ouvert* is a time for thoughtful music and outrageous commentary.

At 4 AM loud speakers boom out the opening of Carnival. Bands of people, covered in colored mud and grease, take to the streets, along with individual protesters and commentators on the state of the world. Steel bands join the fray and music is made with the clanging and banging of anything that will make noise – brake drums are a favorite. This is the place for history, for traditions like role reversals and political satires (Bill Clinton and Monica were

Making music the old way.

favorite characters in '99; Viagra, too, was a hot theme). As dawn becomes day, revelers depart the streets for a thorough cleanup and a few hours rest before the parade of mas bands begins at 11 AM.

Carnival

J'Ouvert is the one really rough-and-tumble part of Carnival, and it is certainly a time that you need to be careful. Jewelry should be left at your hotel, and you should carry just a small amount of money. Go with a group, or stay in the more controlled areas if you want to avoid problems. And don't forget to wear clothes you won't miss, as you can't escape a bit of mud or paint.

Monday Mas

At 11 AM, traditional costumed figures again took to the streets, dancing and chipping their way along, followed by the military bands, and finally by heavily costumed mas bands. As the day drew to a close, people took to the streets in party mode, with and without costumes.

We began Monday at Victoria Square, a shaded park where there is an enclosure with stadium-style seating right on the street facing all the action. Monday's somewhat motley procession was led by the King of Carnival, whose elaborate costume was now in tatters. Everyone was having a good time, and many people paraded by in whatever costume they dreamed up for themselves.

The grandstand at Victoria Park is open to the public for a small entrance fee, but is fenced to separated spectators from the crowds. It's a great place to take a break from the strong sun. At midday it was very hot and a lot of people dancing in costume looked to be wearying, but they were incredibly hardy souls. They were chipping and we thought they were going to keep on chipping until they fell down dead. It was remarkable.

Carnival Monday was one of my favorite days. I never saw such a wonderful hit-or-miss collection of costumes and good feelings in my life. It was absolutely terrific. So haphazard; the groups were half together, going approximately in the same direction, and everyone was having a good time, me especially.

Good food might be hard to come by. You might have your hotel pack something for you. Soft drinks are available everywhere, as are bottles of rum.

Carnival Tuesday
Parade of the Bands, Savannah Grandstand

Stassi took the tape recorder for the first hour or so while I ran with the camera. I got back and found him dazed, but very happy, and I didn't understand until I heard the tape that he made. Here's a partial transcript.

"There's a 40-foot stage completely full of young men and women all dressed in scanty costumes with bangles and beads. All of a sudden the whole stage changes color with the addition of each new band, from teal to black, from gauze to sparkles. They rush out, break from the barrier and they're on the stage. The songs collide and they are all dancing and jumping and strutting their stuff.... The frenetic activity, the dancing, and flag-waving is unbelievable."

People in the bands were all ages, all shapes, and all colors. Even early in the morning we saw people just a little tuckered out. They had been partying now for days, but today's celebration was just beginning and the incredibly loud music kept everyone going. The Grand Stand may seem a restrained place to see the parade of bands because you are looking at a stage rather than being in the street, but truly this is the place to be on Tuesday. The bands were about to be judged, so they were all putting on the best show they could – dancing with abandon. After about five bands passed, men swept the stage of all the baubles and bangles that flew off before the next band burst on stage.

The winner of the title King of Carnival, with the band "Savage Garden," came on stage at around 9:45 AM. His costume, "Let There Be Light," had been totally renewed. I snuck down to the stage entrance to watch him don the elaborate costume, for which he needed the help of several assistants; it was really something to see. It takes very special people to compete for King and Queen.

Just before Peter Minshall's band, "The Lost Tribe," arrived the stage was cleaned again. There were thousands of people in this mas band and they are all beautifully costumed. A tractor-trailer-sized truck filled with musicians

"The Lost Tribe," Peter Minshall's Band, Carnival '99.

Carnival

drove alongside the stage, providing the music to spur the band's enthusiasm. I was tantalized by the costuming; it was elegant and unique. There were no sparkles, but veils and turbans and yards and yards of gauze.

Ornate costumes don't always make a band stand out. "Some Love Ends in Hell" arrived on stage, with blood-red bodies and horns and a lot of real dirt; people were painted red and blue or a mixture of the two and were wearing all sorts of parts and pieces of costumes. They had their horns or a tail and off they went. A man passed by with a bucket of paint ready to help anybody join in. Someone went by in a devil costume painted all black, followed by another. It was absolutely chaotic and wonderful. I thought this was much more traditional costuming and I loved it.

Bryan "Tico" Skinner's band, "Some Love Ends In Hell," Carnival '99.

"Dynasty" was another fabulous band. Different from Minshall's, whose costume variations were very subtle, band leaders Ian McKenzie and Mike Antoine designed costumes depicting variations on the theme "Dynasty of the People." The costumes were not integrated as well as Minshall's, but they were stunning, and the dancing was some of the best we saw. Members of this band obviously worked out in anticipation of this day.

Dynasty's elaborate and wonderful white-costumed section, waving white flags bordered with gold, danced with incredible enthusiasm, and the liveliness of the flag-waving made a show that was outrageous. "Caribbean Pride," the next band section, was dressed in green and black and also danced with phenomenal energy. The entire Dynasty band had more than 2,000 people and each of them, personally, seemed committed to winning, if their dancing was any evidence. The "Patriots" section was red, white, and black, followed by a section called "Sovereign," conveying the power of leadership, dressed in gold and black with feather headdresses. These people hit the stage running. They hit the stage and they were "on."

After a while the bands became mesmerizing, too exciting and too beautiful and, after just a few hours, I became almost jaded, thinking, "What could they possibly do next?" Each band was more exciting than the last; the costumes and the dancers were wonderful.

■ Competitions & Titles

To give you some sense of the number of competitions involved in Carnival and the organizational miracle that it all is, here is a list of some of the titles that can be won:

- **Band of the Year Award – Masquerade:** This is a competition for the best-designed costumes, music, and dance for a masquerade band. To be eligible the band as a group must pass several judging venues. In the streets the bands may be disorganized, but for judging places, like at the Savannah, all that chaos evolves quickly into a synchronized flow of gyrating bodies.

- **Calypso Monarch – Music:** This is the oldest calypso competition and the lyrics are usually based more on social commentary than songs in other competitions.

- **Chutney Soca Monarch – Music:** Best soca with a dash of chutney.

- **Junior Band of the Year – Masquerade:** This is the children's version of Band of the Year.

- **King and Queen of Carnival – Masquerade:** The stars of mas camps compete in extremely elaborate costumes, some with fireworks, and all fabulous. The costumes are huge, some 25 feet high and 30 feet wide, and most have wheels attached to assist the competitor in dancing and moving.

- **Medium Bands – Masquerade**.

- **Panorama Finals – Music:** Steel bands are wheeled onto the Savannah stage and, with enormous energy, they play their best to win.

- **People's Choice Award – Masquerade**.

- **Road March Monarch – Music:** The winner is the songwriter whose work is most often played at judging points. 1999 was the year for women, as Sanell Dempster won the Road March title for her song "The River," played with the band Blue Ventures.

- **Small Bands – Masquerade**.

- **Soca Monarch – Music:** Wild and outrageous, a party music version of Calypso, this competition is definitely one of "crowd appeal."

CARNIVAL SCHEDULE OF EVENTS

Before Carnival Week

- Chutney Soca Monarch Finals
- Extempo
- Junior Calypso Finals

Wednesday

- **Individuals competition** with conventional and traditional costumes, Queen's Park Savannah at 8 PM.

Thursday

- **Calypso (Kaiso) Finals competition**, Queen's Park Savannah, at 8 PM.
- **South King & Queen's Finals**, Skinner Park, San Fernando at 8 PM.

Friday

- **Carnival King and Queen Finals**, Queen's Park Savannah at 8 PM.
- **Steel Pan**, South Quay, 7 PM.
- **Soca Monarch**

Saturday

- **Junior Parade of Bands** (Kiddies Carnival), Queen's Park Savannah, at 8 AM.
- **National Panorama Finals**, (Steel Band), Queens Park Savannah at 7 PM.

Sunday

- **Traditional Mas**, Victoria Square, Woodbrook, Port of Spain, at 1 PM.
- **Dimanche Gras**, Queen's Park Savannah, at 8 PM.

Monday

- *J'Ouvert*, Victoria Square, around the Queen's Park Savannah, and the streets of Port of Spain beginning at 4 AM.
- **Parade of the Bands**, Adam Smith Square, Victoria Square, Queen's Park Savannah, and the streets of Port of Spain at 11 AM.
- **Pan on the Road**, streets of Port of Spain at 11 AM.

■ **Monday Night Mas**, Adam Smith Square, Victoria Square, and the Savannah, Port of Spain at 8 PM (an informal people's mas).

Tuesday

■ **Pan on the Road**, streets of Port of Spain at 11 AM.

■ **Parade of the Bands** (full costume), Queen's Park Savannah at 9 AM.

■ **Las Lap**, evening in the streets of Port of Spain.

The Following Week

■ **Champs in Concert**, Queen's Park Savannah, Port of Spain at 8 PM. Carnival winners in all categories show up for this final festival – if you missed Carnival itself, don't miss this.

■ Tickets & More Information

Tickets are usually available only a few days before each event and cost in the range of $20. For ticket availability and up-to-date information on Carnival, contact the **National Carnival Commission**, Queen's Park Savannah, Port of Spain, ☎ 627-1530, 627-5051/8 or 627-5354/60.

Visit **TIDCO**'s Web site to learn more about Carnival: www.visitTNT.com/ToDo/Events/Carnival/.

CARNIVAL DO'S AND DON'TS:

■ *Do* drink lots of water, juice, or soft drinks.

■ *Do* use a liberal amount of a good sunscreen.

■ *Do* pace yourself (if possible).

■ *Do* stay downtown as close to the Savannah as possible.

■ *Do* wear a hat and very comfortable shoes.

■ *Don't* say we didn't warn you; you are going to have the time of your life!

Carnival

Yachting

This section of our guide is written for yacht owners. It was not an anticipated chapter when we planned our first guide on Trinidad, but we thought it especially valuable information back then and it's become even more relevant now.

We've seen boat yards in the UK, Holland, Barcelona, Palma de Majorca, Portugal, the US and the Caribbean, and we had an opportunity to look over the yacht facilities in Trinidad. We are so favorably impressed by the yacht services and boat repair prices here that we had to let you know. In just a few years, the yacht services industry and the marinas have greatly expanded, and chic hotels and restaurants are now part of the yachty scene too.

A Safe Haven With Services

Until the last few years, Trinidad and Tobago was not a popular Caribbean destination for the sailing crowd. It is the most southerly of the Caribbean countries and its attractions were not widely known. In 1995, with the extreme season of hurricanes, Trinidad found itself home to hundreds of yachts seeking shelter. Once there, yacht owners discovered not only the delights of visiting Trinidad and Tobago, but also found a marvelous resource for boat repair, maintenance, and storage. Suddenly the country's southerly location became a major advantage – it is out of the active Caribbean hurricane zone.

In 1990, there were only a handful of non-local yachts in the Chaguaramas harbors and storage facilities in the northwestern corner of Trinidad. By 1995, that number had grown to 2,500, but most of the yachts were in storage or undergoing repairs. That has now changed, as Trinidad has become an appealing destination apart from its yacht services facilities, and there are a variety of new, secure anchoring and mooring areas, though they are becoming more crowded.

Even more yachts are expected in the future. To assist in welcoming arrivals, the *Trinidad and Tobago Boater's Guide*, published by Jack Dausend, is being distributed at marine centers free of charge. It is a directory of available services and provides summary information on marinas and boat repair yards in the Chaguaramas area.

At present, Chaguaramas has six marinas with associated yacht repair services, and the Trinidad and Tobago Yacht Club with marina services only.

The allure for the yacht traveler was readily apparent after the 1995 hurricane sason. Trinidad's location – outside the active hurricane zone – is just a start, however, in really seeing the opportunities that it presents to the boating community.

Finding haul-out facilities where they can not only manage small boats, but also boats of 175 tons or more, is surprising. This, coupled with their expert shipwrights, sailmakers, mechanics, painters, etc., means they have full-service facilities. Their skills, labor, and professionalism will all please you in comparison with work you may have done in other countries. Insurance, which in other areas may have been prohibitively expensive, may now be affordable thanks to Trinidad's favorable location. Your intended month stay-over for minor repairs might easily turn into a total overhaul or refurbishing, especially when the savings you might realize in labor alone will be 50% over other countries.

The skilled tradesmen you will find in shipyards, combined with Trinidad's well-established industrial and manufacturing sector, will assure that parts and services are first-rate. Professionalism abounds in yard foremen. The skill of the tradesmen and laborers and the wealth of top-notch equipment they work with will ensure quality work and will make your stay for repairs very productive and easier than expected.

Best of all is Trinidad's most valuable resource – its people. The yard foremen are knowledgeable, the tradesmen are professional, and the laborers friendly and receptive. These human advantages, coupled with the sophistication of the technical sector, will serve your yachting needs no matter how large or small your yacht is. The differences of the facilities should help you find an exact fit for your needs.

After your yacht's repairs are underway, don't forget to take in some of the sights of this richly beautiful and varied country. Trinidad alone is full of adventure with a wide variety of things to see and do, and a visit to Tobago might make a great vacation from the yacht. The 20-minute flight to the island is not expensive and a few days' stay would be a nice break. Tobago currently has no facilities for yachts, but anchoring-off is allowed in some areas: Store Bay, Mount Irvine, Man-O-War Bay, and Courland Bay are a few of the favorites. Gas and water are available at Charlotteville on the extreme eastern end of the island.

Services

■ Range of Yards

The five well-established yards with haul-out services, together with the new CrewsInn facilities, offer you a wide range of choices to meet your specific needs. Yards range from full-service haul-out facilities, where all services will be found on the premises, to yards that offer a laid-back relaxed atmosphere where you can do the work yourself and contract out when need be. Wherever you end up, you will no doubt feel that you have found "the yard" for you.

Those of you who do not want to commit to using only on-site contractors at a particular yard will find most yards flexible in allowing you to hire outside contractors. Most yards will even provide you with a list of accredited tradesman who will supply estimates and work with you independently. This can be a very appealing alternative, allowing you to hire those who will best meet your specific needs.

For services that may not be available at the yard you choose, such as special machining needs, you can contract with support industries in the area or in San Fernando. (San Fernando is the heart of the oil and gas industry.) Yards in Trinidad can also supply marine-quality materials, from stainless steel to locally grown teak. For those who know how difficult a haul-out can be when you can't get machining or special materials for those unforseen repairs, Trinidad is a pleasure. Welding aluminum and stainless

Yachts at Chaguaramas.

Yachting

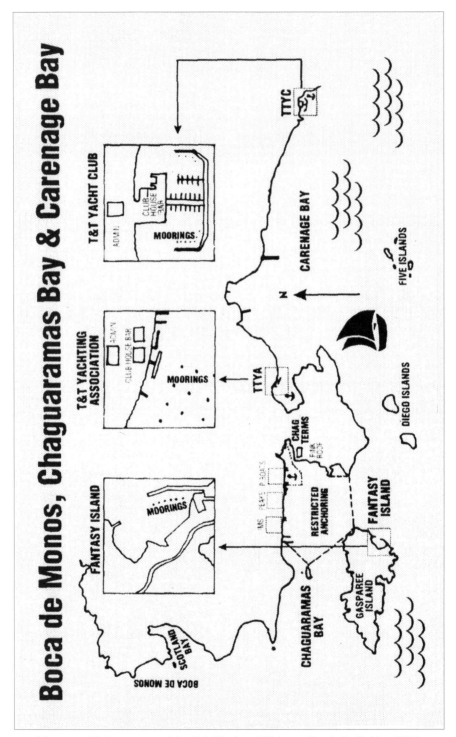

Map provided courtesy of the Trinidad and Tobago Boater's Guide, 1996;
Jack Dausend, Publisher.

steel is second nature for Trinidad's craftsmen – their oil and gas industry has been around since 1910.

Boats in transit in Trinidad receive a special benefit – service is free of tax or VAT. Before you order and buy, we recommend you verify your in-transit status with the chandlery you are using to assure that you are not charged tax.

Thanks to our shrinking world, special orders can be shipped to you in only four working days by Fed Ex, the best of the available carriers, from Miami or elsewhere. You may find yourself settling in for some significant work, like a couple of our friends from Florida who sailed to Trinidad for a haul-out. After finding prices so reasonable compared to their home base in the US, they had a container shipped from the States (VAT excluded, thanks to their in-transit status) and spent the better part of a year doing a complete overhaul.

■ Customs & Immigration

Your arrival will be facilitated thanks to Trinidad and Tobago's private port facility at Chaguaramas Terminals, Ltd., ☎ 627-5680. In the past customs and immigration had to be done in Port of Spain along with commercial traffic.

■ Directory of Facilities

The following is a listing of Trinidad's yachting facilities. All prices quoted are subject to change; please verify with the yard or service of interest to you.

IMS (Industrial Marine Services)

Location: First Ave. South, Chaguaramas
Yard Manager: Brian Govia
Yard Foreman: Kent Yohannson
Phone: ☎ 634-4328
E-mail: imsyachts@tstt.net.tt
Radio: VHF channel 68
Hoist capacity: 70-ton Travelift

Description: *Full-service haul-out and storage facility, teak and wood shop, chandlery, fiberglass/osmosis repair, sandblasting, welding, corrosion protection, paint shop, sailmaker, rigger, office services, restaurant and bar, hot showers, security, and laundry.*

Note: *There are discounts of 10% on advance payments of storage over six months. IMS is associated with Blue Waters Inn in Tobago under its parent company, Tucker Group.*

Yachting

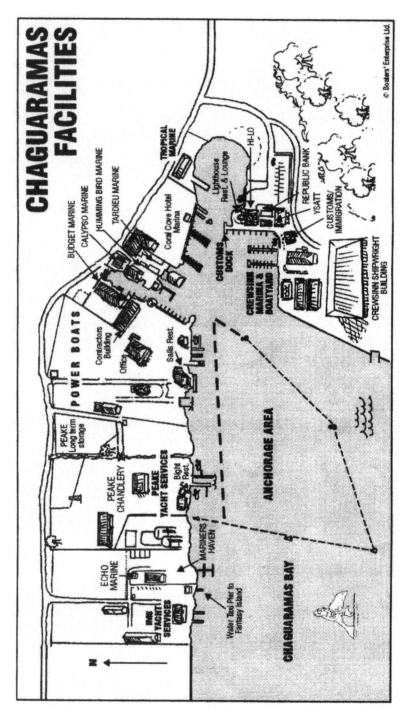

Map provided courtesy of the Trinidad and Tobago Boater's Guide - 1999;
Jack Dausend, Publisher.

Comment: This is a smaller, full-service yard, where you will get more personalized service. Here you can take care of nearly all your needs on premises.

Peake Yacht Services, Ltd.

Location: Lot #5, Western Main Rd., Chaguaramas
Yard Manager: Franz Maingot
Yard Foreman: Augustus "Radix" Henry
Phone: ☎ 634-4420, fax 634-4387
E-mail: pys@cablenett.net
Radio: VHF channel 69
Hoist Capacity: 150-ton Travelift (up to 31-foot beam)

Description: *Haul-out and storage facility, marine grade services, in-water berths, chandlery, welding, sandblasting, woodworking, fiberglass repair, painting, office services, water and electricity, fuel, laundry, showers, bar and restaurant, satellite TV, small hotel, and security.*

Note: *Discounts of up to 10% are offered for advance payments on storage.*

Comment: *Peake Yacht Services prides itself on quality and professionalism. If you are contracting work to be done in your absence in this full-service yard, you can probably sleep (almost) comfortably, knowing the job will get done within specifications. Peake Yacht Services seems to run about as well as their air conditioners, which you'll see run just fine... ah! They also run The Bight Hotel & Restaurant; see listings on pages 71 and 80.*

Power Boats Mutual Facilities Ltd.

Location: Chaguaramas Bay
Yard Foreman: Bernard Border
Phone: ☎ 634-4303, fax 634-4327
E-mail: pbmfl@powerboats.co.tt
Radio: VHF channel 72
Hoist Capacity: 50-ton Acme

Description: *Haul-out and storage facility, in-water berths, chandlery, welding, fiberglass repair, woodworking, local teak, painting, office services, water and electricity, fuel, laundry, bar and restaurant, grocery, security, showers, and apartments.*

Note: *There are discounts for stays of three months or more, paid in advance.*

Comment: *Power Boats' main work is with sailing yachts, but they will give the personal and knowledgeable help you need regardless of the kind of boat you have. Power Boats backs con-*

tracted work 100%, and they will usually arrange at least three estimates for you. They charge a flat 10% of labor costs, for which they will settle any disagreements or disputes. I doubt you could be anything but satisfied with this well-equipped, well-run yard, and we heard nothing but compliments regarding the hands-on care and assistance. They are getting quite a following from satisfied repeat customers.

Trinidad & Tobago Yachting Association (TTYA)

Location: Chaguaramas Bay
Phone: ☎ 634-4210 or 634-4519, fax 634-4376
Radio: VHF channel 68
Hoist Capacity: 15-ton Travelift; maximum length 45 feet, maximum beam 15 ft.

Description: *Full-service haul-out yard, moorings, repair shed, office services, water and electricity, laundry, bar and restaurant, security, and a good anchorage.*

Comment: *This is a private yacht club and sailing school. Most boats anchor out in the partially sheltered anchorage, which has a mud sand bottom. Approximate minimum draft is eight feet, and 40 feet is pretty much the maximum boat size. There is space for approximately 50 foreign boats. Each boat owner takes care of his own workers and tools, though arrangements can be made to use the on-premises work shed. This is a very laid-back, unhurried place, so if you need odds and ends done and are comfortable doing the work yourself, this could be just the place for your smaller boat.*

Trinidad & Tobago Yacht Club

Location: Carenage Bay next to Pt. Cumana
Club Manager: Mr. Power
Phone: ☎/fax 637-4260
Radio: VHF Channel 68

Description: *There are 60 in-water berths, fuel dock (gas, diesel, water), cable TV, Interserv link-up, telephone, laundry, showers, office services, security, bar and restaurant. It's very close to Port of Spain. This is a private club, but foreigners can get a temporary membership. Each person on board pays approximately $10 per week or $25 per month to use the facilities.*

Comment: *This was the first yacht facility in Trinidad. There are slips for about 45 boats with water and electricity, as well as hot showers. Slips cost around $15/day or $260/month. The club's main advantage is its proximity to Port of Spain. The anchorage is not as protected as you'll find in Chaguaramas, but the club has a warm and friendly atmosphere. You will meet a lot of travelers. It's* *a good stop for a happy hour get-together on Wednesdays and Fridays. Most people from Trinidad keep their boats here.*

The CrewsInn Marina & Boatyard

Location: Point Gourde, Chaguaramas Bay

Boatyard and Port Operation Manager: Johan Van Druten

Marina: ☎ 634-4384 or 634-4385, fax 634-4175; radio VHF channel 77; E-mail crewsinn@trinidad.net.tt

Boatyard: ☎ 634-4384/634-4385 (ask for boatyard), fax 634-4828; E-mail boatyard@tstt.net.tt

Hoist Capacity: 200-ton Travelift (32-foot maximum beam)

Draft and Size Limitations: The marina accommodates boats up to 100 feet long and with a draft of 35 feet. There is a 900-foot commercial dock with water and fuel.

Description: *Trinidad's first full-service marina, boat yard, and shopping and hotel complex. There is a 2.7-acre covered shipwright building, a four-acre haul-out yard, and associated workshops. On the site you'll also find a Trinidad and Tobago customs office, grocery store, marine supply shop, pharmacy, retail shops, bank, a restaurant/bar with entertainment, and a hotel. The marina, open since mid-1996, offers 65 in-water berths with water, electricity, cable TV, and telephone hookups. For more information, see the CrewsInn listings in the* Trinidad *chapter, under* Where To Stay *and* Where To Eat.

Comment: *This is the newest and most luxurious of Trinidad's full-service yacht facilities. Whether you are visiting on your yacht or having work done, this is a top-of-the-line place.*

Yachting

Guide Services

Trinidad

 There are a few well-known guided destinations in Trinidad, like Caroni Bird Sanctuary, but there are many places to see and explore without the services of a guide. Driving the island is the best way to get a sense of its diverse environments and extraordinary wealth of animal and bird life. Renting a car will enable you to explore far and wide on your own.

AUTHOR TIP

If you are reluctant to drive, hire a taxi driver like **Krishna Arnie***. We found him by simply flagging a taxi in Port of Spain and asking if he'd like to be our driver for the day. For $50 he drove us for a solid eight hours. He was not only a good driver, but an interesting person, showing us features of his country that a professional guide might ignore. Krishna will be happy to hear from you, though he is usually available only on weekends. His number is ☎ 671-2517.*

Tourism, as we've said before, is relatively new to Trinidad. Though guide services exist and are quickly improving, they may not yet be the quality you are expecting. Most guided tours are not inexpensive; they will cost up to $100 per person per day, so choose your destinations and guides carefully.

For bird watchers especially, we would suggest you contact **Asa Wright Nature Centre**. They lead tours not only on their own land, but also to Caroni, Blanchisseuse, and Nariva. We were very impressed by their articulate and informed staff. Another good choice for a bird watching guide is Mr. Nanan of **Nanan's Tours**. You may hire him personally for a private tour and you won't be disappointed.

CAUTION

Be sure to ask to see your guide's license and make sure it is up to date.

Trinidad is blessed with a significant number of rivers for such a small island. Some of the newer guide services are specializing in sports oriented adventures, exploring Trinidad's rivers and its more inaccessible coastal areas.

■ Bird Watching

ASA WRIGHT NATURE CENTRE, Spring Hill Estate, MM 7½, Blanchisseuse Rd., Arima; ☎ 667-4655, fax 667-0493. Highly recommended for bird watching guides. See detailed information on Asa Wright on pages 68 and 95.

NANAN'S BIRD SANCTUARY TOURS, 38 Bamboo Grove Sett. No. 1, Butler Highway, Valsyn; ☎ 645-1305. Nanan's company is best known for morning and afternoon boat tours of Caroni Swamp. The boats hold 30 people and the twice-daily tours run early in the morning and in late afternoon. The tour costs $10 per person, and they will provide transportation to and from your hotel for an additional $20 to $25 per person. During our recent trip to Trinidad we met two bird watchers from California who were very enthusiastic about their private tour with Mr. Nanan. They paid $120 for a 12-hour day, exploring special places with unique sightings.

■ Land, Coastal & River Tours

KAYAK CENTRE, Williams Bay, Chaguaramas; ☎ 633-7871, fax 628-1404. Owner Merryl See Tai leads kayak tours of the north coast dealing with surf zones (in and out through the surf) with two- to six-foot faces. He also does combined kayak and land tours such as Paria waterfall where, from the landing site, you will hike about 1½ hours up to the falls.

CARIBBEAN DISCOVERY TOURS LIMITED, 9B Fondes Amandes Rd., St. Ann's, Port of Spain; ☎ 624-7281, fax 624-8596, Web site www.tradepoint.tidco.co.tt/cdt. Guide Steven Broadbridge specializes in river and wetland tours and enjoys a fine local reputation. He also leads tours of the rain forests, caves, waterfalls, mud-volcanoes, temples and mosques, and historical buildings. Multi-talented Steven is also a published photographer, and is sensitive to the needs of visitors with this interest.

WILDWAYS, 10 Idlewild Rd., Knightsbridge, Cascade, Port of Spain; ☎/fax 623-7332, e-mail wildways@trinidad.net, Web site www.wildways.org. This is currently the only guide service offering overnight camping/hiking trips, as well as ocean and inland river kayaking and bike touring. They seem to be more sports oriented than most of the other companies, rating their adventures by difficulty and required expertise.

■ Music Tours

Contact **Hayden Browne** through his sister at ☎ 637-9513. See a full description under *Music*, page 34.

Tobago

Tobago has many long established and very professional scuba diving and snorkeling shops. New ones are coming on the scene as word has spread of the unique dive sites in Tobago. There are also innumerable land tour guides, though you should exercise some care in your selection. There is much to see on the island and much to learn, but we were not always impressed with the guides' training and expertise. Though friendly and entertaining, they did not seem particularly knowledgeable about local plants, animals or birds.

Guided tours seem a little expensive for what you get. When first in Tobago you might find it worthwhile to rent a car or hire a driver and make a circuit of the island. It's a good way to get oriented and have a sense of what you'd like to explore further. Remember, Tobago is small, so it's hard to get terribly lost. And there's always someone by the side of the road to point you in the right direction. Here is a list of available guide services by category.

■ Diving/Snorkeling

AQUA MARINE DIVE, LTD., Blue Waters Inn, Speyside; ☎ 660-4341, fax 639-4416, e-mail amdtobago@trinidad.net, Web site www.bluewaters-inn.com. Snorkeling and scuba diving services are available for everyone ranging from novice to very experienced divers. PADI certification courses with four open-water dives cost $450. Advanced courses, such as search and recovery, night and deep diving are also taught. Rental equipment is available.

DIVE TOBAGO, LTD., Pigeon Point, Crown Point; ☎ 639-0202, fax 639-7275/639-2727. Right next to the Conrado Hotel, Dive Tobago will give you a three-hour Resort Course for $55. It includes 1½ hours of instruction by the shore, followed by a 1½-hour trip to a nearby reef with a fully trained diver. You'll not be left alone, so it is safe and a wonderful way to learn if scuba diving is for you. Each person is taught individually, and receives a dive master-signed certificate stating they've completed a resort course. Dive Tobago was highly recommended by an English friend, Frank Reast. He had always wanted to try diving and loved the experience.

MANTA DIVE CENTER, Pigeon Point, Crown Point; ☎ 639-9209, fax 639-0414, e-mail mantaray@tstt.net.tt. They offer a variety of courses, both for novices and experienced divers, and they are perfectly situated for convenient dive trips to Buccoo Reef. Owners Amanda and Sven are open to whatever particular diving interest you want to explore.

SANCTUARY VILLA RESORT DIVE/ACCOMMODATION PACKAGES; ☎ 639-9556, fax 639-0019, e-mail info@sanctuaryvillas.com. The cost is reasonable, if their dive program and locations are what you are looking for. Contact them for up-to-date information, since they are expanding options all the time.

TOBAGO DIVE EXPERIENCE, Manta Lodge, Speyside; ☎ 660-5268, fax 660-5030. This is a full-service dive company offering PADI and NAUI certification and advanced courses. They have equipment rentals and offer various dive packages.

TOBAGO DIVE MASTERS, PO Box 351, Scarborough; ☎ 639-4347 or 639-4697, fax 639-4180. Ellis John, owner and manager, has his dive shop in Speyside. They offer PADI certification, glass-bottom boat rides, and transportation to and from all hotels. They are highly recommended by a friend of ours who is an experienced diver.

■ Fishing

DILLON'S FISHING CHARTER, Pigeon Point; ☎ 639-8765 days, 639-2938 evenings. On his 38-ft. Bertram with in-board twin diesels, Captain Stanley Dillon and his mate will take you for a full or half-day of fishing in the waters off Tobago, where the fish are plentiful. Dillon has 30 years of boating and fishing experience, and his boat is equipped with a fighting chair and belts. He'll set and bait your lines for you. Full-day charters with lunch are $500; half-day charters from 8 AM to noon are $300. Expected

Roger Joseph cleaning fish at Pigeon Point.

catches are blue marlin, dorado (dolphin fish), wahoo, and yellowfin tuna. The charter is for a maximum of six persons, but if you have fewer people, ask for a discount. If you wish, the chef at **Dillon's Seafood Restaurant** in Crown Point will prepare your day's catch that evening. To assure a day of fishing it is best to reserve in advance of your arrival in Tobago.

HARD PLAY, Friendship Estate, Canaan; ☎ 639-7108, fax 639-7788, e-mail hardplay@tstt.net.tt. You can go to sea with Captain Gerard "Frothy" De Silva in search of fish on one of his three boats – a 38-ft. Sport Fisher Original, a 31-ft. Bertram Sport Fisherman, or a 31-ft. Formula 3 Coastal Fisherman. Full-day charters, including lunch and soft drinks, cost $550 and give you an opportunity to catch blue marlin, sailfish, wahoo, white marlin, dorado, and tuna. Half-day charters are $325, with expected catches of dorado, kingfish, barracuda, and more. The charter is for a maximum of six persons; you may negotiate prices for smaller parties.

If you are truly seaworthy and adventurous, and would like to experience fishing 20 to 25 miles out in a 25-ft. launch, just talk to any fisherman at Pigeon Point, or ask there for Lincoln Yates, who will help you make arrangements.

■ Other Watersports

WINDSURF TOBAGO, ☎/fax 639-3846, e-mail windsurftobago@wow.net, Web site www.windsurftobago.com. Pigeon Point Beach in Crown Point provides an unequaled tranquil and lovely location. Focusing his business on windsurfing groups, owner John Pollard can provide a lot of equipment and emphasizes safety. Individuals may not always find equipment available on any given day, but give it a try. John specializes in providing packages that include accommodations, windsurfing, and transfers.

MT. IRVINE WATERSPORTS, Mt. Irvine Bay Beach; ☎ 639-9379, fax 639-4721, e-mail wetsports@pobox.com. Owners Bertrand Bhikarry and Kay Seetal will fix you up with everything you'll need for snorkeling, kayaking, waterskiing, windsurfing, surfing, diving, and boat or fishing charters. You won't find jet skis though; they are committed to preserving the island's idyllic nature. Guided bird watching and nature tours are also available. Credit cards or cash are fine and don't hesitate to negotiate on prices for groups or multiple rentals. Take a moment to read Bertrand's essay about pulling a seine on page 167.

■ Land Tours & Bird Watching

HOSKIN ANTOINE, 44 Sangsters Hill, Scarborough; ☎ 639-4138. Hoskin specializes in small groups of up to eight people; and he's a good man to hire for a day's tour of the island. Interesting and reliable, Hoskin is a very congenial person.

RICARDA SOLOMON, at Hotel Coconut Inn, Bon Accord; ☎ 639-8493. Though Ricarda organizes a variety of interesting tours, she personally leads off-road motorcycle tours of the island's old sugar mills. For $60/person, including the motorcycle, you'll ride through rain forests and see places most guides will never take you. Ricarda is a German woman who came to Tobago years ago. She knows the island well and she loves to ride. Born to be wild!

DAVID ROOKS NATURE TOURS, Scarborough; ☎/fax 639-4276, e-mail rookstobago@trinidad.net, Web site www.trinidad.net/rookstobago. An older German resident of Tobago, David leads a variety of land tours including the rain forest and Little Tobago. Make sure he'll personally be leading the tour you sign up for, and be aware that usually you'll be part of a large group.

SIMON MCLETCHIE TOURS, Store Bay Local Rd., Bon Accord; ☎ 639-0265, fax 639-0265. Led personally by Simon McLetchie, you can't help but have a wonderful time. Nicknamed Sio, he is the essence of a Tobagonian. Sio is 6' 2", powerfully built, and as sweet and gentle a person as you could imagine. He's also very well informed and devoted to his island and all it has to offer. He'll share it with you most sincerely, as he did with us.

Whether you go to the rain forest, waterfalls, or to find "alligators," Simon is our pick for the best man. He is exquisitely able to spot birds in the most unlikely places, while driving and answering one of your questions. He'll identify the birds and tell you all about their habits. He is also knowledgeable about local plants, including medicinal ones, and he's a wealth of local lore. Including lunch at a restaurant, the tours run $60 per person for two to four people, and $45 per person for groups of five or more. Simon prefers personal tours and will not guide more than 12 people at a time, as he believes it does not give a fair experience to all. You may have trouble getting him to take you home, as we did; he really loves his work and there's always just one more bird he wants to show you!

Simon McLetchie and Stassi on the road.

■ Off-Island Tours

AJM TOURS UNLIMITED, in Crown Point at the airport; ☎ 639-0610, fax 639-8918, e-mail ajmtours@trinidad.net. This is the place to go to arrange a brief trip to the nearby Grenadines or to Venezuela and Angel Falls.

Eco-Tourism & The Environment

Eco-tourism is an appealing phrase and is the buzz word for much of the tourism industry's advertising these days. Unfortunately, it often sounds better than it is. Travel marketing is big business and phrases like eco-tourism sell travel programs like hotcakes. Sadly, eco-tourism does not mean that environmentally sound standards have been established, or if they will be enforced even if laws have been written. The environment is the selling point and it is being used up just as quickly as tickets can be sold.

In traveling, even ecologically concerned people want to get as close to the natural wonders of this world as they can. Because of this, many of those wonders are suffering and some are being destroyed altogether. *Newsweek* magazine had an article titled *Beware of the Humans* in their 2/5/96 issue, reporting just some of the abuses in eco-tourism. Even caring people are being drawn into situations where the very environment they want to explore and protect is overburdened by the sheer number of its visitors.

■ Questions To Ask

Before deciding to stay at an eco-hotel, ask what they are doing to protect the environment. Are they saving rainwater, using drip irrigation on the property, recycling gray water and treating wastewater before it enters the ocean, and using solar water heaters? Just what does eco-hotel mean? Too often you will be told that they are ecologically conscious because they don't wash your sheets and towels every day. Just think what a financial savings this is for them. Are they putting those savings to work for the environment in other ways? It's doubtful. Though changing linens less frequently is a good idea, is it enough?

Businesses in Trinidad and Tobago are not immune to the lure of the money to be made in eco-tourism. You will see advertisements for eco-hotels and eco-tours but, in our opinion, not much of what we saw qualified as ecologically responsible. At one hotel, we met a Canadian couple just checking in, and we asked why they had chosen this hotel over all the others. They told us they had found it listed on the Web as an "eco" hotel. So much for truth in advertising. If they had asked any questions, they might have stayed elsewhere.

It is just as important to ask questions before taking an eco-tour. Ask what special expertise the guides have and what controls have been put in place to protect the environment. When you are taken to a newly created preserve, ask what is being preserved and exactly how. Ask what the maximum number of visitors per day is and what permissions commercial guides are required to have before leading groups to the site.

■ Carrying Capacity

One of the concepts that should be central to eco-tourism is sustainability, or carrying capacity. In other words, the number of visitors that can be safely accommodated. Safely accommodated means maintaining the quality of the environment for its native plants and animals while ensuring the quality of the experience for visitors. Pointe-à-Pierre, in Trinidad, has made this concept a part of their overall educational program. Wisely, they have chosen to limit the number of visitors to this wildfowl preserve so naturalists may enjoy what is there, while the number of visitors does not overburden the site.

■ Unmindful Tourism

Trinidad and Tobago are beautiful. The natural environment of both of these islands offers a tremendous variety of vegetation and a wealth of animal life, both above and below the sea. Tobago, more than Trinidad, has become a popular Caribbean vacation getaway, and some of the problems that has created are only now becoming evident. Tobagoins often talk to us of their feelings about developing tourism. Fishermen and divers complain about the consequences of excessive exploitation of the reefs. They are concerned not only because their livelihoods are being affected, but because this is their home, and it is suffering.

Tourists unwittingly take reef tours that damage the very thing they came to see. At Buccoo Reef, boatmen routinely hand out reef walking shoes. Visitors, unthinkingly, don the shoes and go for a stroll on the reef, killing the very thing they came a long way to see. Divers unmindfully handle coral or, worse, break off pieces as souvenirs. Fishermen are dismayed when yachts sail into one of the beautiful bays and drag their anchor chains on the delicate reefs. Waste dumped by yacht owners near reefs has already caused over-fertilization and damage. And it is not only the seas and reefs that are being ruined. Forest trails have become less attractive because tourists absentmindedly break branches, pull leaves off plants, and pick wildflowers as they meander along, admiring the birds and wildlife.

AUTHOR TIP

There is much that you can do by simply taking time to think. One of our own observations is that appreciating the wonders of nature is best done with a clear head. Don't combine eco-tourism and alcohol.

Both Stassi and I have a deep affection for Trinidad and Tobago and hope visitors will be as careful there as they are at home. When traveling, remember that you are in someone else's home. Keeping that in mind will make us all better neighbors.

■ Recycling

In many areas of the States, recycling has become as common as trash, but American visitors in Tobago routinely put recyclable glass bottles in the trash. Trinidadian companies are more environmentally conscious. Old rum bottles are commonly re-labeled and used for roasted peanuts and they can be used many times. Smaller bottles are re-used for sauces and you'll commonly see recycled bottles on the shelves at supermarkets in Trinidad and Tobago. Plastic containers are not recycled in Tobago because the cost of shipping them to the treatment facility in Trinidad is prohibitive, but in Trinidad they are collected and recycled at the Laventille/Fernandez compound.

HOW YOU CAN HELP THE ENVIRONMENT

■ Take quick showers. Even relatively clean, fresh water decreases the salinity of the surrounding sea water, increasing algae and impairing the growth of coral, which is very sensitive to changes in salinity.

■ Do not walk on reefs under any circumstances. If you dive or snorkel, don't take souvenirs from under the water.

■ Buy recyclable glass bottles when you can, and avoid plastic bottles completely. Bring recyclable bottles back to the store where you bought them. If you are unable to do so, at least put bottles and aluminum cans in a bag and give them to the hotel maid.

■ If you are on a yacht, find out where you can deposit your waste on land where it will be properly treated, and don't dump your bilges into the seas.

■ Limit your use of electricity. Turn off lights and air conditioning when not in use.

■ In the forests, keep to the trails and leave the foliage and wildflowers where they are.

■ Needless to say, but we're saying it anyway, don't leave litter behind you.

■ When you hear the word "eco," be wary of what you're being sold.

Eco-Tourism

Bibliography

Aboriginal and Spanish Colonial Trinidad, A Study in Culture Contact, Linda A Newson. Academic Press, Ltd., London, 1976.

The British in the Caribbean, Cyril Hamshere. Harvard University Press, Cambridge, 1972.

Callaloo, Calypso & Carnival, The Cuisines of Trinidad and Tobago, Dave Dewitt & Mary Jane Wilan. The Crossing Press, Freedom, CA, 1993.

Calypso Callaloo, Early Carnival Music in Trinidad, Donald R. Hill. University Press of Florida, Gainesville, FL, 1993.

Caribbean Beat, Publication of BWIA, January/February, 1999.

Class Alliances and the Liberal Authoritarian State: The Roots of Post-Colonial Democracy in Jamaica, Trinidad and Tobago, and Surinam, F.S.J. Ledgister. Africa World Press, Inc., Trenton, NJ, 1998.

A Continent of Islands, Searching for the Caribbean Destiny, Mark Kurlansky. Addison-Wesley Publishing Company, 1992.

Drawings of the Island's Past, Gerald G. Watterson. Published by Gerald G. Watterson, St. James, Trinidad, 1993. This small book of drawings focuses on the old gingerbread homes and churches, many of which were destroyed by Hurricane Flora in 1963. It is available at the library in Scarborough, Tobago.

History of the People of Trinidad and Tobago, Eric Williams. Andre Deutsch Limited, London, 1963.

The Independence Experience, 1962-1987, edited by Selwyn Ryan, Institute of Social and Economic Research. The University of The West Indies, St. Augustine, Trinidad, 1988.

Isles of the Caribbean, Robert L. Breeden, Editor, Special Publications Division. National Geographic Society, 1980.

KAISO! The Trinidad Calypso, A Study of the Calypso as Oral Literature, Keith Q. Warner. Three Continents Press, Washington, D.C., 1985.

MotMot Times, Sept/Dec 1998, *Happy New Year*, Simonese Cruickshank, and *Is There a Doctor in The House*, T.S., The Tourism Department, Scarborough, Tobago.

Race Relations in Colonial Trinidad 1870-1900, Bridget Brereton. Cambridge University Press, 1979.

Rodale's Scuba Diving, Tobago – *Carnival of Currents*, Jan./Feb. 1997, Keith Phillips.

A Short History of The West Indies, J.H. Parry and P.M. Sherlock. MacMillan St. Martin's Press, London, Third Edition, 1956.

Tobago "Melancholy Isle," Volume I, 1498-1771, Douglas Archibald. West Indiana Ltd., Port of Spain, Trinidad and Tobago, 1987.

The Trinidad Carnival Mandate for a National Theatre, Errol Hill. University of Texas Press, Austin, TX, 1972.

Trinidad Ethnicity, Kevin A. Yelvington, Editor. The University of Tennessee Press, Knoxville, 1993.

The West Indies & The Guianas, D.A.G. Waddell. Prentice-Hall, Inc., Englewood Cliffs, NJ, 1967.

Useful References

■ Sources

Good resources for books on Trinidad and Tobago's local animals and plants can be found at the following places:

- Asa Wright Nature Centre, Trinidad
- Pointe-à-Pierre, Trinidad
- Man-O-War Bay Cottages, Charlotteville, Tobago
- Tobago Library, Scarborough, Tobago

■ Of Interest to Naturalists

A Birder's Guide to Trinidad and Tobago, William L. Murphy. Peregrine Enterprises, 1995.

Birds of Trinidad and Tobago: A Photographic Atlas, Russell Barrow.

Birds of the West Indies (Peterson Field Guide), James Bond, et al. Houghton Mifflin, 1993.

A Guide to the Birds of Trinidad and Tobago, Richard ffrench. Cornell University Press, 1991.

The Nature Trails of Trinidad, Richard ffrench and Peter Bacon.

The Trinidad and Tobago Field Naturalists Club Trail Guide, describes trails on the islands and provides maps.

■ History & Culture

From Columbus to Castro: The History of the Caribbean 1492-1969, Dr. Eric Williams. Vintage Books, 1984. One of the better histories of the Caribbean.

A House for Mr. Biswas, V. S. Naipaul. Knopf, 1995. A good resource for insight into the life of an East Indian.

Sharks and Sardines: Blacks in Business in Trinidad & Tobago, Selwyn D. Ryan.

Muslimeen Grab for Power, Selwyn D. Ryan. 1991.

■ Calypso

Calypso & Society in Pre-Independence Trinidad, 1990, Gordon Roehler.

Carnival, Canboulay and Calypso: Traditions in the Making, John Cowley. Cambridge University Press, 1996.

The Political Calypso: True Opposition in Trinidad and Tobago, 1962-1987, Louis Regis. University Press of Florida, 1998.

Bibliography

www.hunterpublishing.com

Hunter's full range of travel guides to all corners of the globe is featured on our exciting Web site. You'll find guidebooks to suit every type of traveler, no matter what their budget, lifestyle, or idea of fun. Full descriptions are given for each book, along with reviewers' comments and a cover image. Books may be purchased on-line using a credit card via our secure transaction system.

Adventure Guides – There are now over 40 titles in this series, covering such destinations as Jamaica, the Yucatán, New Hampshire, Florida, Virginia, Texas, and the Alaska Highway. Aimed at the independent traveler who enjoys outdoor activities (rafting, hiking, biking, skiing, canoeing, etc.), all books in this signature series have complete information on places to stay and eat, sightseeing, in-town attractions, transportation and more!

Alive Guides – This ever-popular line of books takes a unique look at the best each destination offers: fine dining, jazz clubs, first-class hotels and resorts. In-margin icons direct the reader at a glance. Top sellers include *The Cayman Islands*; *St. Martin & St. Barts*; *Antigua, Barbuda, St. Kitts & Nevis*; *Cancún & Cozumel*; and *The Virgin Islands*.

Hunter's Romantic Weekends series offers myriad things to do for couples of all ages and lifestyles. Quaint places to stay and restaurants where the ambiance will take your breath away are included, along with fun activities that you and your partner will remember forever. Among the romantic destinations covered: Virginia, Maryland & Washington, DC; Georgia & The Carolinas; Texas; New England; Central & Northern Florida; and America's Southwest.

One-of-a-kind travel books available from Hunter include *Best Dives of the Western Hemisphere*; *The Jewish Travel Guide*; *The African-American Travel Guide*; *Golf Resorts*; and many more.

Index

A

Abercromby Inn, Port of Spain, 64-65

Accommodations: Arnos Vale, 132, 136, 143-145; Atlantic Coast of Tobago, 137-139; Blanchisseuse, 64, 69-71; Bon Accord, 128, 130; for Carnival, 63; Chaguaramas, 64, 71; Charlotteville, 142; cooking facilities, 63; cooking tools, 41; Crown Point, 126-131; Grand Rivière, 73; Las Cuevas, 72; location, 63-64; Maracas Bay, 72; Mayaro, 72; meal plans, 124; Mid-Caribbean Coast, 132-137; North Caribbean Coast, 139-140; Port of Spain, 63, 64-68; reservations, 124; Scarborough, 137-139; Speyside, 140-141; Tobago, 123-145; Trinidad, 62-73; Tunapuna, 73

Adventure Farm and Nature Reserve, Tobago: bird watching, 156, 160; sightseeing, 160

Adventures and sports: Tobago, 173-179; Trinidad, 101-104

African Trophies, Port of Spain, 114

Agouti, 25

AIDS hot line, 42

Airlines, 51-52

Airport transfers, 62-63, 124

AJM Tours Unlimited, 220

Alicia's Guest House, Port of Spain, 66-67

Alma's kiosk, Tobago, 151

Aloe, 30

Amoco Renegades (band), 33, 34

Anchorage Restaurant, Chaguaramas, 79; nightlife, 112

Antoine, Hoskin (guide), 219

Aqua Marine Dive, Ltd., guides, 217

Arawak Indians, 10, 11

Area code, 47

Argyle Waterfall, Roxborough, 157, 182

Arima, Trinidad: accommodations, 68-69, 95-96; driving tours, 105-108; horse racing, 104; nature center guides, 216

Aripo, Trinidad, caves, 95, 101

Arnie, Krishna (guide), 215

Arnos Vale, Tobago, 121; accommodations, 132, 136, 143-145; bird watching, 156; dive sites, 177; nightlife, 184; restaurants, 152; sightseeing, 160-163; snorkeling, 178

Arnos Vale Hotel Resort, Tobago, 132

Art, Tobago, 187-188

Asa Wright Sanctuary, Trinidad: accommodations, 68-69, 95-96; bird watching, 25, 85, 95-96; guide services, 215, 216; snakes, 26

Atlantic Coast, Tobago, 122; accommodations, 137-139; beaches, 172-173; restaurants, 153-155; sightseeing, 157-158

Azee's Hotel and Restaurant, Trinidad, 72

B

Back Bay Beach, Tobago, 169

Backyard Batik Shop & Cafe, Crown Point, 150

Bacolet, Tobago, 122; beaches, 172; driving tours, 180; nightlife, 185; restaurant, 154; shopping, 187; surfing, 179

Bambú, 115, 187

Banks and money, 37; service charges, 45; tipping, 45; VAT, 45

Battis, Cornell (market), 150

BC sugar processing plant, Trinidad, 90

Beaches: Tobago, 168-173; Trinidad, 98-101, 106, 109; warning, 99

Bed and breakfasts (host homes), 64

Belandra Beach, Trinidad, 109

Belle Garden, Tobago: accommodations, 138-139; restaurant, 155; sightseeing, 158; tennis, 173

Bight, Chaguaramas, accommodations, 71; restaurant, 80

Biking, Tobago, 40, 174
Billy, Marvin (guide), 88
Bird watching: binoculars for, 41; guide services, 216, 219-220; Tobago, 26-27, 156-157, 160, 163-166; Trinidad, 25, 56, 85, 87, 89-90, 95-97
Black Rock, Tobago, 121; accommodations, 133-134; cafe, 152
Blanchisseuse, Trinidad, 55, 60; accommodations, 64, 69-71; beaches, 99; driving tours, 105-108; fishing, 104; restaurants, 80
Blue Crab, Scarborough, 153
Blue Horizon, Mt. Irvine, 132-133
Blue Waters Inn, Speyside, 140
Boater's Guide (Dausend), 205
Boating, Tobago, 178-179
Boca de Monos, yacht services, 208
Bocas Islands, 61, 91-94, 111
Bon Accord, Tobago: accommodations, 128, 130; diner, 151; nightlife, 184
Botanical Gardens: Port of Spain, 81-82; Scarborough, 163
Breakfast Shed, Port of Spain, 77
Brechin Castle, Trinidad, 90
Broadbridge, Steven (guide), 103
Browne, Hayden (guide), 34, 216
Buccoo Reef, Tobago, 158-159; diving, 175, 177; snorkeling, 178
Buccoo, Tobago, 121; accommodations, 135; beaches, 169; restaurants, 152-153; Sunday block party, 186
Buffalo trees, 30
Business, 9
BWIA Invaders (steel band), 34

C
Café Callaloo, Crown Point, 150
Caiman, 158
Calypso, 35-37, 114
Calypso Revue, Port of Spain, 37; nightlife, 112
Camping: guide services, 216; Tobago, 145; Trinidad, 73
Canaan, Tobago: fishing guides, 218; nightlife, 185; restaurant, 154

Canoe Bay Beach Park, Tobago: camping, 145; sightseeing, 163-164
Carenage Bay, yacht services, 208
Carera Island, 91
Caribbean Discovery Tours Limited, Port of Spain, 103, 216
Caribbean Islands, map, 6
Carib Indians, 10-12
Carnival, 48-49, 189-203; accommodations, 63; calinda, 191; competitions and titles, 201; Dimanche Gras, 196-197; do's and don'ts, 203; fêtes, 193; history, 189-192; information, 203; J'Ouvert, 197-198; main events, 195-200; masquerade, 193-195; Monday Mas, 198; Panorama, 195; schedule of events, 201-203; steel bands, 33-34, 195; stick-fighting, 191; tickets, 203; today, 192-193; Tuesday, 198-200
Caroni Swamp, Trinidad: bird watching, 25, 56, 87; guide services, 216
Cascade, Trinidad: accommodations, 68; squash, 103
Cashew trees, 29
Castara, Tobago, 121; accommodations, 139; beaches, 171; dive sites, 177
Caves: Aripo, Trinidad, 95, 101; Crown Point, Tobago, 159; Gaspar Grande Island, 92; Lopinot, Trinidad, 96
CDA, see Chaguaramas, Trinidad
Celery Bay Beach, Tobago, 171
Centipede Island, 91
Chacachacare Island, 91, 102
Chaguaramas, Trinidad, 61; accommodations, 64, 71; beaches, 98, 100; CDA, 93-94, 102, 111; fishing, 104; golf, 102; hiking, 102; kayaking, 103, 216; military museum, 94; nightlife, 112, 114; restaurants, 79-80; windsurfing, 104; yachting services, 200-213
Charlotteville, Tobago, 123; accommodations, 142; beaches, 171-172; cafe, 156; dive sites, 176; driving tours, 181, 183; sightseeing, 164

Cholson Chalets, Charlotteville, 142

Chutney soca music, 36

Climate, 38-39

Club Flag's, Port of Spain, nightlife, 112-113

Cocoa, 29, 85, 157-158, 182

Coconut Inn, Tobago, accommodations, 128

Coconuts, 28

Coco Reef Resort, Crown Point, 126-127; tennis, 173

Coco's Hut Restaurant and Bar, Blanchisseuse, 80

Cocrico, 26

Conrado Beach Resort, Tobago, 127-128

Cooking tools, 41

Copra Tray Restaurant and Bar, Tobago, nightlife, 184

Coral reef exploitation, 222-223

Courland Bay, Tobago, accommodations, 136-137

Couva, Trinidad, sugar factory, 90

Credit cards, 37, 62

CrewsInn, Chaguaramas, 71

CrewsInn Marina and Boatyard, 213

Crime, 39-40

Crown Point, Tobago, 120; accommodations, 126-131; beaches, 168-169; biking, 174; diving, 217; driving tours, 180-181; map, 120; nightlife, 185; restaurants, 150-151; sightseeing, 158-159

Crusoe's Cave, Crown Point, 159

Crystal Palace, Scarborough, 185

Culloden Bay, Tobago, 171

Culloden Reef, Tobago, dive site, 177

Customs and immigration, 43, 47, 207

D

Darmoo, Ramish (ferry), 92

Deep-sea fishing, Trinidad, 104

Delaford, Tobago, 122; accommodations, 138; beaches, 172-173; sightseeing, 158

Demographics, 8-9

Devil's Woodyard, Trinidad, 85

Diego Martin Estate and Waterwheel, Trinidad, 94

Dillon's Fishing Charter, Tobago, 218

Dillon's Seafood Restaurant, Pigeon Point, 218

Dive Tobago, 217

Diving, Tobago, 174-178; guide service, 217-218

Double D's Delight, Lowlands, 153-154

Driving, 53; gasoline, 54; on left side, 53, 104; license, 54; tours in Tobago, 180-184; tours in Trinidad, 104-112

Drugs, 40

Duchy of Courland, 13

Duncan, Lorris (wood carver), 187

E

East Coast, Trinidad, 62, 85, 108-109

Economy, 7-9; demographics, 8-9; oil, 7-8; tourism, 8; yacht services industry, 8

Eco-tourism, 221-223

Eco-tourism at Buccoo Reef, 159

Edith Falls, Trinidad, 94, 102

Electricity, 47

Eleven Degrees North, Crown Point, 150-151

El Tucuche, Trinidad, 101

Embassies, 40

Emergencies, 42

Emperor Valley Zoo, Port of Spain, 82

Englishman's Bay, Tobago, 171

Environment, 221-223; carrying capacity, 222; recycling, 223; reef exploitation, 222-223

Events and holidays, 48-52

Exodus (steel band), 34

F

Facts, 47

Fauna and flora, 23-31

Ferry service, 52-53

Film and cameras, 41

First Historical Café and Bar, Tobago, 155, 182

Index

Fishing: guide services, 218-219; Tobago, 178-179; Trinidad, 104

Flora and fauna, 23-30

Food: and beverages, 76; fast, 76; local dishes, 75, 146; MSG, 76; Tobago, 145-150; Trinidad, 74-76; *see also* Restaurants

Fort George, Trinidad, 94

Fort Granby, Tobago, 14

Fort James, Plymouth, 163

Fort King George, Scarborough, 164

Francis, Elwyn (guide), 92

French Fort, Tobago, bird watching, 156, 164

G

Gail's Café, Charlotteville, 156

Gaspar Grande Island (Gasparee), 92

Gingerbread Villa, Plymouth, 133

Ginger lilies, 30

Golden Star, Crown Point, 185

Golf: Tobago, 173-174; Trinidad, 102

Gommangalala, 27

Gordon Bay Beach, Tobago, 171

Grafton Beach Resort, Black Rock, 133-134; kayaking, 179; squash, 173

Grafton, Tobago: accommodations, 144-145; beaches, 170; bird watching, 156, 163

Gran Couva, Trinidad, 85

Grand Rivière, Trinidad: accommodations, 73; beaches, 101; driving tour, 110

Grenadines, tours, 220

Guanapo Gorges and Yarra River, Trinidad, 101-102

Guide services, 215-220; bird watching, 216, 219-220; diving/snorkeling, 217-218; fishing, 218-219; land, coastal and river tours, 216, 219-220; music tours, 216; off-island tours, 220; steel bands, 34; Tobago, 217-220; Trinidad, 215-216; watersports, 219

H

Handicap access, 62

Hard Play, Canaan, fishing guides, 218

Harry Balti (restaurant), Crown Point, 151

Health emergencies, 42

Health and fitness clubs: Tobago, 174; Trinidad, 103

Hibiscus, 30

Hiking: guide services, 216; Tobago, 173; Trinidad, 101-102

Hillsborough Beach, Tobago, 172

Hillsborough Dam, Tobago, 158; bird watching, 156; driving tour, 181-182

Hilton Hotels: Port of Spain, 66; Tobago Plantations, 137

Hira, Tobago Fine Art, 188

History, 9-23; of government, 6-7; of calypso, 35; of Carnival, 189-192; Crown Colony status, 12; 15th-18th centuries, 10-14; 19th century, 14-18; PNM, 20-23; of steel bands, 31-32; twentieth century, 18-23

Hitchhikers, picking up, 54

Hitchhiking, Tobago, 119

Holiday Inn, Port of Spain, 65-66

Holidays and events, 48-52

Hong Kong City Restaurant, Port of Spain, 77

Horseback riding, Tobago, 179

Horse racing, Trinidad, 104

Host homes (bed and breakfasts), 64

Hotel Coconut Inn, motorcycling tours, 174

Hot Shoppe, Port of Spain, 77

Houses to rent, Tobago, 143-145

I

Ice cream, Toco, Trinidad, 109

Immigration and customs, 43, 47, 209

Immortelle trees, 26

IMS (Industrial Marine Services), 209-211

Indigo, Port of Spain, 77

Information: Carnival, 203; special interests, 44; tourist, 46

J

Jemma's Tree House Restaurant, Speyside, 156, 183
Jimmy's Holiday Resort, Crown Point, 128
Johnny's, Port of Spain, 77
Johnston Apartments, Crown Point, 129

K

Kaiso (calypso), 35
Kaiso House, 37
Kapok Hotel, St. Clair, 67
Kariwak Village, Crown Point, 129-130; health and fitness facilities, 174
Kayaking: guide services, 216; Tobago, 179; Trinidad, 103
King Peter's Bay Beach, Tobago, 171
King's Bay Beach, Delaford, 172-173
King's Bay Waterfall, Delaford, 158
KP Resorts, Buccoo, 135

L

La Brea, Trinidad, Pitch Lake, 56, 88-89, 112
La Fantasie, Port of Spain, 77
Lagoon Lodge, Bon Accord, 130
Laguna Mar Nature Lodge, Blanchisseuse, 69-70
Lambeau, Tobago, horseback riding, 179
Lamp shades, 41
Language, 5, 47
L'Anse Noir, Trinidad, 110
Lapeyrouse Cemetery, Port of Spain, 83
Las Cuevas, Trinidad, 106; accommodations, 72; beaches, 99
La Tartaruga Restaurant, Buccoo Bay, 153
Leatherback turtles, 27-28
Le Grand Courlan, Black Rock, 134; spa, 174
Les Coteaux Cultural Theater, Tobago, 185
Library, Tobago, 122
Lighthouse, Toco, Trinidad, 109
Lighthouse Restaurant, Chaguaramas, 80
Little Bay Beach, Tobago, 171
Little Tobago Island, 183; bird watching, 156, 164-165
Lizard, twenty-four-hour, 27
Lopinot historic site, Trinidad, 96
Lowlands, Tobago: art, 187-188; restaurant, 153-154
Lush, Canaan, nightlife, 185

M

Macqueripe Beach, Chaguaramas, 100
Madoo, James (guide), 87
Magnificent Seven, Port of Spain, 83
Main Ridge Forest Reserve, Tobago, 182; bird watching, 156, 165-166
Manchineel trees, 30
Mango Valley, Trinidad, 94
Manicou (opossum), 25
Man-O-War Bay, Charlotteville, beach, 171-172
Man-O-War Bay Cottages, Charlotteville, 142
Manta Dive Center, guides, 217
Manta Lodge, Speyside, 140-141; diving, 217
Manzanilla, Trinidad, 62; beaches, 100; driving tours, 108-109
Maps, list, viii
Maracas Bay, Trinidad: accommodations, 72; beaches, 98, 99, 106; driving tours, 105-108; hiking, 102; restaurants, 81
Maracas Waterfall, Trinidad, 97
Maraval, Trinidad: accommodations, 68; golf, 102; shopping, 115
Marcia's Diner, Bon Accord, 151
Marianne River, Trinidad, 106
Mario's Pizza, Port of Spain, 78
Mas Camp Pub, Port of Spain, nightlife, 113
Mason Hall, Tobago, 182
Matelot, Trinidad, 110; beaches, 101
Matura, Trinidad, beaches, 101, 109
Mau Pau, Port of Spain, nightlife, 113

Mayaro, Trinidad, 62; accommodations, 72; beaches, 100; driving tours, 108-109
McLetchie, Simon, tours, 219-220
Medicinal plants, 30
Metaire system, 14
Mid-Caribbean Coast, Tobago, 121; accommodations, 132-137; beaches, 169-170; restaurants, 152-153; sightseeing, 160-163
Miss Jean's, Miss Esmie's, Miss Trim's, Miss Joycie's, Alma's and Sylvia's (kiosks), Tobago, 151, 170
Money and banks, 37; service charges, 45; tipping, 45; VAT, 45
Monkeys, 25
Monsoon, Port of Spain, 78
Moon Over Bourbon Street (MOBS), Port of Spain, nightlife, 113
Moriah, Tobago, 182
Morshead's, R.T. (market), 149
Motmot Ridge and the Observatory, Tobago, 143-144
Motorcycling, Tobago, 174
Mount St. Benedict, Trinidad, bird watching, 97
Mt. Irvine, Tobago, 121; accommodations, 132-135; beaches, 170; dive sites, 177; golf, 173; restaurants, 152; shopping, 187; snorkeling, 178; surfing, 179; tennis, 173; watersports, 219; windsurfing, 179, 219
Mt. Plaisir Estate Hotel, Grand Rivière, 73
Mt. Pleasant, Tobago, restaurant, 153
Mud Volcanoes, Trinidad, 84
Murchison Trace, Tobago, 166
Music, 31-37; calypso, 35-37; parang, 32; steel bands, 32-35
Music tours, 216

N

Nanan's guides, 87, 215, 216
Nariva Swamp, Trinidad, 85
Natalie's Bake and Shark, Maracas Bay, 81
National Museum, Port of Spain, 83
Naturalist Beach Resort, Castara, 139

Nature, 24-30; and environment protection, 221-223; flora and fauna, 23-30; guided tours, 216, 219-220; leatherback turtles, 27-28; medicinal plants, 30; plants, 29-30; Tobago, 25-26; Trinidad, 25-26, 85; *see also* Bird watching
Neal & Massy Trinidad All Stars (band), 34
Ned, Jason (artist), 188
Newspapers, 43
Nightlife: Tobago, 184-186; Trinidad, 112-114
Normandie Hotel, Port of Spain, 67-68; nightlife, 113
North Caribbean Coast, Tobago, 121; accommodations, 139-140; sightseeing, 163
Northeast Trinidad, 61; beaches, 101; driving tours, 109-111
Northern Range, Trinidad, 55, 105
North Star/Bougan Villa, Blanchisseuse, 70
Northwest Trinidad, 91-94

O

Off-island guided tours, 220
Oil, 7-8
Old Donkey Cart House Inn and Restaurant, Tobago, 137-138, nightlife, 185; restaurant, 154
Old Police Station, Port of Spain, 83-84
Olivierre, Evette (guide), 74, 99, 106
Opossum (manicou), 25
Oropuche Swamp, Trinidad, 56
Ottley, Lloyd (market), 150

P

Packing tips, 41, 47
Palm Tree Village Hotel, Lambeau, horseback riding, 179
Panorama (steel band competition), 33
Papillon Restaurant, Mt. Irvine, 152
Parang music, 32
Paria Beach, Trinidad, 99
Paria Waterfall, Trinidad, 86, 106

Parlatuvier, Tobago, 121; accommodations, 140; driving tour, 182-183, 184; restaurant, 156; sightseeing, 163

Par-May-La's Inn, Port of Spain, 65

Parrots, 182

Passports and visas, 47

Patino's, Buccoo, 152-153

Patrage, Port of Spain, 78

Paw paw fruit, 30

Pax Guest House, Tunapuna, 73

Peacock Mill, Canaan, 154; nightlife, 185

Peake Yacht Services, Ltd., 211

Pelican Inn Hotel, Cascade, 68

Pelican Inn Pub, Port of Spain, 78

Pelican Squash Club, Trinidad, 103

Phase II (band), 33, 34

Phone cards, 44-45

Photography, 41

Pier One, Chaguaramas, nightlife, 114

Pigeon Point, Tobago: accommodations, 127-128; beaches, 168; Buccoo Reef, 158-159; diving, 217; fishing charters, 218; restaurant, 218; shopping, 187-188; windsurfing, 179

Piparo, Trinidad, 84

Pirate's Bay Beach, Charlotteville, 172

Pitch Lake, La Brea, Trinidad, 56, 88-89

Pizza Boys, Port of Spain, 78

Planning your trip, 37-54

Plantation Beach Villas, Grafton, 144

Plants, medicinal, 30

Pleasure Pirates, Tobago, 185

Plymouth, Tobago, 121; accommodations, 133; sightseeing, 163

PNM (People's National Movement), 20-23

Pointe-à-Pierre Wildfowl Trust, bird watching, 25, 56, 89-90

Port of Spain, Trinidad, 60; accommodations, 63, 64-68; driving tours, 105-112; guide services, 216; health and fitness clubs, 103; kayaking, 103; map, 61; nightlife, 112-113; restaurants, 77-79; shopping, 114-115; sightseeing, 81-84; tennis, 103

Poui trees, 25

Power Boats Mutual Facilities Ltd., 211-212

Prescriptions, 42

Princess Building Grounds, Port of Spain, 103

Q

Queen's Park Savannah, Port of Spain, 84

Quenk (wild pig), 25

R

Rafters, Port of Spain, 78-79

Rainbow Resorts, Crown Point, 130-131

Rain forest, Tobago, 165-166, 219-220

Rapso music, 36

Recycling, 223

Red House, Port of Spain, 84

Reef tours, 222-223

Religion, 43

Restaurants: Atlantic Coast of Tobago, 155; Blanchisseuse, 80; Chaguaramas, 79-80; Crown Point, 150-151; Maracas Bay, 81; Mid-Caribbean Coast, 152-153; Parlatuvier, 156; Port of Spain, 77-79; Speyside, 156; Tobago, 150-156, 218; Trinidad, 77-81

Restrite Sea Gardens Guest House, Delaford, 138

Richards, Hugh (sandal maker), 186-187

Richard's Bake and Shark, Maracas Bay, 81

Richmond, Tobago, 122

Richmond Great House Inn, Belle Garden, 138-139, 182; dining, 155; sightseeing, 158; tennis, 173

Riverside Restaurant, Parlatuvier, 156

Road March King, 36

Rooks, David, nature tours, 219

Roti, 75

Rouselles, Bacolet, 154

Rovanel's Resort, Crown Point, 131

Roxborough, Tobago, 122; bird watching, 156; driving tours, 181-183; sightseeing, 157-158

Royal Palm Suite Hotel Ltd., Maraval, 68

Rum distillery tour, Trinidad, 90

S

Sacketeers Hiking Club, Trinidad, 101-102

Saddle, Trinidad, 94, 107

St. Andrew's Golf Club, Maraval, 102

St. Clair, Trinidad: accommodations, 67; restaurant, 79

St. Giles Island, bird watching, 156, 166

St. Madelin, Trinidad, sugar factory, 90

Salybia Falls, Trinidad, 102

Sanctuary Villa Resort, Tobago, 136, accommodations, 144-145; diving, 217-218

Sandals, handmade, 114, 186-187

San Fernando, Trinidad, 56, 112

Sangre Grande, Trinidad, 86

San Juan Estate, Trinidad, 85

San Souci, Trinidad, 110

Scarborough, Tobago, 122; accommodations, 137-139; diving, 218; driving tours, 180-182; food market, 149; library, 122; nature tours, 219; nightlife, 185; restaurants, 153-154; shopping, 188; sightseeing, 163-164; tennis, 173

Scarlet ibis, 25, 87

Scarlet Ibis wreck, diving, 177

Scuba, Tobago, 174-178

Seafood, Tobago, 147

Second Spring Bed & Breakfast Inn, Blanchisseuse, 70

Seine, pulling, 166-168

Service charges, 45, 62

Sesame candy, 147, 186

Sewdass Sadhu Shiv Mandir temple, Trinidad, 91

Sex, 42

Shark and bake, 75

Shark oil, 109

Shirvan Watermill Restaurant, Mt. Pleasant, 153

Shopping: Tobago, 186-188; Trinidad, 114-115, 186-188

Sightseeing: Charlotteville, 164; Crown Point, 158-159; Port of Spain area, 81-84; Scarborough, 163-164; Speyside, 164-165; Tobago, 156-168; Trinidad, 81-97

Silvia's kiosk, Tobago, 151

Singing Sandra (musician), 36

Snakes, 25, 26

Snorkeling, 41, 132, 162, 178, 184, 217-218

Soca music, 36

Soccer, Trinidad, 103

Solomon, Ricarda (guide), 174, 219

Spas, Tobago, 174; Trinidad, 103

Spectrum (stadium), Trinidad, 111

Speedboat racing, Trinidad, 104

Spektakula Forum, Port of Spain, 37; nightlife, 114

Speyside, Tobago, 123; accommodations, 140-141; diving, 175-177, 217-218; driving tours, 181-183; restaurant, 156; sightseeing, 164-165

Sportfishing, Tobago, 179

Squash: Tobago, 173; Trinidad, 103

Steel bands, 31-35; at Carnival, 33-34, 195; guide, 34; history, 31-32; instruments, 34-35; Panorama, 33; pan yards, 34; tuning, 35

Stews, 75-76

Stone Haven Bay Beach, Tobago, 170

Stone Haven Villas, Tobago, 126

Store Bay Beach, Tobago, 168-169; shopping, 186

Studley Park, Tobago, restaurant, 155

Sugar Aloes (musician), 36

Sugarcane, 30

Sugar factory tours: Tobago, 160-162; Trinidad, 90-91

Sunblock, 42

Sunday block party, Buccoo, 186

Sundeck Suites, Port of Spain, 66

Surf Country Inn, Blanchisseuse, 70-71; restaurant, 80

Surfing: Tobago, 179; Trinidad, 104

Sylvester, Antoinette (ice cream), 109

T

Tamana Trail and Bat Cave, Trinidad, 86

Tara Beach House, Scarborough, 139

Tatoo (armadillo), 25

Taxes, 45, 47, 62

Taxis: Tobago, 119; Trinidad, 59-60, 62

Telephones, 44-45, 47

Tennis: Tobago, 173; Trinidad, 103

Theater, Tobago, 185

Thom, Renwick (lobsters), 147

Tiki Village Restaurant, St. Clair, 79

Time zone, 47

Tipping, 45

Tobago, 116-188; accommodations, 123-145; adventures and sports, 173-179; animals and birds, 25-26, 156-157, 160, 163-166; art, 187-188; beaches, 168-173; biking, 40, 174; boating, 178-179; camping, 145; diving, 174-178, 217-218; driving tours, 180-184; fishing, 178-179, 218-219; food, 145-150; getting here and getting around, 117-123; golf, 173-174; grocery shopping, 148-150; guide services, 217-220; hiking, 173; history in 15th-18th centuries, 12-14; history in 19th century, 14-15; horseback riding, 179; kayaking, 179; library, 122; map, 116; nightlife, 184-186; orientation, 117; people and culture of, 4; pulling a seine, 166-168; restaurants, 150-156, 218; shopping, 186-188; sightseeing, 156-168; squash, 173; surfing, 179; tennis, 173; theater, 185; why to visit, 2-3; windsurfing, 179, 219; yacht anchoring-off sites, 206; see also Trinidad and Tobago

Tobago Plantations, Ltd., accommodations, 125-126, 137

Toco, Trinidad, 61; beaches, 101; driving tours, 109-111; lighthouse, 109; surfing, 104

Top O'Tobago, Arnos Vale, 136, 145

Top Ranking Hillview Guest House, Speyside, 141

Toucan Inn and Bonkers, Crown Point, 151

Touring: guide services, 216, 219-220; Tobago, 180-184; Trinidad, 104-112

Tourism, 8

Tourist information, 46

Transportation, 52-54

Traveler's checks, 37

Trees: flowering, 26; poisonous, 29-30; special, 29-30

Trinidad, 55-115; accommodations, 62-74; adventures and sports, 101-104; animals and birds, 25, 56, 85, 87, 89-90, 95-97; beaches, 98-101, 106, 109; camping, 74; driving tours, 104-112; fishing, 104; food, 74-76; getting here and getting around, 59-62; golf, 102; guide services, 215-216; hiking, 101-102; history in 15th-18th centuries, 10-12; history in 19th century, 15-18; horse racing, 104; kayaking, 103; maps, 55, 56-58; nightlife, 112-114; orientation, 55; people and culture of, 4-5; restaurants, 77-81; shopping, 114-115; sightseeing, 81-97; squash, 103; surfing, 104; tennis, 103; why to visit, 1-2; windsurfing, 104; see also Trinidad and Tobago

Trinidad Hilton, Port of Spain, 66

Trinidad Maracas Bay Hotel, 72

Trinidad and Tobago: business in, 9; coral reef tours, 222-223; costs, 42; crime, 39-40; economy, 7-9; environmental protection, 221-223; flora and fauna, 23-30; geography, 5; government, 6-7; health care, 42; history, 9-23; holidays and events, 48-51; immigration and customs, 43, 47; language, 5, 47; looking ahead, 23; maps, 43; music, 31-37;

nature, 24-30; newspapers, 43; People's National Movement (PNM), 20-23; planning your trip to, 37-54; religion, 44; service charges, 45; telephones, 44-45, 47; television, 45; tipping, 45; tourist information, 46-47; in 20th century, 18-23; VAT, 45; voting rights in, 18-19
TTYA (Trinidad & Tobago Yachting Association), 212
Tunapuna, Trinidad: accommodations, 73; bird watching, 97
Turtle Beach Hotel, Courland Bay, 136-137; beach, 171; tennis, 173
Turtles, leatherback, 27-28

U
Upper Blanchisseuse, Trinidad, 106

V
Valencia, Trinidad, 109
VAT (value added tax), 45
Venezuela, tours, 220
Veni Mangè, Port of Spain, 79
Visas and passports, 47

W
Watersports, guides, 219; *see also specific activities*
Water supply, 47
West Mall, Trinidad, 111, 115
Where to eat, *see* Restaurants
Where to stay, *see* Accommodations
Whitehall, Port of Spain, 83
Wildways guide services, 216
Windsurfing: Tobago, 179, 219; Trinidad, 104
Witco Desperadoes (steel band), 34
Woodford Square, Port of Spain, 84

Y
Yacht services industry, 8, 205-213; customs and immigration, 209; facilities directory, 209-213; map, 208; restaurants, 111; Tobago anchoring-off sites, 206; Yacht Club, 212-213; yachting association (TTYA), 212; yards, 207
Yates, Lincoln (guide), 219

Z
Zoo, Port of Spain, 82
Zoom Caribbean, Tobago, 114, 187

Photo by Douglas Spranger

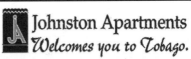